Access to medicines in the Democratic Republic of the Congo and the United Republic of Tanzania from a least developed country perspective

Europäische Hochschulschriften Recht

European University Studies in Law

Publications Universitaires Européennes de Droit

Band/Volume 6692

Dady Mumbanika Mbwisi

Access to medicines in the Democratic Republic of the Congo and the United Republic of Tanzania from a least developed country perspective

Right to modern and traditional medicines

PETER LANG

Bibliografische Information der Deutschen Nationalbibliothek
Die Deutsche Nationalbibliothek verzeichnet diese Publikation in der Deutschen Nationalbibliografie; detaillierte bibliografische Daten sind im Internet über http://dnb.d-nb.de abrufbar.

Zugl.: Erlangen, Nürnberg, Univ., Diss., 2022

n 2
ISSN 0531-7312
ISBN 978-3-631-88759-2 (Print)
E-ISBN 978-3-631-88762-2 (E-PDF)
E-ISBN 978-3-631-88763-9 (EPUB)
DOI 10.3726/b20081

Peter Lang – Berlin · Bern · Bruxelles · New York · Oxford · Warszawa · Wien

Diese Publikation wurde begutachtet.

www.peterlang.com

Table of contents

Acronyms and Abbreviations

Afr. J. Legal Stud	African Journal of Legal Studies
Afr J Tradit Complement Altern Med	African Journal of Traditional, Complementary and Alternative Medicines
AHRLJ	African Human Rights Law Journal
AIDS	Acquired Immune Deficiency Syndrome
Art.	Article
ARVs	Antiretroviral drugs
AU	African Union
BMI	Business Monitor International
BMJ	British Medical Journal
CEDAW	Comittee on the Elimination of Discrimination Against Women
CESCR	Committee on Economic, Social and Cultural Rights
CHRGG	Commission for Human Rights and Good Governance
CRC	Convention on the Rights of the Child
CRDS	Centre de Recherche en Droit Social
DPM	Direction de la Pharmacie et du Médicament
DRC	Democratic Republic of the Congo
ECOSOC	Economic and Social Council
EPU	Editions Publibook Université
GA	General Assembly
HIV	Human Immunodeficiency Virus
HRQ	Human Rights Quarterly
ICCPR	International Covenant on Civil and Political Rights
ICESC	International Covenant on Economic, Social and Cultural Rights
IMT	Institut de Médecine Tropicale
Int J Complement Alt Med	International Journal of Complementary and Alternative Medicine
Md. J. Int'IL	Maryland Journal of International Law and Trade
MHPs	Modern Health Personals
MSD	Medical Stores Department
NEMLIT	National Essential Medicine List for Tanzania
NGOs	Non-Governmental Organisations

NHRC	National Human Rights Commission
OAU	Organization of African Unity
Para	Paragraph
PER / PELJ	Potchefstroom Electronic Law Journal
PEV	Programme Elargi de Vaccination
PNDS	Plan National de Développement Sanitaire
PNMLS	Programme National Multisectoriel de Lutte contre le Sida
PNTS	Programme National de Transfusion Sanguine
QUAMED	Quality Medicine for All
R. Const	Registre Constitutionnel
SADC	Southern African Development Community
SAJHR	South African Journal on Human Rights
SNAME	Système National d'Approvisionnement en Médicaments Essentiels
TFDA	Tanzania Food and Drugs Authority
THPs	Traditional Health Practitioners
TM	Traditional Medicine
TMPs	Traditional Medicine Personals
TRIPAIX	Tribunal de Paix
UDHR	Universal Declaration of Human Rights
UN	United Nations
UNICEF	United Nations Children's Fund
URT	United Republic of Tanzania
WHO	World Health Organization

Acknowledgements

Attempting to provide an exhaustive inventory of the help I received during the many years devoted to the conception, writing, and completion of this thesis would be a risky and incomplete task. Therefore, I am thankful to all people who participated in completing this work in one way or another. Mainly, I am grateful to my supervisor Prof. Dr. Markus Krajewski, for his guidance, insightful comments, and critical observations, which contributed to the improvement of my dissertation. Despite his multiple occupations and responsibilities, Markus kindly fulfilled his role of Supervisor (Doktorvater), even beyond the sole scientific and academic spheres. My gratitude goes to Prof. Dr. Andreas Funke, who replied to my request for potential supervision, centering my attention on Prof. Krajewski. My thanks go to the Friedrich-Ebert Foundation for financial support, which fully funded my doctoral research.

My special thanks to Prof. Dr. Yves Junior Manzanza, who motivated me to undertake my doctoral studies in Germany and shared the official website from Prof. Andreas Funke. I also thank Prof. Dr. Laura Clerico, who kindly admitted me to her seminar as part of my admission requirement to the doctorate program and agreed to review and evaluate my dissertation.

I am also grateful to Prof. Dr. Ndjoko Karine Loset, who motivated me to obtain an external Ph.D. student status in one of the universities in the Netherlands before applying for a NUFFIC grant in 2013. Also, I am grateful to Prof. Dr. Fons Coomans for kindly agreeing to be my supervisor and supporting my application to Maastricht university's law school and the NUFFIC program. Unfortunately, destiny decided otherwise. In my application process as an external Ph.D. student at Maastricht University, I also received significant assistance from Dr. Jennifer Selling, who acted as a co-supervisor in providing valuable comments on my proposal. Thank you very much, Jennifer. Special thanks to my parents Marc Mumbanika Musag'i and Sophie Ngunza, for their tireless support and moral and spiritual accompaniment. Especially my father has constantly advised me to be patient and follow in the steps of Prof. Yves Manzanza who also completed his Ph.D. in Germany. Furthermore, I am thankful to my family, consisting of my wife Berthie Niary and my two kids, Marc Berdinho and Brady Dadinio, for their patience and love. My thanks also go my brothers and sisters, Marie-Louise, Ismael, Agapy Manzanza, Clara, Kenda, and Madeleine, for their love and support. I am also grateful to all my Congolese professors and teachers for their encouragement, especially Kumbu JM, Omeonga, Nzundu, Ngwabika, Mulengi, and Kangulumba.

Last but not least, my profound thanks to my friends, namely Rhode, Fiston Kafulu, Dadou Boto, Mimie Malu, Assaam, Kweta, and Guy Kipulu, for their encouragement and support.

I. General introduction

People in the least developed countries, such as the Democratic Republic of the Congo (DRC) and the United Republic of Tanzania (URT),[1] need medicines more than anyone else. In addition to common diseases that can affect everyone's health irrespective of location, Congolese and Tanzanian people face peculiar ailments in the African environment, such as neglected tropical diseases, malaria, cholera, yellow fever, and Ebola.[2] Furthermore, people's ability to access medicines of good quality that are available and accessible for all is doubly affected by the countries' status and their socioeconomic status.[3] Regarding the country's status, the DRC and URT are among the world's poor countries,[4] facing the problem of poverty which renders them incapable of providing the necessary amenities, infrastructure, and resources that facilitate the full enjoyment of the right to health,[5] including access to medicines of good quality. The country's developmental level is a crucial factor upon which depends the full implementation of access to medicines as part of the right to health.[6] Without relieving least developed countries of their

1 Least developed countries, including the DRC and URT, have low levels of income and face severe structural impediments to sustainable development. See United Nations Conference on Trade and Development: The least developed countries Report, 2019, xii.

2 Ministère de la santé publique, Plan National de Développement Sanitaire 2016-2020: vers la couverture sanitaire universelle, 2016 (hereinafter PNDS 2016-2020), 27. Ministry of Health and Social Welfare, Health Sector Strategic Plan July 2015 – June 2020, 2015, 16. See also Maria Jurua, "Access to drugs at risk: securing access to medicines for least developed countries," *Africa Development*, 42, no. 1, (2017):107.

3 David Coburn and Elaine S. Coburn, "Health and health inequalities in a neo-liberal global world," in *The economics of health equity*, eds. Di McIntyre and Gavin Mooney (Cambridge: Cambridge University Press, 2007), 15.

4 The DRC and URT are among the world's poor countries. See the Democratic Republic of the Congo, National report submitted in accordance with paragraph 15 (a) of the annex to Human Rights Council Resolution 5/1, 2009, para 124 (b), and the United Republic of Tanzania, combined initial, second and third periodic reports submitted by States parties under articles 16 and 17 of International Covenant on Economic, Social and Cultural Rights, 2009 (hereinafter URT's Report to the CESCR, 2009) para 165.

5 African Commission on Human and Peoples' Rights, Communication 241/01: Purohit and Moore vs. Gambia (henceforth Gambia Case), 2001, para 84.

6 Committee on Economic, Social and Cultural Rights General Comment No. 14: The Right to the Highest Attainable Standard of Health (Art. 12), 2000 (henceforth General Comment 14), para 12. UN Human Rights Office of the High Commissioner,

obligations regarding the right to health, States and other entities in the position to assist should grant them international assistance and aid,[7] allowing them to implement access to medicines within their jurisdictions. It is essential to stress that the development level of a given State also affects or influences adopted implementation measures. For example, in the URT and DRC, there is no compulsory universal health coverage or good legal conditions that allow individuals to claim access to medicines before the courts.[8]

The citizens of URT and DRC lack sufficient means to afford existing available medicines, despite their lower health status and higher needs for medicine.[9] Financial constraints also hinder individuals' capability to claim access to medicines through complaint procedures before human rights treaty bodies, such as the African Commission of Human and Peoples' Rights,[10] and the African Court of Human and Peoples' Rights.[11] Other factors that impede access include the shortage of medicines within public health facilities, the absence of medication for African diseases, the high price of available drugs of good quality, the presence of bad quality medicines,[12] and the irrational use of medicines through self-medication. Overall, people's access to medicines of good quality in the least developed countries, including the URT and DRC, is limited.[13] While taking into

---

Access to Medicines in the context of the Right to Health, 2015, para 9, and African Commission on Human and Peoples' Rights, Principles and Guidelines on the Implementation of Economic, Social and Cultural Rights in the African Charter on Human and Peoples' Rights, 2011 (henceforth African Commission's Guidelines on ESCRs), para 15.

7 African Commission's Guidelines on ESCRs, para 45.

8 Existing laws on courts and tribunals in the DRC do not organize the exercise of human rights jurisdiction regarding access to medicines. Whereas in the URT, access to medicine is not a justiciable right under the Constitution.

9 The problem of access to medicine rises up when it comes to low-income countries where the population has lower economic status and lower health status. Ahmadiani Saeed, and Shekoufeh Nikfar, "Challenges of access to medicine and the responsibility of pharmaceutical companies: a legal perspective," *DARU Journal of Pharmaceutical Sciences*, (2016):2.

10 African Charter on Human and Peoples' Rights, 1986 (hereinafter African Charter), art 56.

11 Protocol to the African Charter on Human and Peoples' Rights on the establishment of an African Court on Human and Peoples' Rights, 2004 (henceforth African Court Protocol), art 5.

12 Hiroko Yamane, *Interpreting TRIPS globalisation of intellectual property rights and access to medicines* (Oxford: Hart Publishing, 2011), 281.

13 For peoples living in poverty, the full enjoyment of the right to the highest attainable standard of physical and mental health is becoming increasingly remote. See Human Rights Council Resolution 12/24. Access to medicine in the context of the right of

account the country's developmental level, the present study deals with the legal protection of access to medicines as an essential component of the human right to health.

A. Justification of the legal approach for access to medicines in DRC and URT

The legal dimension of a human right to health, including access to medicines, is based on its recognition as a legitimate standard within international and domestic laws.[14] A human rights-based approach[15] to medicines considers States, namely the DRC and URT, as duty bearers, responsible for meeting their legal obligations in that regard through implementation measures consistent with human rights, on the one hand. It also considers individuals as rights holders, entitled to make claims for redress of violation of their right to health, on the other hand.[16] Indeed, both the DRC and URT are committed to the legal protection of access to medicines at the international and domestic levels through the ratification of human rights treaties and the adoption of laws and regulations.

At the international level, for instance, the DRC and URT are Member States of the United Nations Organization (UN),[17] the African Union (AU),[18] and the Southern African Development Community (SADC),[19] the constitutive Charters of which make provisions for the protection of human rights and health-related issues through individual and collective efforts.[20] More importantly, they have ratified specific human rights instruments adopted within the framework of these organizations, which expressly protect the right to health, including access to medicines, from different perspectives. The International Covenant on Economic, Social and

---

everyone to the enjoyment of the highest attainable standard of physical and mental health, A/HRC/RES/12/24, 2009 (henceforth Human Rights Council Resolution 12/24).

14 John Tobin, *The right to health in international law* (Oxford: Oxford University Press, 2012), 47.

15 United Nations Research Institute for Social Development, The human rights-based approach to social protection, Issued Brief 02, 2016, 1, file:///C:/Users/Besitzer/Google%20Drive/My%20PHD%20THESIS/IB2-Human-rights-based-approach.pdf (accessed November 11, 2018).

16 Ibid.

17 Charter of the United Nations, 1945 (hereinafter UN Charter).

18 Constitutive Act of the African Union, 2001 (hereinafter the AU Constitutive Act).

19 Treaty of the Southern African Development Community as amended, 1993 (hereinafter SADC Treaty).

20 See UN Charter, arts 55 and 56, SADC Treaty, and art 5 (i), and AU Constitutive Act, arts 4 (m) and 14 (1)(f).

Cultural Rights,[21] provides for the right to the enjoyment of the highest attainable standard of physical and mental health while the African Charter provides for the right to enjoy the best attainable state of physical and mental health.[22] Further ratified treaties cover access to health services for all,[23] children's health care, and universal access to HIV AIDS treatment.[24]

The human rights treaties entitle individuals to lodge complaints before established supervisory bodies for any violation of the right to access medicines by the State parties concerned.[25] Furthermore, as duty-bearers, the governments of the DRC and URT are under treaty's obligations to implement access to medicines either through individual efforts only[26] or through both individual and collective efforts, including international assistance and cooperation.[27] These implementation measures shall ensure the availability, accessibility, and acceptability of access to medicines and provision for remedies in case of its violation.[28]

At the domestic level, each country has its human rights protection system. In the DRC, for instance, as the supreme law of the land, the DRC Constitution protects all the categories of human rights, whether civil and political rights (CPRs), economic, social, and cultural rights (ESCRs), and collective rights.[29] The Constitution provides for the right to health under article 47, which reads as follows, "the right to health and food security is guaranteed. The law establishes fundamental principles and organization rules relating to public health and food security." It is plausible to argue that the concept of the "right to health" is inclusive of access to medicines. Furthermore, the DRC Constitution consecrates the monist approach, in which ratified human treaties have precedence over national laws other than the Constitution.[30] Like under ratified human rights treaties, the DRC Constitution

---

21 International Covenant on Economic, Social and Cultural Rights, 1976 (hereinafter ICESCR), art 12.

22 African Charter, art 16.

23 Southern African Development Community Protocol on Health as amended, 2004 (henceforth SADC Health Protocol), arts 11 and 12.

24 Southern African Development Community Protocol on Gender and Development as amended, 2008 (henceforth SADC Gender Protocol), arts 11 and 27.

25 African Charter, arts 47 and 55, African Court Protocol, art 5, Protocol on Tribunal in the Southern African Development Community, 2011 (hereinafter SADC Tribunal Protocol), art 15 (2), and the Optional Protocol to the International Covenant on Economic, Social and Cultural Rights, 2013 (hereinafter Optional Protocol to ICESCR), arts 2 and 10.

26 African Charter, arts 1 and 16.

27 ICESCR, arts 2 and 12, SADC Protocol on Health, art 2 (b).

28 General Comment 14, paras 12 and 59.

29 Constitution de la République Démocratique du Congo telle que révisée à ce jour, 2006 (hereinafter DRC Constitution), Title II.

30 Ibid. arts 153 and 215.

subjects the implementation of the constitutional right to health to a range of implementation measures,[31] including the enactment of the law on public health. Using the current DRC Constitution as a starting point, one can regroup existing implementation measures on access to medicines into two main categories. The first category includes laws and regulations adopted before the coming into force of the DRC Constitution, including at the colonial time. They mainly comprise the 1933 Ordinance on the practice of pharmacy,[32] the 1952 Decree on the practice of medicine,[33] the 1958 Ordinance on the exercise of medicine and application modalities,[34] the 1972 Ordinance Law on the exercise of pharmacy,[35] and the 1972 Ordinance on the implementation of the 1972 Ordinance Law.[36] Other measures include the 1991 Ordinance Law establishing the National Board of Pharmacists[37] and the 2002 Decree on the exercise of traditional medicine.[38] The second category comprises some laws and policies adopted after the coming into force of the DRC Constitution, such as the Public Health Law,[39] the Law on people living with HIV (the HIV Law),[40] the Law on the rights of the Child,[41] and the Law on the rights of women,[42] the National Strategy of Strengthening Health System,[43] and

31 Ibid. arts 47 and 202.

32 Ordonnance N° 27 bis Hyg. sur l'exercice de la pharmacie au Congo-Belge, 1933 (hereinafter 1933 Ordinance).

33 Décret portant art de guérir au Congo -Belge, 1952 (hereinafter 1952 Decree).

34 Ordonnance 71-8 sur l'exercice de l'art de guérir et les conditions et modalités d'application, 1958. (henceforth 1958 Ordinance).

35 Ordonnance-Loi 72-046 sur l'exercice de la pharmacie, 1972 (hereinafter 1972 Ordinance-Law).

36 Ordonnance 72-359 portant mesures d'exécution de l'Ordonnance-Loi 72-046 du 14 Septembre 1972 sur l'exercice de la pharmacie, 1972 (hereinafter the 1972 Ordinance).

37 Ordonnance-Loi 91-018 portant création d'un ordre des pharmaciens en République du Zaïre, 1991 (hereinafter 1991 Ordinance-Law).

38 Arrêté Ministériel N° 1250/ CAB/MIN/S/CJ/KIZ/32/2002 portant organisation de l'exercice de la profession de praticien de la médecine traditionnelle, 2002 (hereinafter Traditional Medicine Decree).

39 Loi N° 18/035 fixant les principes fondamentaux relatifs à l'organisation de la santé publique, 2018 (hereinafter Public Health Law)

40 Loi N° 08/011 portant protection des droits des personnes vivant avec le VIH/SIDA et des personnes affectées, 2008 (hereinafter HIV Law).

41 Loi N° 09/001 portant protection de l'Enfant, 2009 (hereinafter Children Law).

42 Loi N° 15/013 portant modalités d'application des droits de la femme et de la parité, 2015 (hereinafter Women Law).

43 Ministère de la Santé Publique de la RDC, Stratégie de Renforcement du Système de Santé, 2006.

the 2011-2015 Health Plan of Action.[44] The Constitution vests all the courts and tribunals with a common and general human rights jurisdiction.[45]

Like in DRC, the 1997 URT Constitution is the primary legal text that protects all human rights in the URT.[46] Unlike the DRC Constitution, the URT Constitution's Part III relating to basic rights and duties does not contain any provision dealing explicitly with the right to health or the specific right of access to medicines. Instead, Part II on fundamental objectives and directive principles of State policy refers to, among others, the right to social welfare at times of sickness, the protection of other human rights following the Universal Declaration of Human Rights (UDHR), and the eradication of disease,[47]which can cover access to medicines. However, unlike basic rights, directive principles of State policy are not judicially enforceable.[48] Following the country dualist tradition,[49] courts in the URT can only apply ratified human rights treaties after their domestication or incorporation into the municipal law.[50] To implement the treaty and constitutional provisions on access to medicines, including the protection of public health,[51] the URT has adopted an important number of legislations, regulations, and programs. These include the 2003 Tanzania Food, Drugs, and Cosmetics Act, the 1982 Disabled Persons Act, the 2007 Environmental Health Practitioners Act, the 2007 Health Laboratory, Practitioners Act, the 2008 Mental Health Act, and the 1999 National Health Insurance Fund Act. They further include the 2002 Traditional and Alternative Medicines Act, the 2008 HIV and AIDS Act, the 2009 Public Health Act, the 2011 Pharmacy Act, the 2009 Law of the Child Act, and the 1998 Health Sector Reform Programme. All these implementation measures have in common the fact that their enactment is posterior to the 1977 URT Constitution.

However, despite the above legal framework, access to medicines in the DRC and URT remains still a very challenging concern, especially in rural areas.[52]

---

44 Ministère de la Santé Publique de la RDC, Plan National de Développement Sanitaire 2011-2015, 2010 (hereinafter PNDS 2011-2015).

45 DRC Constitution, art 150.

46 The Constitution of the URT as amended, 1977 (hereinafter URT Constitution).

47 Ibid. arts 7 and 9 (a), (f) et (i).

48 Ibid. art 7 (2).

49 Ibid. art 63 (3) (e).

50 Committee on the Elimination of Discrimination against Women, concluding observations on the combined seventh and eighth periodic reports of the United Republic of Tanzania, 2016 (hereinafter CEDAW Concluding observations to URT), para 10 (a).

51 Art 30 (2) (b) of the URT Constitution calls for the enactment of the law on public health.

52 Tanzania Global Health Initiative Strategy 2010-2015, (2011): 7, and PNDS 2011-2015, paras 125-127.

Without undermining the impact of a country's poverty on people's access to medicines, the present study examines the extent to which the existing human rights law applicable to the DRC and URT addresses the questions of quality, availability, accessibility, and enforcement of access to medicines.

B. Selection of the countries

The country studies are selected based on their similarities and differences in respect of their applicable human rights law on access to medicines. To begin with elements of similarities, a common issue to the DRC and URT is that their constitutional provisions on the right to health are not well known to the general public, including experts in the field. Indeed, contrary to the protection of the right to health under the Constitution of the Republic of South Africa, which is presented as a shining example in Africa,[53] some studies on the constitutional protection of the right to health in Africa ignore, if not underestimate, the relevant provisions of the DRC Constitution and URT Constitution.[54] Furthermore, in addition to being poor countries facing similar economic, social and structural problems, both the DRC and URT have the same treaty's obligations regarding access to medicines at the international, African, and SADC levels. Finally, like the Traditional Medicine Act on the practice of traditional medicine in the URT, the Public Health Law in the DRC recognizes traditional medicine (TM) as an essential component of the national health system.

However, the legal systems from the DRC and URT, including some legal aspects regarding the protection of access to medicines, are different. For instance, the DRC follows a continental European legal tradition with elements of French

53 Matthew Kavanagh, "Constitutionalizing health: Rights, democracy and the political economy of health policy," *Publicly Accessible Penn Dissertations*, 2017, https://repository.upenn.edu/edissertations/2863 (accessed April 12, 2018), Moses Mulumba, David Kabanda, and Viola Nassuna, "Constitutional provisions for the right to health in east and southern Africa," *Centre for Health, Human Rights and Development, Regional Network for Equity in Health in East and Southern Africa* (2010): 11, Andra Le Roux-Kemp, "The recognition of health rights in constitutions on the African continent: a systematic review," *African Journal of International and Comparative Law 24*, no. 1, (2016): 153.

54 According to Danwood Chirwa, the DRC does not belong to the list of African States that recognize ESCRs directly in the bill of rights of their constitutions. For his part, Le Roux-Kemp argues that the URT Constitution does not include any ESCRs, including health-related rights, neither as basic rights nor as directive principles of state policy. See Danwood M. Chirwa, "Access to medicines and health care in Sub-Saharan African: A historical perspective," *Md. J. Int'IL 31* (2016): 37, and Le Roux-Kemp, "Recognition of health rights," 144.

and Belgian law whereas the URT is a member of the Common Law family. In addition, Congo's legal system adopts a monist approach with regard to the relationship between international and domestic law,[55] whereas Tanzania is a dualist country strictly separating international and domestic law.[56] Consequently, unlike under the DRC law, where civil courts and tribunals can directly apply ratified human rights treaties,[57] under the domestic law of URT, the courts can only apply domesticated human rights treaties.[58] Furthermore, unlike the DRC Constitution, which provides for an explicit constitutional right to health, the URT Constitution deals with health-related rights, including access to medicines, as part of the directive principles of State policy through the protection of other human rights and the right to social welfare. Moreover, unlike under the DRC Constitution, where access to medicines is theoretically justiciable, the URT Constitution does not make it judicially enforceable. Therefore, how these differences play out when it comes to the implementation of the right to health and access to medicines is of interest.

C. Research questions

Four main questions form the backbone of the present thesis. The first question relates to the legal basis for access to medicines in the DRC and URT, consisting of domestic laws and ratified human rights treaties. The second question looks at whether differences in the constitutional references to the right to health and the country's monist or dualist approach towards ratified human rights treaties also lead to different results in implementing access to medicines within the country studies. The third question examines whether the scope of the right to health protected under ratified human rights treaties and domestic laws is sufficiently enough to include TM. Finally, the fourth question looks at the extent to which the comparative approach can allow the country studies to learn from each other in improving access to medicines within their respective jurisdictions.

D. Study hypotheses

The present study is built upon the following hypotheses. First, the DRC and URT are committed to the legal protection of modern and traditional medicines and have already taken some relevant implementation measures in that regard. However, they need other legal steps for adequate access to medicines, including

55 DRC Constitution, art 215.

56 URT Constitution, art 63 (3). See also the United Republic of Tanzania, Consolidated 2nd to 10th periodic reports to the African Commission of Human and People's Rights, 2006 (henceforth URT's Report to the African Commission, 2006).

57 DRC Constitution, art 153 in fine.

58 CEDAW Concluding observations to URT, 2016, para 10 (a).

adopting new laws and regulations and amending some existing laws. Moreover, despite the potential for an explicit constitutional right to health[59] under the DRC Constitution and its monist approach towards ratified human treaties, the DRC appears in many respects similar to the URT as a dualist State which protects access to medicines as a non-justiciable right. Likely, despite the inferior status of the constitutional right to health and the country dualist approach towards human rights treaties under the URT Constitution, the URT seems in many respects as a country with an explicit constitutional right to health in its implementation of some aspects of access to medicines. Finally, without government political will in implementing access to medicines, the differences regarding the constitutional protection of the right to health and the country's monist or dualist approach would remain theoretical without concrete improvement of people's enjoyment of their right to medicines.

E. Methodology

The primary method used in this study is desktop research based on written sources. Used materials were collected by visiting libraries, searching the internet, including the official websites of the African Commission, African Court, SADC, UN, AU, treaty bodies, and national health Ministry of the URT and DRC. In addition to the field study conducted in DRC, I have obtained some electronic versions of documents through email communications from URT contacts. Like any other legal doctrine, collected materials consist of normative and authoritative sources.[60] Normative references consist of, among other things, statutory texts, Constitutions, regulations, and human rights treaties. Authoritative sources comprise mainly case law that is not binding precedents, scholarly legal writings, and the jurisprudence and works of the CESCR, the African Commission, the African Court, and the SADC Tribunal.

The study has used descriptive, normative, empirical, and comparative approaches to interpret collected materials. The descriptive approach consists of describing the research object, which is the applicable human rights law on access to medicines in DRC and URT as it stands or reads today.[61] Regarding ratified

59 A specific and explicit constitutional reference to the right to health can lead to a greater relevance through the implementation and revision of laws and policies. See Katrina Perehudoff, B. Toebes, and H. Hogerzeil, "Essential medicines in national Constitutions: Progress since 2008," *Health and Human Rights Journal 18*, (2016): 151.

60 Mark Van Hoecke, "Legal doctrine: which method (s) for what kind of discipline?," in *Methodologies of legal research. Which kind of method for what kind of discipline?* ed. Mark Van Hoecke (Oxford: Hart Publishing, 2013), 11.

61 Jan M. Smits, *The mind and method of the legal academic*, (Camberley: Edward Elgar, 2012), 9 and 11.

human rights treaties by the DRC and URT, their interpretation shall be consistent with the ordinary meaning of the treaty´s terms, objects and purpose.[62] Therefore, internal law provisions should not justify the State's failure to implement its duly ratified human rights treaties.[63] For their part, while the normative approach indicates how the law should read through normative judgments or criticisms,[64] the empirical approach looks at what the law does, through its application and consequences[65] on Congolese and Tanzanian societies concerning access to medicines. Finally, the comparative approach helps identify and explain both similarities and differences in the applicable laws on access to medicine in DRC and URT, with a view to taking advantage of the main practical benefits of comparative law, namely its use as an aid to the legislators of the country studies.[66] If one proceeds cautiously and intelligently, other countries'experience can help to choose the solution that best suits one's legal tradition.[67]

F. Sources

The present study uses both primary and secondary sources. Primary sources protect the right of access to medicines and set up State's obligations to that at the international and domestic levels. They mainly include ratified human rights treaties providing for access to medicines and enforcement mechanisms, namely the ICESCR, the Optional Protocol to ICESCR, the African Charter, the African Court Protocol, the SADC Treaty, SADC Health Protocol, SADC Gender Protocol, SADC Tribunal Protocol, the Constitutions, laws and regulations of the country studies. These primary sources are interrelated to one another. For instance, the African Commission, the African Court, the SADC Tribunal, and the CESCR use the treaty that institutes them as applicable law. Concerning the African Court, its jurisdiction covers other relevant human rights instruments ratified by the States concerned, such as the ICESCR, the SADC Gender Protocol, and the SADC Health Protocol.[68] Moreover, each treaty body can draw inspiration from, consult, or consider, as subsidiary measures, other ratified human rights treaties.[69] At the

62 Vienna Convention on the Law of Treaties, 1969, art 31 (1).

63 Ibid. arts 26-27.

64 Smits, *The mind and method*, 9.

65 Ibid. 9 and 28.

66 Legislators worldwide have found that they cannot produce good laws on many matters without the assistance of comparative law. See K. Zweigert and H. Kötz, *An introduction to comparative law*, 3rd ed. Translated by Tony Weir (Oxford: Oxford University Press, 1998), 16.

67 Ibid.

68 African Court Protocol, art 7.

69 Optional Protocol to ICESCR, art 8 (3), African Charter, art 60, and SADC Tribunal Protocol, art 21.

domestic level, approved human rights treaties become part of the domestic legal arena of DRC and URT through the monist[70]and dualist approaches[71] followed by the country studies. Consequently, courts can apply them upon ratification in the DRC[72] and after their domestication in the URT.

Secondary sources serve as useful interpretative tools for the human right of access to medicine and the State's obligations provided by primary sources. They include, among others, relevant documentation emanating from the UN bodies, specialized agencies, funds, programs, and mechanisms, and other international organizations, including from regional rights systems, any observations, comments or reports by the State Party concerned, legal precedents, and doctrine, and rules of public international law.[73] In sum, these sources go beyond the traditional sources of general public international law as listed under the International Court of Justice Statute, which also apply to the international human rights law.[74]

G. Delimitation of the study

The present study examines the legal protection of access to medicines under the applicable human rights law to the DRC and the URT, the nature of the State's obligations to that, and existing enforcement mechanisms. Regarding the spatial delimitation, the study covers two African countries, namely the DRC and URT. The URT maintains a dual legal system that applies respectively to the United Republic (Mainland Tanzania) and Tanzania Zanzibar.[75] However, the study focuses only on the United Republic's legal system for two main reasons. First, the URT Constitution applies to both Mainland Tanzania and Tanzania Zanzibar as the supreme land law.[76] Therefore, the validity of the Constitution of Zanzibar depends on its consistency with the URT Constitution.[77] Secondly, unlike Tanzania Zanzibar's parliament, the parliament of Mainland Tanzania can adopt laws that also apply to Tanzania Zanzibar.[78]

70 DRC Constitution, Title VI.

71 URT Constitution, art 63 (3)(e).

72 DRC Constitution, art 153 in fine.

73 Optional Protocol to ICESCR, art 8 (3), African Charter, art 6, SADC Tribunal Protocol, art 21.

74 Christine Chinkin, "Sources," in *International human rights law*, eds. Moeckli, Shah, Sivakumaran, 2nd ed, (Oxford: Oxford University Press, 2014), 76 and 89.

75 URT Constitution, arts 1 and 4.

76 Ibid. art 152 (3).

77 Ibid. art 64 (8).

78 Ibid. art 64 (4).

H. Contributions to knowledge

Affordable access to medicines is a key element of the human right to enjoy the highest attainable standard of physical and mental health (the right to health). Despite the international and domestic legal recognition of the right to health and the relevance of access to medicines in this context, the implementation of the right is far from universal. In fact, millions of people, in particular in the least developed countries, lack access to medicines and are therefore deprived of the right to enjoy the highest attainable standard of physical and mental health. The reasons for this are manifold. Apart from the limited resources available to the States and the lack of sufficient means of the affected people to afford medicines, political and legal structures also contribute to the deprivation of access to medicines and hence the right to health.

While there is no shortage of scholarly literature on the right to health in general, little research has been undertaken with a focus on the specificities of the legal framework in African countries, including an investigation into domestic constitutional and statutory regimes of these countries. The present study partly fills in the gap by assessing access to medicines in two Sub-Saharan African countries, namely the DRC and the URT. It addresses the multilevel framework of the protection of the human right to health in these two countries, showing the challenges least developed countries face when implementing the right to health and providing access to medicines. The study also portrays the different layers of the above framework, beginning at the global, the African continental, and the regional levels of the SADC, and the domestic constitutional and statutory law. Thus, this approach allows for an interesting comparative perspective on different legal regimes protecting the right to health.

The thesis combines this general inquiry into the right to health with a specific focus on TM, including access to TMs. Considering TM is an innovative angle and addition to studies on the human right to health. In fact, TM is often overlooked in mainstream scholarship despite its immense practical importance for many people worldwide, especially in the DRC and the URT. Addressing TM in the context of the human right to health and analysing its challenges from a human rights perspective, therefore, constitute an important contribution to human rights scholarship.

I. Chapter outlines

Chapter I serves as a general introduction to the study and is followed by four chapters. Chapter II examines the protection of medicines under the international human rights law, which consists of ratified human rights treaties by the DRC and URT at the global, African continental, and SADC levels. It partly answers the overall question relating to the legal basis for access to medicines in DRC and URT. The chapter argues that ratified human rights treaties constitute a principal legal basis for access to medicines within the country studies.

Chapter III discusses the protection and implementation of access to medicines under the domestic laws of the DRC and URT. This chapter connects with Chapter II as it focuses on domestic laws as another essential legal basis for access to medicines in the DRC and URT. The chapter responds to the research question relating to the differences based on the constitutional protection of the right to health and the monist or dualist approach towards ratified treaties to implement access to medicines. To this end, it examines the constitutional protection of the right to health, discusses the relationship between the constitutional and treaty right of access to medicines, and existing implementation measures on the quality, availability, accessibility, and justiciability of access to medicines.

Chapter IV deals with the protection of TM. It relates to the study question on the scope of the right to health under ratified treaties and domestic laws. Its underlying idea is that both constitutional and treaty provisions on the right to health do not expressly distinguish between modern and traditional medicines. Therefore, chapter IV interprets the human right to health to include TM as well. The chapter also examines the indirect protection of TM through the human rights to cultural life and natural resources using an interdependency human rights approach.

Chapter V provides the general conclusion. In addition to summarizing the study, it responds to the research question on the comparative approach's potential advantages throughout this study. It consists of concluding observations and recommendations. Accordingly, concluding remarks identify legal obstacles to an adequate implementation of the existing human rights law on access to medicines in DRC and URT. The chapter further contains recommendations to the obstacles which if adopted, can improve access to medicines within the country studies' jurisdictions. The reform proposals shall include common measures for both countries and State-specific measures. Accordingly, common measures shall deal with commonly identified obstacles, if any, within the applicable law of these two countries. In contrast, specific measures shall address the state-specific deficiencies and consider the other State's positive aspects in the same area while changing what needs to be changed.

II. Access to modern medicines under the international human rights law

The present chapter examines the protection of access to medicines under the international human rights law, which comprises global, African, and SADC human rights laws.

A. Access to medicines under the global human rights law

People's efforts to protect their health since humanity[79] constitute the basis for the gradual protection of health by States at the domestic, regional, and international levels.[80] Without undermining global efforts on health-related matters, including under the Covenant of the League of Nations,[81] the present section considers the UN Charter as the starting point for the States' commitment to health-related issues at the global level. The UN Charter contains several references to the notion of human rights.[82] However, it does not list their content, nor does it use the expression of the right to health or access to medicine. Instead, article 55 of the UN Charter urges the UN to promote international economic, social, health, and related problems. Whereas article 57 calls for establishing specialized agencies by intergovernmental agreement, the primary instruments should define their international responsibilities in health and related fields. In this context, the Constitution of the World Health Organization[83] establishes the World Health Organization as the UN specialized agency responsible for health and related problems. Before focussing on the protection of access to medicines under the ICESCR, the section provides a brief history of the recognition of health and access to medicines under the global human rights law, and describes the concept of medicines.

---

79 Martyn Sama and Vinh-Kim Nguyen, *Governing health systems in Africa*, (Dakar: Council for the Development of Social Science Research in Africa, 2008): 3.

80 For more details about the historical recognition of health as a human right, see Brigit Toebes, *The right to health as a human right in international Law* (Cambridge: Intersentia, 1999), 7-15, Holger Hestermeyer, *Human rights and the WTO: The case of patents and access to* medicines (Oxford: Oxford University Press, 2007), 83-84.

81 For instance, articles 23 (f) and 25 of the 1919 Covenant of the League of Nations refer to health and disease.

82 See the Preamble to the UN Charter and its articles 1, 13, 55, 62, 68, and76.

83 The Constitution of the World Health Organization, 1946 (hereinafter WHO Constitution).

1. Brief history towards the recognition of health and access to medicines as human right at the global level

The recognition of access to medicines as a human right at the global level is inherent to the right to health. The WHO Constitution is the precursor instrument for recognizing health as a human right globally. It defines for the first time the words health and the right to health. According to the WHO Constitution, health is "a state of complete physical, mental and social well-being and not merely the absence of disease or infirmity." However, while some commentators describe this definition of health as vague,[84] others interpret it as entailing the State's obligation to ensure individuals' good health.[85] The counter-argument to the first criticism is that the WHO's definition of health remains the most commonly used and usually referred to in the context of the right to health.[86] The WHO Constitution refutes the second criticism in making an explicit distinction between the abstract concept of health and the right to health. To this end, it states that "the enjoyment of the highest attainable standard of health is one of the fundamental rights of every human being without distinction of race, religion, political belief, economic or social condition." If States cannot ensure a state of complete physical, mental and social well-being, they can at least implement the enjoyment of the highest attainable standard of health. Some critics argue that this definition of the right to health is not binding because it forms part of the WHO Constitution's preamble.[87] It is worth recalling that the preamble helps interpret the main WHO objective, which is to attain the highest possible level of health.[88] Although the WHO's provision on the right to health does not expressly mention modern medicines, its full implementation depends on, among others, health services and facilities, including pharmaceutical products,[89] which cover medicines.

Two years following the adoption of the WHO Constitution, the UN General Assembly adopted the UDHR as the mother of all human rights norms.[90] Its article

84 For details about criticism against the WHO's definition of health, see Toebes, *The right to health*, 20-25

85 Danwood M. Chirwa, "The right to health in international law: its implications for the obligations of state and non-state actors in ensuring access to essential medicine," *SAJHR 19*, no. 4, (2003): 545.

86 Toebes, *The right to health*, 20-25.

87 Gabriel Alexander Baumstark, *The human right to health and its relation to the WTO*, (Stuttgart: Boorberg, 2016), 21-22, and Holger Hestermeyer, "Access to medication as a human right," *Max Planck UNYB*, (2004), 145-6.

88 WHO Constitution, art 1.

89 Ibid. art 2 (c), (e), (u).

90 Johannes Morsink, *Inherent human rights: philosophical roots of the Universal Declaration*, (Philadelphia: University of Pennsylvania Press, 2009), 18.

25, which serves as the leading legal reference regarding the right to health by scholars,[91] treaty bodies,[92] and specialized agencies,[93] protects the right to medical care within the ambit of the right to an adequate standard of living.[94] Access to medical care under the UDHR is broad enough to include medicines. Based on the UDHR, subsequently adopted international human rights treaties also make provisions for the right to health. As the first binding human rights instrument,[95] the International Convention on the Elimination of all Forms Racial Discrimination,[96] like the UDHR, protects the right to medical care, in addition to the right to public health. Its content covers modern medicines.[97] For its part, the ICESCR, like the WHO Constitution, protects everyone's right to enjoy the highest attainable standard of physical and mental health[98]while expressly omitting the social dimension of health.[99] The content of article 12 of the ICESCR comprises medicines as well.[100] Similar to the UDHR, which talks about medical care, the Convention on the Elimination of All Forms of Discrimination Against Women protects women's access to health care services,[101] the content of which includes medicines.[102] Like

91 Baumstark, *Human right to health*, 23.

92 General Comment 14, para 2, and Committee on the Elimination of Discrimination Against Women (CEDAW), General recommendation N°. 24: Article 12 of the Convention (Women and Health), 1999, para 4.

93 World Health Organization and Office of the United Nations High Commissioner for Human Rights, the right to health, Fact Sheet N°31, 2008.

94 Gerd Oberleitner, "Right to health," in *Understanding human rights: manual of human rights education*, ed. Wolfgang Benedek (Graz: European Training and Research Centre for Human Rights and Democracy, 2012), 151.

95 Ineke Boerefijn, *The reporting procedure under the Covenant on Civil and Political Rights. Practice and procedures of the Human Rights Committee* (Cambridge: Intersentia, 1999), 157, Maite San Giorgi, *The human right to equal access to health care* (Cambridge: Intersentia, 2012), 12.

96 International Convention on the Elimination of all Forms Racial Discrimination (ICERD), 1969, art 5 (e) (iv).

97 State parties to the ICERD report on the implementation of the right to health, including health services. See for instance, combined eighth and ninth periodic reports submitted by Kenya under article 9 of the Convention, 2021, p. 26.

98 ICESCR, art 12.

99 In drafting article 12 of the Covenant, the Third Committee of the United Nations General Assembly did not adopt the definition of health contained in the preamble to the Constitution of WHO. General Comment 14, para 4.

100 Ibid. paras 12 and 43.

101 Convention on the Elimination of All Forms of Discrimination Against Women (CEDAW), 1981, art 12.

102 Women's right to health covers services, including medicines and medical care, which prevent, detect and treat illnesses specific to women. See CEDAW Committee,

the WHO Constitution, the Convention on the Rights of the Child[103] and the Convention on the Rights of Persons with Disabilities[104] grant their beneficiaries the right to enjoy the highest attainable standard of health. The content of this right is broad enough to include medicines.[105] Finally, like the UDHR and the ICERD, the International Convention on the Protection of all Migrant Workers and Members of their Families protects the right to receive medical care,[106] which is broad enough to cover medicines. Alongside these human rights treaties, further conventions, declarations, and resolutions address the health of persons and medicines,[107] essential drugs or medicines,[108] primary health care,[109] and access to treatment and care.[110]

The content of these human rights instruments supplements each other to the extent that some provisions are similar, while others contain some minor language differences. Furthermore, given that the right to health under the ICESCR applies to everyone, including children, women, persons with disabilities,[111] its content considers various aspects of the right to health protected in other both general and specific human rights instruments, such as the UDHR, the ICERD, the CEDAW, and CRC.[112] Article 12 of the ICESCR includes essential primary health care and

---

General recommendation N°. 24: Article 12 of the Convention (women and health), 1999 (hereinafter CEDAW General recommendation 24), paras 11 and 12 (d).

103 Children's right to health includes health care services. See Convention on the Rights of the Child (CRC), 1990, art 24.

104 Convention on the Rights of Persons with disabilities, 2008, art 25.

105 Essential medicines are part of children's right to health. See Committee on the Rights of the Child, General comment N°. 15 on the right of the child to the enjoyment of the highest attainable standard of health (art 24), 2013.

106 International Convention on the Protection of the Rights of all Migrant Workers and Members of their Families, 2003, art 28.

107 WHO Framework Convention on Tobacco Control, 2005, art 14 (2) (d). See also UN Human Rights Council, Resolution 12/24 on access to medicine in the context of the right of everyone to the enjoyment of the highest attainable standard of physical and mental health, A/HRC/RES/12/24, 2009.

108 UN General Assembly Resolution A/RES/55/2, United Nations Millennium Declaration, 2000, para 20, UN Security Council Resolution 1308 on the Responsibility of the Security Council in the Maintenance of International Peace and Security: HIV/AIDS and International Peace-keeping Operations, 2000 (hereinafter UN Security Council Resolution 1308). See also Declaration of Alma-Ata on International Conference on Primary Health Care, Alma-Ata, 1978 (henceforth Alma-Ata Declaration), para VII.

109 Alma-Ata Declaration, para VII

110 UN Security Council Resolution 1308.

111 General Comment 14, paras 21-27.

112 Ibid. para 2.

essential medicines defined in the Alma-Ata Declaration and the WHO.[113] Similarly, the content of the right to health under the CEDAW,[114] the CRC,[115] and the Human Rights Council Resolution 12/24[116] considers the right to health protected in other human rights instruments.

The above human rights instruments are relevant for protecting access to medicines in the DRC and URT from various perspectives. For instance, the CESCR, the African Commission, the African Court, or the SADC Tribunal can use them either as sources of law or as interpretative tools while dealing with health issues that involve DRC or URT.[117] Moreover, the DRC[118] and URT[119] consider the State's obligations under the WHO Constitution[120] in implementing the Covenant's right to health. Besides, the UDHR enjoys a special status under the Constitutions of the DRC and URT.[121] In sum, in implementing access to medicines at the domestic level, the DRC and URT can learn from these instruments in one way or another.

---

113 Ibid. para 43.

114 The CEDAW Committee notes the emphasis that the UDHR, the ICESCR, the CRC, and CEFRD place on the right to health and the conditions that enable good health to be achieved. See CEDAW General recommendation 24, para 4.

115 The Committee on the Rights of the Child expressly adopts the definition of health given by the WHO Constitution and the primary health care approach of the Alma-Ata Declaration in interpreting children's right to health under article 24 of the CRC. See Committee on the Rights of the Child, General Comment No. 15 on the right of the child to the enjoyment of the highest attainable standard of health (art 24), 2013, para 4.

116 The Resolution considers the protection of the right to health in the UDHR, the CESCR, and the UN Millennium Declaration. See Human Rights Council Resolution 12/24.

117 Optional Protocol to ICESCR, art 8 (3), African Charter, art 60, African Court Protocol, art 3, and SADC Tribunal Protocol, art 21.

118 In implementing the right to health under the ICESCR, the DRC mentions the adoption of a national strategic tobacco control plan in compliance with the WHO Framework Convention on Tobacco Control. See, Sixième rapport périodique soumis par la République Démocratique du Congo en application des articles 16 et 17 du Pacte, attendu en 2013, 2019 (hereinafter DRC's 2019 Report to the CESCR), para 86.

119 As a WHO Member State, the URT annually reports to the World Health Organization. See the URT's 2009 Report to the CESCR, para 129.

120 WHO Constitution, art 3 and chapter XIV.

121 The DRC Constitution explicitly refers to the UDHR in its preamble and article 45. For its part, Article 9 (f) of the URT Constitution urges State authority and its agencies to preserve and uphold human dignity following the spirit of the UDHR.

2. The concept of medicine and the right to health

None of the human rights treaties providing the right to health at the global, regional, and sub-regional levels mention or define "medicine or drug". Similarly, the African CESCR and the African Commission, which mention essential drugs and essential medicines in General Comment 14[122] and Resolution 141,[123] do not define these two concepts. Despite various studies dealing with access to medicine, the existing scholarly literature proceeds with a tacit understanding of medicine.[124] For a few studies that attempt to define medicines,[125] like the African Commission and the CESCR,[126] they only rely on the definition of essential medicines or drugs provided by the WHO. According to the WHO, essential drugs are "those that satisfy the health care needs of the majority of the population.[127] This definition does not say what a drug is. It is important to recall that the WHO decided to use "essential medicines" as an alternative to essential drugs. It describes essential medicines as those that satisfy the priority health care needs of the population.[128] This definition does not help to understand the concept of medicines. Instead, it stresses the goal and role of essential medicines.

It is worth noting that there is no universal definition for medicines. However, a working definition is of practical interest as it permits distinguishing medicines

122 General Comment 14, para 12 (a).

123 African Commission Resolution 141 on Access to Health and Needed Medicines in Africa, Abuja, 2008 (henceforth African Commission Resolution 141 or Resolution 141).

124 Scholars consider understanding the concept of medicine or drug as self evident. See Laura Niada, The human right to medicines in Sub-Saharan Africa, Thesis, University of Westminster, 2010, available Thesis NADIA LAURA.pdf, accessed 18 June 2020, Raju, K.D., Patent linkages and its impact on access to medicines: challenges, opportunities for developing countries. In: Correa, C.M., Hilty, R.M. (eds) Access to medicines and vaccines (Cham: Springer, 2022): 329-369, Kohler, J.C., Makey, T.K. "Why the COVID-19 pandemic should be a call for action to advance equitable access to medicines." *BM Med* 18, 193 (2020): 1-3, Urias Eduardo and Ramani Shyama V., "Access to medicines after TRIPs: is compulsory licensing an effective mechanism to lower drug prices? A review of the existence evidence." *Journal of International Business Policy*, (2020): 367-384.

125 Although the book title talks about medicines, the author defines only essential medicines. Sellin, Jennifer Anna, *Access to Medicines. The Interface between Patents and Human Rights: Does one size fit all?* (Cambridge: Intersentia, 2014), 24-26.

126 General Comment 14, para 12 (a), and Resolution 141.

127 World Health Organisation, Report of the Expert Committee: the selection and use of essential medicines, in WHO technical report series 914, 2002 (henceforth WHO Report on essential medicines), 14.

128 Ibid. 16.

from other pharmaceutical preparations while separating them from different types of drugs. The working definition also differentiates medicines used in human health from those for animals' health.[129] A combined definition provided by the WHO and the domestic laws of the DRC and URT will fill in this gap. According to the WHO, the term "medicines" is more commonly used to describe pharmaceutical preparations used in clinical health care practice.[130] It means that medicines are part of pharmaceutical preparations, which serve the purpose of clinical health care, such as treating, diagnosing, or controlling diseases. Like the WHO's definition, medicine under the Pharmacy Act in the URT is a synonym for a pharmaceutical product.[131] It means any substance or mixture of substances manufactured for the treatment of diseases or use in the diagnosis or prevention of diseases, disorders, or abnormal physical or mental state, or the symptoms thereof, in man or animal. The phrase clinical health care practice in the WHO's definition means to include treatment, diagnosis, and prevention of diseases, and disorders under the Pharmacy Act. Furthermore, unlike the WHO's description, the Pharmacy Act makes it explicit that medicine is used in man and animal health. Similar to the Pharmacy Act, the Decree regulating the trade of pharmaceuticals in the DRC[132] defines medicine as any substance or composition presented as having curative or preventive properties concerning human or animal diseases. Therefore, one can use medicine to establish a medical diagnosis or restore, correct, or modify human or animal physiological functions.[133] Like under the Pharmacy Act, medicine is a substance or composition that serves to cure, prevent, or diagnose human or animal ailments. Thus, in this thesis, (conventional or modern) medicine means any pharmaceutical product used to treat, prevent, control, and diagnose human diseases, excluding medicine used in animals' health. For its part, drugs will be used as a synonym of medicine only to the extent that they serve the purpose of clinical health care, excluding, therefore, any drugs associated with narcotic or illicit substances.[134]

The expression right to access medicine is a derivative right of the right to health. Therefore, in this dissertation, the right to health should be used as a shorthand expression for the right to "the enjoyment of the highest attainable standard of physical and mental health," the right to "enjoy the best attainable state of physical and mental health," the right to "health care," and "health services and universal

129 Medicines also treat and prevent diseases in animals. See Regulation (EU) 2019/6 of the European Parliament and of the Council on veterinary medicinal products and repealing Directive 2001/82/EC, 2018, art 4 (1).

130 WHO Report on essential medicines, 13.

131 Pharmacy Act, art 2.

132 Decree on the trade of pharmaceuticals, art 1 (22).

133 Ibid.

134 WHO, Report on essential medicines, 13.

HIV and AIDs treatment" protected in the ICESCR, the African Charter, the SADC Treaty, the SADC Health Protocol, and the SADC Gender Protocol. Under the domestic laws, the right to health refers to the rights to "health" and "social welfare in case of sickness," and "other human rights" argued in the DRC's and the URT's Constitutions.

3. Protection of access to medicines under the ICESCR

The present section discusses the protection of access to medicines under article 12 of the ICESCR as part of the right to health. It further outlines the nature of the State´s obligations with respect to access to medicines and the enforcement mechanism to that.

a. Access to medicines as part of the right to health

Article 12 of the ICESCR reads as follows,

> The States Parties to the present Covenant recognize the right of everyone to the enjoyment of the highest attainable standard of physical and mental health. The steps to be taken by the States Parties to the present Covenant to achieve the full realization of this right shall include those necessary for the provision for the reduction of the stillbirth-rate and of infant mortality and for the healthy development of the child, the improvement of all aspects of environmental and industrial hygiene; the prevention, treatment, and control of epidemic, endemic, occupational and other diseases, the creation of conditions which would assure to all medical service and medical attention in the event of sickness.

Compared with the WHO's threefold dimension of health, article 12 under discussion does not explicitly cover the social aspect of health.[135] In providing for "the enjoyment of the highest attainable standard of physical and mental health under article 12, State parties cannot guarantee absolute physical and mental health. Due to the covenant silence on the definition of the concept "highest attainable standard of physical and mental health," commentators suggest that the right to health herein protected lies somewhere between the too-demanding idea of a right to be healthy and the too-limited idea of a right merely to health care.[136] Though article 12 does not expressly use the word access to medicines, it protects medicines

---

135 General Comment 14, para 1. See also Morsink, *Inherent human rights*, 247.

136 Jonathan Wolf, "The content of the human right to health," in *Philosophical foundations of human rights*, eds. Rowan Cruft, S. Matthew Liao, and Massimo Renzo (Oxford: Oxford Scholarship Online, 2015), 492, Kimberley Brownlee, "Do we have a human right to the political determinants of health?," in *Philosophical foundations of human rights*, eds. Rowan Cruft, S. Matthew Liao, and Massimo Renzo (Oxford: Oxford Scholarship Online, 2015), 502, Morsink, *Inherent human rights*, 186.

as part of the highest attainable standard of living for physical and mental health. An illustration is the objectives assigned to the steps that States shall take for the full realization of the right to health under article 12 (2). For instance, the reduction of the stillbirth rate and infant mortality, which is linked to the rights to life and full and free development of human personalities,[137] cannot fully be achieved without appropriate access to medicines. The same applies to the role of medicines in the prevention, treatment, and control of diseases as an integral, vital, and indispensable part of the therapy.[138] Finally, the creation of conditions for medical service and medical attention in the event of sickness implies the availability of, and accessibility to, medicines as an essential component of both medical service and medical attention. This assertion is further supported by the CESCR's General Comment 14 on the normative content of article 12 of the ICESCR, as discussed in the next section.

aa) General Comment 14 and article 12 of the ICESCR

The CESCR provides the essential normative elements of article 12 of the ICESCR through the General Comment 14. It is worth recalling that neither the ICESCR nor the Economic and Social Council resolution 1985/17 of 28 May 1985 establishing the CESCR expressly provides the CESCR's competence to issue general comments. This legal gap is filled in through a combined reading of the ECOSOC resolution 1987/5[139] as endorsed by the GA resolution A/RES/42/102,[140] and the ECSCR report on the second session.[141] According to the CESCR's report on the second session

> The Committee would endeavor through its general comments to make the experience gained so far through the examination of these reports available for the benefit of all States parties in order to promote their further implementation of the Covenant; draw the attention of the States parties to insufficiencies disclosed by a large number of reports; suggest improvements in the reporting procedures and stimulate the activities of the States parties, the international organizations, and the specialized agencies concerned in achieving progressively and effectively the full realization of the rights recognised in the Covenant.[142]

137 Morsink, *Inherent human rights*, 248.

138 Hestermeyer, "Access to medication," 104.

139 Resolution 1987/5 26, May 1987.

140 Adopted on 7 December 1987, the resolution A/RES/42/102 endorses the invitation to the CESCR by the ECOSOC to make general comments in the light of the Human Rights Committee. See resolution 42/102, paras 5-6.

141 Committee on Economic, Social and Cultural Rights, Report on the second session, 1988, paras 366-369.

142 Ibid. para 369.

It follows from this quote that the aim of the general comment is to assist State parties to adequately implement all the Covenant's rights, including through the improvement of their periodic reports. Despite the controversy about their legal nature,[143] general comments constitute the most suitable of the CESCR´s tools to clarify the normative content of the Covenant and provide the most comprehensible and clear survey of the CESCR's position.[144] Therefore, any study on access to medicine under the ICESCR and the nature of State's obligations to that should consider the CESCR's interpretation of the relevant provisions through its General Comment 14.[145] Based on the CESCR's experience in examining States parties' reports on the right to health over many years, the General Comment 14 exclusively deals with article 12 of the ICESCR.[146] It contains five parts dealing respectively with the normative content of article 12, States parties' obligations, violations and implementation at the national level, and the obligations of non-State actors.[147]

bb) Essential normative elements of article 12

As part of article 12 of the ICESCR, medicines shall be available, accessible, acceptable, and of good quality.[148] Availability means that medicines are available in sufficient quantity within each State party. Accessibility comprises non-discrimination, physical, economic, and information accessibility. Physical accessibility implies the possibility for all sections of the population, including vulnerable and marginalized groups, to access medicines in both urban and rural areas.[149] Focus on rural areas is due to the fact that, in most cases, health services are often available in urban areas. At the same time, most people, including vulnerable and marginalized groups, live in rural areas. Economic accessibility requires that medicines are affordable for all. Since access to medicines is not free of charge,[150] the principle

---

143 Some authors argue that State parties are directly bound to the Covenant rather than to the general comments. See Baumstark, *Human right to health*, 25-26. Whereas others think that, even though general comments are not legally binding, they can still be used as interpretative tools. See, Markus Krajewski, "Human rights and austerity programmes," *SSRN*, 2013, https://ssrn.com/abstract=2199625 (accessed January 15, 2019).

144 Magdalena Sepúlveda, *The nature of the obligations under the International Covenant on Economic, Social and Cultural Rights* (Cambridge: Intersentia, 2003), 41.

145 Ibid., 73. See also Krajewski, "Human rights and austerity," 6.

146 General Comment 14, para 6.

147 General Comment 14.

148 Ibid. para 12.

149 Ibid. para 12 (b) (ii).

150 The only exception may be drawn from article 12 (2) of the CEDAW, which suggests that States parties shall ensure to women appropriate services in connection with pregnancy, confinement, and the post-natal period, granting free services where necessary.

of equity in user fees demands that poorer households should not be disproportionately burdened with health expenses as compared to richer households. For its part, acceptability requires that medicines are respectful of the culture of individuals, minorities, peoples, and communities.[151] Quality demands that medicines are unexpired and are scientifically and medically appropriate. In addition, medicines should be of decent quality, and should be rationally used while their storage should be in clean, dry and well-sanitized areas.[152] All these four elements supplement each other and should go hand in hand. However, sometimes, they come into conflict with each other from different perspectives. According to Hestermeyer,[153] for the sake of medicines' quality, their availability can be severely limited during the lengthy trials necessary for their safety and effectiveness. Furthermore, even after the completion of trials, the financial accessibility of people, especially in poor countries, is affected due to the fact that manufacturers of medicines will often offset the trial cost.[154]

b. The nature of the State's obligations

The full implementation of article 12 of the ICESCR depends on the Covenant's general provisions, namely articles 2, 3, 4, and 5. Article 2 provides general obligations for implementing all the Covenant's rights. For their part, articles 3 to 5 constitute the underlying principles guiding all ESCRs' implementation and amount to the State's obligations.[155] However, the present section focuses on the general and specific duties of State parties under articles 2 and 12 of the ICESCR. It further considers their interpretation by the CESCR through its various issued General Comments, the clarification, and guidance to help State parties meet their human rights obligations.[156]

aa) General obligations

Article 2 consists of paragraphs 1, 2[157] and 3.[158] This subsection focuses on article 2 (1), which reads as follows,

---

151 General Comment 14, para 12 (c).

152 Report of the Special Rapporteur on the right of everyone to the enjoyment of the highest attainable standard of physical and mental health, 2013, paras 55, 57 and 61, General Comment 14, para 12 (d).

153 Hestermeyer, "Access to medication," 105-106.

154 Ibid.

155 Committee on Economic, Social and Cultural Rights, General Comment No. 16: The equal right of men and women to the enjoyment of all economic, social and cultural rights (art 3 of the ICESCR), 2005, para 2.

156 Krajewski, "Human rights and austerity," 6.

157 Art 2 (2) of the ICESCR deals with the principle of non-discrimination.

158 The inclusion of article 2 (3) was proposed by the delegate of Indonesia to protect the rights of the nationals of former colonies which had recently gained independence at the time of drafting, in which there were powerful economic groups of

> Each State Party to the present Covenant undertakes to take steps, individually and through international assistance and cooperation, especially economic and technical, to the maximum of its available resources, with a view to achieving progressively the full realization of the rights recognized in the present Covenant by all appropriate means, including particularly the adoption of legislative measures.

Four main points may derive from this Covenant's provision. First, it sets forth each State party's main obligation which is: achieving progressively the full realization of all the Covenant's rights, including access to medicines. This obligation considers the difficulties involved in any country,[159] by referring to, among others, available resources. At the same time, it cannot serve as an excuse for States to engage only in negligible steps towards the realization of ESCRs claiming lack of resources.[160] In other words, from the entry into force of the ICESCR, each State party should make continuous efforts towards the full realization of each Covenant's right. As Coomans points out, the idea of progressive realization in article 2(1) at hand embodies a dynamic element, which means that realization does not stop when the State has reached a certain level.[161]

Secondly, to attain the above principal obligation, the provision calls for taking steps by all appropriate means, including the adoption of legislative measures. Explicit mention to the legislative measures illustrates those reasonable means, which shall extend to policies, judicial, administrative, and financial measures.[162] No matter the nature of the steps to be adopted, what counts is their capability to be appropriate and achieve the intended goals. These steps are supposed to be "deliberate, concrete and targeted as clearly as possible towards meeting the obligations recognized in the Covenant."[163]

Thirdly, the reference to the undertaking of steps individually, coupled with the notion of available resources within a State party, emphasizes that the protection of access to medicines remains and remains mainly the domestic business of each State party as an attribute of its sovereignty. Finally, since resources include those available within the international community,[164] it is each State party's duty to expressly seek international assistance and cooperation from and with other State parties, intending to implement access to medicines.[165]

---

non-nationals in control of important sectors of economy. Sepúlveda, *Nature of the obligations*, 414-415.

159 CESCR General Comment No. 3: The nature of States Parties' obligations (art 2, para. 1, of the Covenant), 1990 (hereinafter General Comment 3), para 9.

160 Krajewski, "Human rights and austerity," 12.

161 Fons Coomans, "Identifying the key elements of the right to education: A focus on its core content," *Child Rights Information Network*, (2007): 2.

162 General Comment 3, para 9.

163 Ibid. para 2.

164 Ibid. paras 13 and 14.

165 ICESCR, arts 17 (2), 22 and 23.

bb) Specific obligations under article 12

The first specific obligation deriving from article 12 of the ICESCR is the legal recognition of the right to health under all the State parties' domestic laws.[166] For State parties to the ICESCR, including the DRC and URT, article 12 of the ICESCR constitutes one of the legal bases for protecting the right to health within their jurisdictions. To this end, article 27 (2) of the ICESCR states that the ICESCR enters into force three months after the date of the deposit of its instrument of ratification or instrument of accession by the State concerned. The entry into force of a treaty such as the ICESCR has legal consequences upon the State parties. It binds all State parties and obligates them to perform all the provisions of the ICESCR in good faith.[167] The second specific obligation relates to protecting the child's right to health, including access to medicines, before and after birth. The same duty extends to the pregnant woman's right to health due to efforts aiming to reduce stillbirth-rate and infant mortality. The third specific obligation concerns everyone and aims to prevent, treat and control diseases. Applied to medicines, it implies that drugs are crucial for preventing, treating and controlling diseases. The last specific obligation links to the third one and also applies to everyone in the event of sickness. It consists of creating conditions that assure all medical service and medical attention in the event of illness. Its full realization necessitates the delivery of medicines. This obligation fits well with a narrowly defined threshold of the right to health and is probably the step most readers think of when it comes to the human right to health care.[168]

In sum, article 12 (2) of the ICESCR considers each State party's latitude to decide the nature of steps to be taken in order to achieve the full realization of access to medicines. Without undermining the other State obligations provided under the Covenant, the establishment of an appropriate national health system is of paramount importance in implementing this Covenant's provision. Alongside the specific obligations of State parties under article 12 of the ICESCR, the CESCR has developed the trilogy approach and the minimum core obligation as discussed below.

cc) Obligations to respect, protect and fulfil

Like all human rights, access to medicines gives rise to the obligations to respect, protect and fulfil.[169] The duty to respect includes refraining from denying or limiting equal access for all persons to health services and abstaining from enforcing

166 Samantha Besson, "Human rights and constitutional law: patterns of mutual validation and legitimation," in *Philosophical foundations of human rights*, eds. Rowan Cruft, S. Matthew Liao, and Massimo Renzo (Oxford: Oxford Scholarship Online, 2015), 289. See also URT's Report to the CESCR, 2009, para 109.

167 Vienna Convention on the Law of Treaties, art 26.

168 Morsink, *Inherent human rights*, 249.

169 General Comment 14, para 33.

discriminatory practices as a State policy. For its part, the obligation to protect entails the State's responsibility to regulate the practice of medicine by non-state actors through controlling medicines' marketing, and ensuring that medical practitioners and other health professionals meet appropriate standards of education, skill and ethical codes of conduct.[170] The responsibility to protect considers the fact that in providing health care services, individuals perform a part of the State's sovereignty.[171] Therefore, it is the State's responsibility to use price controls for the medicine to discourage any monopolistic pricing that can lead to the excessive cost of drugs[172]and fight the sale of drugs of poor quality.[173] However, due to the lack of technical capacity, financial and human resources, some developing countries' regulators still rely on outdated methods and processes for enforcement of quality control.[174] As a result, substandard and falsified medicines in these countries can be the only ones to reach the poor.[175]

Finally, the duty to fulfil that includes the obligation to facilitate, provide and promote, requires States to undertake actions that create, maintain, and restore the population's health, including local production of medicines.[176] Based on the idea that the adoption of positive steps contributes to greater enjoyment of rights, ESCRs, including access to medicines, are the prime example of rights where "not doing anything is not an option."[177]

In sum, the above CESCR's typology of State's obligations is a useful conceptual device to identify different ways State parties can and must discharge their obligations specific to international human rights law.[178] Failure to comply with these three obligations through commissions[179] and omission[180] amounts to the Covenant violation.

170 Ibid. para 35.
171 Chirwa, "The right to health," 561-562.
172 Special Rapporteur Report 2006, para 75, and Special Rapporteur Report 2013, paras 20-21.
173 World Health Organisation: Counterfeit medicines, Fact Sheet N°275, 2006 (hereinafter WHO Fact Sheet 275), 1-2.
174 Special Rapporteur Report 2013, para 65.
175 See WHO Fact Sheet 275, and Special Rapporteur Report 2006, para 72.
176 Special Rapporteur Report 2013, para 14.
177 Frédéric Mégret, "Nature of obligations," in *International Human Rights Law*, eds. Moeckli, Shah, Sivakumaran, 2nd ed, (Oxford: Oxford University Press, 2014), 103.
178 Ibid. 103-104.
179 General Comment 14, para 48.
180 Ibid, para 49.

dd) *Minimum core obligation and minimum essential level of access to medicines*

The CESCR undertakes efforts to elucidate the nature of the State's obligations towards ESCRs, including the right to health, described as vague and open-ended.[181]To this end, it has identified a minimum core obligation incumbent upon every State party to ensure the satisfaction of, at the very least, minimum essential levels of each of the rights.[182] Interestingly, providing primary health care and essential drugs constitutes a minimum essential level of the right to health.[183] Given that the word drug sometimes is associated with narcotics or illicit substances, the WHO uses essential medicines[184] as an alternative to essential drugs. Essential medicines satisfy the priority health care needs of the population.[185] Their selection criteria include, among others, public health relevance, evidence on efficacy and safety, and comparative cost-effectiveness.[186] Essential medicines serve the purpose of being available within the context of functioning health systems at all times in adequate amounts, in the appropriate dosage forms, with assured quality and adequate information, and at an affordable price.[187] It is worth noting that each country has the responsibility to define its list of essential medicines.[188] The DRC and URT have each a list of essential medicines.[189]

The thinking behind the minimum core obligation is that the provisions of the ICESCR must have a minimum element of responsibilities without which they could not be considered law.[190] However, the legal consequence of non-compliance with the minimum core obligation seems controversial. For instance, under General Comment 3, State parties can justify the failure to comply with their minimum obligations if they demonstrate that they have used all resources at their disposal to satisfy their minimum duties as a matter of priority.[191] For its part, the General Comment 14 does not allow any State's justifications about non-compliance with

181 Coomans, "Identifying the key elements," 1, Alicia Ely Yamin, "The future in the mirror: incorporating strategies for the defence and promotion of economic, social, and cultural rights into the mainstream human rights agenda," *HRQ*, (2005): 1214.
182 General Comment 3, para 10.
183 Ibid. See also General Comment 14, paras 43 and 44.
184 WHO Report on essential medicines, 3.
185 Ibid.
186 Ibid.
187 Ibid.
188 Ibid.
189 Ministère de la Santé publique de la République Démocratique du Congo: Liste nationale des médicaments essentiels, 2010, the National Essential Medicine List for Tanzania (NEMLIT), 2007, and Ministry of Health and Social Welfare, Standard treatment Guidelines and essential medicines list, 4th ed., 2013.
190 General Comment 3, para 3, Krajewski, "Human rights and austerity," 13.
191 General Comment 3, para 10. See also Hestermeyer, Access to medication, 142-3.

the minimum core obligation, which is non-derogable.[192] Although General Comment 14 urges State parties and other actors to assist and provide international assistance and cooperation, which enable developing countries to fulfil their core obligation, it subjects all State parties, including developed and the least developed countries, to the same minimum core obligations.[193] The CESCR's interpretation of the State's core obligation can appear unrealistic, especially for least developed countries, such as the DRC and URT. One cannot tell, whether, despite their limited resources, the DRC and URT have met to date their core obligations regarding the provision of essential medicines.

The language differences between General Comment 3 and General Comment 14 can justify criticisms against the concept of minimum core obligation by scholars[194] and some national judicial institutions.[195] However, about 30 years since the passing of General Comment 3 and 20 years since General Comment 14 was passed, State parties, including the DRC and URT, do not address the minimum core obligations regarding essential medicines in their reports. Like State's reports, the CESCR's concluding observations are also silent in that regard. While subscribing to the CESCR's approach in General Comment 3, the State's justification for non-compliance with its minimum core obligations regarding essential medicines is of no practical relevance at the current stage of the CESCR's works and practices.

c. *Enforcement mechanisms for access to medicine under the ICESCR*

Thirty-seven years after the coming into force of the ICESCR, the state reporting procedure was the only foreseen protection mechanism for all the Covenant's rights. Compared to the 1976 International Covenant on Civil and Political Rights (ICCPR), the ICESCR was subject to criticism since it lacked an individual communication procedure. However, the coming into force of the Optional Protocol to ICESCR sends back this criticism to the past.[196] Indeed, currently, protection mechanisms for access to medicine under the ICESCR extend to individual and

---

192 General Comment 14, para 47.

193 Ibid.

194 Lisa Forman et al., "Conceptualising minimum core obligations under the right to health: How should we define and implement the 'morality of the depths'," *International Journal of Human Rights*, (2016): 6 and 17.

195 Government of the Republic of South Africa and others vs. Grootboom and others, 2001 (1) SA 46 (CC), paras 32-33.

196 Lilian Chenwi and Danwood M. Chirwa, "Direct protection of economic, social and cultural rights in international law," in *The protection of economic, social and cultural rights in Africa: International, regional and national perspectives*, eds. Danwood Mzikenge Chirwa and Lilian Chenwi (Cambridge: Cambridge University Press, 2016), 40.

inter-State communications, and the inquiry procedure. Except for the state reporting, which is mandatory and binds all the State parties to the ICESCR upon ratification, other protection mechanisms are optional, as they only apply to those State parties that have ratified the Optional Protocol and its prescribed conditions.[197] Moreover, unlike the reporting procedure, other protection mechanisms have in common alleged violation of ESCRs as triggers for their activation.

aa) Mandatory enforcement mechanism: State reporting procedure

Articles 16 and 17 of the ICESCR urge State parties to submit to the UN Secretary-General reports on the adopted measures, and the progress made in achieving the observance of all ESCRs, including access to medicines. These reports also indicate factors and difficulties affecting the degree of fulfilment of the Covenant's obligations. The state reporting mechanism serves as a self-evaluation and oversight procedure.[198] To this end, it provides a basis on which the State party concerned, the CESCR, the UN, and its agencies, and other State parties can effectively evaluate the progress made towards realizing the Covenant's obligations.[199] Due to the increasing backlog of States' reports on the implementation of the ICESCR and upon the UNGA's request to the ECOSOC on the rearrangement of the reporting procedure,[200] State parties submit an initial report two years after the entry into force of the ICESCR, and a periodic report within five years' intervals. While the initial report aims to ensure that the State party has undertaken a comprehensive review concerning national legislation, administrative rules and procedures, and practices to ensure conformity with the Covenant, periodic reports provide information on the progress over time for the practical realization of the relevant rights.[201] Such time periods are necessary since it allows State parties to take measures that progressively lead to the full implementation of the right of access to medicines. However, it still seems not to be enough for State parties, such as the URT and the DRC, which do not submit their periodic reports to the CESCR regularly.[202]

197 Optional Protocol to ICESCR, arts 1 (2), 10 (1) and 11 (1).

198 Chenwi and Chirwa, "Direct protection of ESCRs," 68.

199 Committee on Economic, Social and Cultural Rights, General Comment No. 1: Reporting by States parties, 1981 (hereinafter General Comment 1), and UN GA Resolution A/RES/42/105 on "Reporting obligations of States parties to United Nations instruments on human rights," 1987, para 9.

200 Resolution A/RES/42/105, para 9, ECOSOC Resolution 1988/4, 1988, art 6. See also CESCR, Provisional rules of procedure of the Committee, 1993.

201 General Comment 1, paras 2 and 7.

202 For instance, while the URT submitted its initial report in 1979, its subsequent periodic reports were submitted in 2009. See URT's Report to the CESCR, 2009, para 2. For its part, while the DRC's initial report was submitted only in 1987, its

According to article 16 (2) (a) of the ICESCR, the UN Secretary-General submits to the ECOSOC for consideration received State reports. It is worth recalling that since the adoption by the ECOSOC of Resolution 1985/15 of 28 May 1985, the CESCR has carried out the monitoring functions assigned to the ECOSOC under the ICESCR. The CESCR's power in examining the State reports depends on the submission or not of State reports. In case of non-submission of State reports, the CESCR's power remains toothless since it has no legal means at its disposal to push these States to comply with their Covenant's obligations. All it can do is recommend to the ECOSOC to transmit a reminder to the State party involved.[203] If the State party concerned fails to comply with the ECOSOC's reminder, the CESCR should consider such a failure in its annual report.

In examining the received reports, the CESCR makes suggestions or recommendations to the State party concerned in concluding observations, which specify questions that require urgent attention and the date of the following periodic report's presentation.[204] The concluding observations made by the CESCR provide valuable insights on both general and specific State's obligations concerning the Covenant's right.

(1) DRC's report and the CESCR's concluding observations

The DRC ratified the ICESCR on 1 November 1976 and submitted its initial report only in 1987 without information about article 12 of the ICESCR.[205] Its subsequent periodic reports were submitted respectively in 2007[206] and 2019.[207] Accordingly, the 2007 report mentions article 47 of the DRC Constitution on the right to health as part of article 12 of the ICESCR. Information regarding the implementation of the constitutional right to health includes studies and some government efforts conducted or made before the coming into force of the DRC Constitution.[208] The report acknowledges the role of international assistance in the implementation of the right to health. To this end, it mentions efforts made by some UN agencies such as the United Nations Population Fund, WHO, and the International Committee of the Red Cross in the area of reproductive health, sexually transmitted diseases,

---

subsequent reports were submitted in 2007. See the Democratic Republic of the Congo, Combined second to fifth periodic reports submitted under articles 16 and 17 of the Covenant (hereinafter DRC's Report to the CESCR, 2007), paras 1-4.

203 Rules 59 of the CESCR's provisional rules of procedure, and Resolution 1988/4, art 3.

204 Rules 64 and 78 (1) of the CESCR's provisional rules of procedure

205 This is made explicit by the heading of the report, "Reports submitted by States parties to the Covenant, in accordance with Council resolution 1988 (LX), concerning rights covered by articles 13-15."

206 DRC's Report to the CESCR, 2007, para 4.

207 DRC's Report to the CESCR, 2019.

208 DRC's Report to the CESCR, 2007, paras 245-248.

and HIV/AIDS.[209] The provision of international aid considers the country's developmental level and challenges faced in implementing all the aspects of the right to health.

The report also mentions factors that impede the full realization of the right to health. These include the deterioration of socioeconomic conditions, including health infrastructure, geographical challenges to reach health facilities, and the high cost of medications vis-à-vis low-income levels for the majority of inhabitants.[210]

According to the 2019 report, the government has allocated about 8% of the general budget to the health sector in 2018. Further efforts giving effect to the right to health include the adoption of the 2016-2020 Health National Development Plan, the equipment and rehabilitation of some health facilities, the reduction of the rate of maternal and infant mortality, and treatment for people affected by HIV and AIDs.[211] Interestingly, the report also refers to the pharmacy inspectors in charge of medicines' quality control.[212] However, unlike the 2007 report, the 2019 report does not inform about the encountered challenges in the implementation of the right to health. Moreover, these two reports are silent about the specific measures dealing with access to medicines, such as compliance with the minimum core obligations.

The CESCR has not yet issued its concluding observations to the DRC's 2019 report. Regarding its concluding observations to the DRC's 2007 report,[213] they commend the adoption by the DRC of the new Constitution in 2006, the Child Law, the HIV Law, the Labour Law, and the Mining Code.[214] Although both the reports and the CESCR do not make it explicit, some provisions of these legal instruments are relevant for the enjoyment of access to medicines in the DRC. Moreover, the CESCR identifies the persistent instability and recurrent armed conflicts in some of the provinces in the country, the lack of judicial and other remedies for violations of ESCRs, corruption and mismanagement of international cooperation aid and unbalanced budgetary allocations[215]as principal subjects of concern. These concerns highlight the DRC's non-compliance with its general obligations as argued under the Covenant's articles 2 (1), (2), and 3, which may impact the implementation of access to medicines. The CESCR noted that in some parts of the country, people

209 Ibid. paras 282-283.

210 The source of this information is a study conducted in 2001. Ibid. para 268.

211 DRC's report to the CESCR, 2019, paras 76, and 81.

212 Ibid. para 76.

213 CESCR, concluding observations to the combined second to fourth reports of the Democratic Republic of the Congo, 2009 (hereinafter CESCR concluding observations to DRC, 2009).

214 Ibid. paras 4-5.

215 Ibid. paras 6, 8, 10, 11 and 16.

died from preventable and treatable illnesses, and that most of the health districts were no longer functioning, leaving 37% of the population deprived of any form of healthcare, whilst some people could not access available health services due to user fees.[216]

However, the concluding observations by the CESCR do not consider in an appropriate way the elements of availability, accessibility, and quality of access to medicines. In addition to some requests and recommendations of general nature,[217] the CESCR urged the DRC to allocate 15% of its budget to building a sustainable health system.[218] The DRC's 2019 report to the CESCR, as above discussed, reveals that the government has never fulfilled this recommendation on the budget allocation.

(2) URT's report and the CESCR's concluding observations

The URT ratified the ICESCR on 11 September 1976, and it submitted its initial report in 1979.[219] Unlike the DRC, the URT's initial report expressly dealt with article 12 by providing information on the government's emphasis on preventive and non-preventive services, including provision of free access to medical care.[220] It took about 30 years before the URT submitted a consolidated first to third periodic report in 2009.[221] The report provides information about the allocation of 11% of the general budget to the health sector for 2008-2009, the government effort to tackle mental health, reproductive rights, and the training of health personnel.[222] It further explicitly mentions the National HIV/AIDS Policy, the National Multi-Sectoral Strategic Framework on HIV and AIDS 2008–2012 among implementation measures for the right to health.[223] Moreover, the report reveals that following the Tanzanian "sharing cost policy" regarding access to healthcare, pregnant women, children under five, people with disability, people with HIV, and elderly, have free access to health care services, while vaccinations against dangerous diseases and treatment for these diseases are free of charge for everyone. Furthermore, the report identifies poverty as the main encountered challenge to the implementation of the Covenant's rights, including access to medicines.[224]

---

216 Ibid. para 34.
217 Ibid. paras 37-42.
218 Ibid. para 34.
219 The United Republic of Tanzania, Reports submitted in accordance with Council resolution 1988 (LX) by States parties to the Covenant concerning rights covered by articles 10 to 12, 1979.
220 Ibid.
221 The present report complements pre1990 initial reports and covers those which are overdue since 1990. URT's Report to the CESCR, 2009, paras 1-2.
222 Ibid. paras, 110, 112, 113 and 120.
223 Ibid. paras 119, 122, and 123.
224 Ibid. paras 165-166.

The CESCR has issued its concluding observations in 2012,[225] in which it commends, among other things, the establishment of the Prevention and Combating of Corruption Bureau and the adoption of the Persons with Disabilities Act. However, it condemns the lack of legal and non-legal remedies for violation of ESCRs, the prevalence of corruption, and challenges faced by women in rural and remote areas in accessing health services. In other words, these subjects of concern are inconsistent with the State's obligations to implement all the ESCRs, including access to medicines without discrimination and within the available resources as argued in articles 2, 3, and 12 of the ICESCR. Moreover, the CESCR is concerned about the lack of universal healthcare coverage, the shortage of qualified healthcare professionals, shortages in medical supplies in rural clinics, and difficulties in access to healthcare centres owing to how far they are from villages.[226]

Accordingly, the CESCR urges the URT to intensify steps to ensure universal healthcare coverage, including through allocation of increased resources, adequate provision of medical equipment and staff at health centres, and ensuring coverage of health-care services for rural villages.[227]

In sum, the discussion of the state reporting procedure has indicated that both DRC and URT have already taken different measures to give effect to access to medicines. It has also revealed that the CESCR has identified some subjects of concern in the enjoyment of the right of access to medicines and has made some recommendations accordingly. However, in addition to being incomplete, reports from DRC and URT do not adequately deal with the elements of availability, accessibility, and quality of medicines, nor do they contain information about the State's compliance with its minimum core obligations relating to essential medicines. Like the State parties, the CESCR examines received reports in isolation from the notions that it has developed in its General Comments, such as the core minimum obligations.

bb) Optional enforcement mechanisms

Optional enforcement mechanisms only apply to the State parties that have ratified the Optional Protocol to ICESCR.[228] They include communications, inter-State communications, and the inquiry procedure. Unlike communications, which bind State parties to the Optional Protocol to the ICESCR upon ratification, the inter-State communications and the inquiry procedure are subject to an additional and express declaration from each State party.[229] It is worth recalling that the DRC,

---

225 CESCR, concluding observations on the initial to third reports of the United Republic of Tanzania, 2012 (hereinafter CESCR's concluding observations to URT 2012).

226 CESCR's concluding observations to URT 2012.

227 Ibid. paras 30-34.

228 The DRC and URT are not parties to the Optional Protocol.

229 The declaration can also be withdrawn. Optional Protocol to ICESCR, arts 10 and 11.

unlike the URT, has already signed the Optional Protocol, expressing its intent to access the Optional Protocol in the future. Nevertheless, the accession to the Optional Protocol by DRC and URT gives rise to some concerns when considering their attitude toward individual complaints procedure before the African Court. Indeed, unlike the CESCR, which can only issue views, the African Court is competent to enforce the Covenant's right to health through binding judgments.[230] While the DRC has never recognized the African Court's jurisdiction to receive individual complaints, the URT has withdrawn[231] the authorization allowing the African Court's competence in that regard. Furthermore, as will be seen throughout this study, the URT is among the African States which refuse to implement the African Court's judgments and orders issued against them.[232] One cannot tell why the DRC and URT would allow their citizens to seek remedies regarding the violation of access to medicines through the CESCR's views issued in Geneva while preventing them from obtaining binding judgments and orders from the African Court located in Africa. Also, it is not clear whether African State parties to the Optional Protocol, which permanently fail to implement the African Court's judgments, can comply with the non-binding CESCR's views and recommendations.

The Optional Protocol establishes a trust fund to provide expert and technical assistance to States Parties, with the consent of the State Party concerned, for the enhanced implementation of the rights contained in the Covenant.[233] Being party to the Optional Protocol and getting involved in one of the procedures herein established are the main conditions for benefiting from the trust fund. However, limiting access to the trust fund to State parties to the Optional Protocol conflicts with the subtitle of article 14 of the Optional Protocol dealing with "international assistance and cooperation." Therefore, as part of article 2 (1) of the ICESCR, the trust fund should profit all State parties to the ICESCR, and address all challenges and obstacles relating to the implementation of ESCRs identified in the State's reports.[234] In sum, like some African State parties to the ICESCR,[235] the DRC and URT are urged to become parties to the Optional Protocol.

---

230 African Court Protocol, art 3.

231 Activity report of the African Court on Human and Peoples' Rights: 1 January-31 December 2020, 2021 (henceforth African Court Activity report 2021), para 39.

232 Of the over 100 judgments and orders rendered by the African Court as of February 2021, only Burkina Faso had fully complied with the judgments of the Court. Ibid. para 37.

233 Optional Protocol to ICESCR, art 14 (3).

234 ICESCR, arts 22 and 23.

235 The four African State parties to the Optional Protocol as of December 2021 are Niger, Gabon, Central African Republic, and Cabo Verde.

cc) Execution and enforcement of the CESCR's decisions

The efficacy of the CESCR's decisions resulting from the fulfilment of its supervisory functions depends significantly on its power to enforce them. In the context of the state reporting procedure, the CESCR's decisions take the form of suggestions and recommendations of general nature.[236] It is the responsibility of the State party concerned to implement them voluntarily. In case of non-compliance, however, the CESCR has no power to compel the State party concerned to comply with its recommendations. Instead, it has developed a parallel practice, which consists of requesting the State party, which does not comply with its concluding observations,[237] to report on any action taken in response to its decisions in its subsequent reports. This kind of follow-up weakens the effectiveness of the established protection mechanisms under the ICESCR. As indicated earlier, in the state reporting procedure, State parties can purposely opt not to report at all or partly report without consideration of the CESCR's recommendations from the previous report.

B. Protection of access to medicines under the African human rights law

The DRC and URT are Member States of the African Union, which have ratified various human rights instruments adopted within the framework of this regional organization, including the African Charter. The present section provides a brief historical background towards the recognition of the right to health within the AU framework. It further focuses on the protection of access to medicines under the African Charter.

1. Towards the recognition of health as a human right within the AU framework

The Charter that has created the Organisation of African Unity (OAU) in 1963[238] did not expressly use the concept of human rights nor use that of the right to health. Instead, article II (2) urged all Member States to coordinate and harmonize their general policies, especially in the fields of health, sanitation, and nutritional cooperation. Like the UN Charter, the OAU Charter expressly subjected health issues to the principle of cooperation among all Member States. Moreover, like

236 These refer to the CESCR's decisions resulting from the examination of State's reports. See Rule 64 of the CESCR Rule of Procedure.

237 CESCR's concluding observations to URT 2012, and CESCR's concluding observations to DRC, 2009.

238 The OAU was created by the Organization of African Unity Charter, which was adopted in 1963 (hereinafter OAU Charter).

the UN Charter, the OAU Charter called for the establishment by its Assembly of specialized commissions, including the Health Commission.[239] Since 2000, the Constitutive Act of the AU has replaced the OAU Charter, supplementing, therefore, its shortcomings concerning human rights. The AU Act erects the protection and promotion of human and peoples' rights into both the objective and principle of the AU.[240] Furthermore, like the UN Charter and the OAU, article 14 (1) (f) of the AU Act establishes the Committee on Health, Labour, and Social Affairs as one of the specialized Technical Committees responsible for health-related issues.

Twenty-three years after the adoption of the OAU, the African Charter came into force as the first and foremost African human rights treaty.[241] Article 16 of the African Charter protects every individual's right to enjoy the best attainable state of physical and mental health, including medical attention in case of sickness. African countries have adopted several subsequent human rights instruments dealing with the right to health within the framework of the OAU[242] and the AU either as autonomous human rights instruments or as Protocols to the African Charter. For instance, according to article 14 of the 1999 African Charter on the Rights and Welfare of the Child (Children Charter), every child has the right to enjoy the best attainable state of physical, mental, and spiritual health, including medical assistance, and health care based on primary health care. Although the right to health herein protected is similar to article 16 of the African Charter, the Children Charter additionally considers the spiritual dimension of health and health care. For its part, the Protocol to the African Charter on Human and Peoples' Rights on the Rights of Women in Africa[243] recognizes women's right to health, including sexual and reproductive health and health services. The African Women Protocol uses a different language from the African Charter and the Children Charter. Comparable to the Children Charter, the African Youth Charter[244] deals with the right to enjoy the best attainable state of physical, mental, and spiritual health, including medical assistance, and health care based on primary health care approach. Unlike other

239 Ibid. art xx.

240 See the preamble to the AU Constitutive Act, and its arts 3 (h), 4 (m).

241 Rachel Murray, *Human rights in Africa from the OAU to the African Union*, (Cambridge: Cambridge University Press, 2004), 22, Rashida Manjoo, "Women's human rights in Africa," in *The African regional human rights system: 30 years after the African Charter on Human and Peoples' Rights*, ed. Manisuli Ssenyonjo (Netherlands: Leiden-boston, 2012), 139.

242 Murray, *Human rights in Africa*, 8- 9, 22 and 43, Makau Mutua, "The African human rights system: A critical evaluation," *Human Development Occasional Papers*, (2000): 4-5.

243 Protocol to the African Charter on Human and Peoples' Rights on the Rights of Women in Africa, 2005 (hereinafter African Women Protocol), art 14.

244 African Youth Charter, 2009, art 16.

human rights treaties, such as the Children Charter, the African Charter, and the African Women Protocol, the Youth Charter expressly provides access to treatment for HIV and AIDS. Finally, the Convention for the Protection and Assistance of Internally Displaced Persons in Africa[245] protects the right to medical care and other health services.

The practical relevance of these provisions is that they can serve as interpretative tools of the right to health protected under the ICESCR, the African Charter, and the SADC Treaty in any case that involves DRC and URT. Moreover, as long as the DRC and URT are parties to the above treaties and the African Court Protocol, the African Court is competent to enforce the right to access to medicines.[246] Finally, once duly ratified, the above human rights treaties become part of the domestic law of DRC and URT.

The present study focuses on the right to health as argued under the African Charter, which applies to everyone, including children, women, youth, and internally displaced persons.

2. Protection of the right to health under the African Charter

Several provisions of the African Charter deal with health-related rights. Illustrations include articles 16, 18 (3), and 18 (4) of the Charter. Article 16 provides that

> every individual shall have the right to enjoy the best attainable state of physical and mental health. State parties to the present Charter shall take the necessary measures to protect the health of their people and to ensure that they receive medical attention when they are sick.

This Charter's provision refers to health as the right to enjoy the best attainable state of physical and mental health. For its part, article 18 (3) of the Charter states that "the State shall ensure the elimination of every discrimination against women and also ensure the protection of the rights of the woman and the child as stipulated in international declarations and conventions." This provision covers the right to health through women's and child's rights. However, its scope is limited only to women and children, excluding adult men. Finally, article 18 (4) provides that, "The aged and the disabled shall also have the right to special measures of protection in keeping with their physical or moral needs." The right to special measures of protection is broad enough to include the right to health. Like article

245 African Union Convention for the Protection and Assistance of Internally Displaced Persons in Africa, 2012, art 9.

246 African Court Protocol, art 3.

18 (3), the provision of article 18 (4) covers only some people, namely aged and persons with disabilities.

Without undermining the relevance of all these Charter's requirements, the present section focuses on article 16 of the African Charter, which covers everyone's right to health, including women, children, the aged, and people with disability. The section further outlines the nature of the State's obligations to enable access to medicines and the enforcement mechanisms to that.

a. *Access to medicines under article 16 of the African Charter*

Article 16 of the African Charter does not expressly provide a specific and independent right to access medicines. Instead, it entitles everyone to the right to enjoy the best attainable state of physical and mental health and obligates the State parties to take the necessary measures to protect their people's health and ensure that they receive medical attention when they are sick. A close look at this Charter's provision reveals that, like the ICESCR, article 16 omits the social aspect of the right to health. Moreover, the expression of "the best attainable state of physical and mental health" under article 16 means a state of health that is free from those factors that can affect people's health such as diseases, illnesses, cruel treatment, and injuries.[247] The State's obligation to protect its people's health, including in the event of sickness, reinforces this assertion. The provision of medical attention constitutes an ideal way of protecting people's health.

Read together, article 16 of the African Charter protects access to medicines through the right to enjoy the best attainable state of physical and mental health, the protection of people's health against sickness, and medical attention provision. According to the African Commission, medicines form part of basic services necessary for a minimum health standard under article 16.[248] More importantly, the African Commission has adopted Resolution 141, which exclusively addresses medicines as part of article 16 of the African Charter.[249]

247 Sexual violence, assaults, trauma, and injuries affect people's physical, psychological and mental health. See African Commission on Human and Peoples' Rights, Communication 323/06: Egyptian Initiative for Personal Rights and Interrights vs. Egypt, 2011 (henceforth Egypt Case), para 265.

248 African Commission on Human and Peoples' Rights, Communication 25/89, 47/90, 56/91, 100/93: Free Legal Assistance Group, Lawyers' Committee for Human Rights, Union Interafricaine des Droits de l'Homme, les Témoins de Jehovah/Zaïre, 1993 (hereinafter Zaïre Case).

249 African Commission Resolution 141.

aa) *African Commission Resolution 141 and access to medicines*

Article 45 (1) (b) of the African Charter empowers the African Commission to formulate and lay down principles and rules, which solve legal problems relating to human and peoples' rights. It is within this context that the African Commission adopted Resolution 141, which is entirely dedicated to needed medicines as part of article 16 of the African Charter. Unlike General Comment 14, Resolution 141 expressly refers to the United Special Rapporteur on the Right to Health, as the only external source of interpretation. It does not expressly mention General Comment 14 issued by the CESCR 8 years before its adoption. Nevertheless, due to its similarities with General Comment 14, Resolution 141 will be discussed in comparison with the later, especially, concerning the normative content of the right to health, its essential elements, and the nature of States' obligations, including the minimum core obligations.

bb) *The full scope of access to medicines under article 16 of the African Charter*

Like the normative content of the right to health under General Comment 14, Resolution 141 identifies access to medicines as part of the human right to health. Furthermore, similar to General Comment 14, the full scope of access to needed medicines under Resolution 141 includes availability, accessibility, acceptability, and quality.[250] Availability requires that existing needed medicines are available in sufficient quantities.[251] It further covers new medicines that State parties should develop. Like under General Comment 14, accessibility includes four interrelated components. Firstly, it requires that everyone has access to needed medicines without discrimination. Secondly, it includes the physical accessibility of medicines to all. Thirdly, needed medicines have to be economically accessible or affordable. Fourthly, information about the availability and efficacy of medicines should be accessible. For its part, acceptability requires that needed medicines respect cultural norms and medical ethics. Finally, the quality of medicines supplies implies that available medicines are safe, effective and medically appropriate.[252] However, unlike General Comment 14, which subjects the implementation of these four elements of access to medicines to the State's developmental level, Resolution 141 does not. Besides, unlike General Comment 14, which stresses physical accessibility to medicines for vulnerable groups of society, Resolution 141 remains silent in that regard.

250 Ibid.
251 Ibid.
252 Ibid.

b. The nature of the State's obligations under article 16 of the African Charter

The African Charter provides for the State's obligations regarding the right to health. Although it does not explicitly distinguish between general and specific obligations, one can look at the State's obligations towards the human right to health by using this approach. Accordingly, general obligations refer to those provisions that apply to all the Charter's rights. In contrast, specific obligations refer to those deriving from article 16 of the Charter.

aa) General obligations

Several provisions of the African Charter like articles 1, 2, 3, 25,[253] 26,[254] and 62[255] apply to all the protected rights. Article 1 of the African Charter urges State parties to recognize the rights, duties, and freedoms enshrined in the Charter, and undertake to adopt legislative or other measures to give effect to them. The content of this provision is twofold as far as the State's obligations are concerned. First, it imposes the obligation upon all State parties, including the DRC and URT, to recognize all rights, duties, and freedoms contained under the African Charter. Furthermore, the same obligation binds each State party individually at the domestic level. Secondly, each State party is required to adopt legislative or other measures to implement these guaranteed rights. Like article 2 (1) of the ICESCR, article 1 expressly mentions legislative measures while also calling for adopting other measures. Unlike article 2 (1) of the ICESCR, article 1 under discussion binds each State party to immediately implement all the Charter's rights, including access to medicines, within its own resources. The Charter's founders did not provide for international assistance and cooperation in the implementation of the Charter, nor did they consider the principle of progressive realization. The African Commission interprets the State's obligations regarding ESCRs to comprise the clause of progressive realization and that of available resources, including regional and international aids.[256] Regarding international cooperation, the African Commission reiterates the view that it is incumbent upon developed countries to assist others.[257] However, it is not clear whether this duty only applies to African developed countries parties to the African Charter, if any, or also it concerns developed

---

253 According to article 25, States parties have the duty to promote and ensure through teaching, education, and publication, the respect of the rights and freedoms contained in the Charter.

254 State parties have the duty to establish and improve appropriate national institutions entrusted with the promotion and protection of the Charter rights and freedoms.

255 Article 62 of the African Charter relates to the reporting procedure.

256 African Commission's Guidelines on ESCRs, para 13.

257 Ibid. para 39.

countries from other continents. It is important to recall that the African Commission has emphasized the binding and general nature of article 1 under discussion. To this end, it ruled that

> the African Charter was drafted and acceded to voluntarily by the African States wishing to ensure the respect of human rights on this continent. Once ratified, States Parties to the Charter are legally bound to its provisions. A state not wishing to abide by the African Charter might have refrained from ratification. Once legally bound, however, a state must abide by the law in the same way an individual must.[258]

In other words, a violation of any Charter's provision, such as article 16, automatically entails that of article 1 under discussion.[259] The African Commission further recalled the binding nature of article 1 of the African Charter in subsequent communications.[260] The African Commission's interpretation rebuts the views that the wording and language of article 1 of the Charter deprive it of much of its force.[261]

Regarding articles 2 and 3 of the African Charter, they relate to everyone's equality before the law, equal protection, and the prohibition of any discrimination in the enjoyment of all the Charter's rights, including access to medicines. These two articles are interrelated. According to the African Commission[262] and the African Court,[263] articles 2 and 3 constitute the Charter's anti-discrimination and equal protection provisions. They are non-derogable since they bind the State parties in all circumstances for the full enjoyment of the Charter's rights,[264] including access to medicines.

bb) Specific obligations

Specific obligations regarding access to medicines relate to article 16 of the African Charter. They concern everyone's entitlement to enjoy the best attainable

---

258 African Commission on Human and Peoples'Rights, Communication 137/94-139/94-154/96-161/97: International PEN, Constitutional Rights Project, Civil Liberties Organization and Interights vs. Nigeria, 1998 (henceforth the Saro Case), para 116.

259 African Commission on Human and Peoples' Rights, Communication 147/95-149/96: Sir Dawda k. Jawara vs. Gambia, 2000, para 46, African Court on Human and Peoples' Rights, Application 006/2012: African Commission on Human and Peoples' Rights vs. Republic of Kenya (hereinafter Kenya Case), 2012, para 217.

260 Egypt Case, para 272.

261 Richard Gittleman, "The African Charter on Human and Peoples' Rights: a legal analysis," *Virginia Journal of International Law*, (1986): 688, Christof Heyns, "The African regional human rights system: in need of reform?," *AHRL 2*, (2001): 159.

262 African Commission on Human and Peoples' Rights, Communication 241/01: Purohit and Moore vs. Gambia, 2001 (henceforth Gambia Case), para 49.

263 Kenya Case, paras 137-138.

264 Gambia Case, para 49.

state of physical and mental health, and the State's obligations to protect their people's health and ensure that they receive medical attention when they are sick. A close look at article 16 of the African Charter leads one to identify three types of obligations. First, it is the State's obligation to ensure the concrete enjoyment of everyone's best attainable state of physical and mental health. One cannot fully enjoy his right to health if State parties do not implement the said right. Secondly, it entails the specific obligation to protect people's health through the adoption of necessary measures, without mentioning them. This particular obligation is broad enough to include all kinds of measures, including legislative, judicial, budgetary and other measures, whether preventive or curative. Thirdly, article 16 entails the duty to adopt necessary measures to ensure that people receive medical attention when sick. This obligation seems more specific as it only deals with people's illness or sickness. It implies the idea of an adequate health system, which provides appropriate health care services, including medicines, to tackle diseases, illness, or injury. Like other Charter's protected rights, obligations that derive from article 16 are not expressly subject to any limitation, such as progressive realization or availability of resources. However, the African Commission holds that all ESCRs under the African Charter, including the right to health, are subject to the clause of progressive realization and available resources.[265]

cc) The obligations to promote, protect and fulfil

The African Commission Resolution 141, like General Comment 14, identifies three levels of the State's obligations towards enabling access to medicines. The obligations are namely to promote, protect, and fulfil. It is essential to observe that the content of the duty to promote under Resolution 141 is akin to the obligation to respect in General Comment 14. It consists of refraining from measures that negatively affect access, such as denying or limiting equal access to medicines for marginalized individuals, prohibiting or impeding the use of TM and healing practices that are scientifically sound and medically appropriate. Further, the duty to promote includes refraining from interfering with the provision of humanitarian aid that facilitates the supply of necessary medicines.[266] Unlike the obligation under General Comment 14, the obligation to promote under Resolution 141 extends to the duty to refrain from implementing intellectual property policies that do not take full advantage of all flexibilities in the WTO Agreement on Trade-Related Aspects of Intellectual Property that promote access to medicines.

Like in General Comment 14, the obligation to protect ensures that third parties do not violate people's access to needed medicines. Consequently, it requires appropriate regulatory systems to be put in place that allows access to drugs that

265 African Commission's Guidelines on ESCRs, para 13.
266 African Commission Resolution 141.

have met scientifically relevant quality, safety, and efficacy standards.[267] Moreover, unlike in General Comment 14, the duty to protect expressly includes rational use of medicines and prevents unreasonably high prices for needed medicines in public and private sectors. The duty to protect under Resolution 141 adopts the principle of equity pricing, in which the poor should not pay a disproportionate amount of their income for access.[268]

As far as the obligation to fulfild is concerned, similar to the obligation under the General Comment 14, it requires the adoption of all necessary and appropriate positive measures that promote, provide, and facilitate access to needed medicines, including immediately meeting the minimum core obligations regarding essential medicines. It further includes promoting meaningful participation by affected individuals, and groups in decisions that affect access to medicines, such as regulatory, pricing, and patent decisions, and creating incentives for companies to register needed medicines expeditiously. It is worth stressing that, unlike in General Comment 14, Resolution 141 expressly subjects the obligation to fulfil (take positive measures) to the maximum of the State's available resources, a clause the African Charter does not explicitly provide. Unlike General Comment 14, Resolution 141 does not determine the specific content of the obligations to promote, provide and facilitate access to medicines herein mentioned.

dd) Minimum core obligations

Similar to General Comment 14, Resolution 141 identifies making available essential medicines as part of the State's core obligation. However, unlike the General Comment 14, Resolution 141 deals with the core obligation towards providing essential medicines as part of the obligation to fulfil. It is worth stressing that Resolution 141 does not define the core obligation nor refer to the minimum essential level of access to medicines. The African Commission Guidelines on ESCRs fill in the gap by drawing inspiration from ESCR's General Comment 3. Accordingly, while States parties have an obligation to ensure the satisfaction of, at the very least, the minimum essential levels of each of the Charter's ESCRs, the minimum core obligation demands that no significant number of individuals is deprived of the vital elements of an individual right.[269] It follows that essential medicines fall within the ambit of the minimum essential levels of the right to health. In contrast, the enjoyment of essential medicines by a significant number of individuals amounts to the fulfilment of State's core obligation. Finally, unlike General Comment 14, which subjects the implementation of core obligations by developing

267 Ibid.

268 The duty to protect also stimulates and promotes competition, intellectual property, consumer protection, and other laws to promote access to medicines. Ibid.

269 African Commission's Guidelines on ESCRs, para 17.

countries to international cooperation and assistance,[270] Resolution 141 subjects it to the maximum of the only State's available resources. However, on the ground, like General Comment 14, which does not allow any justification about non-compliance with the core obligations, Resolution 141 subjects State parties to the immediate duty to ensure essential medicines are available to their people. The minimum core obligation under the African Charter exists regardless of resources and is non-derogable.[271]

One can lament that the African Commission, which defines the minimum core obligation in the light of the CESCR's General Comment 3, purposely omits to allow State parties to justify non-compliance with their core obligations for lack of available resources. It is misleading to hold that all African countries, especially the DRC and URT, have already met their core obligation the provision of essential medicines on a non-discriminatory basis, especially for vulnerable or marginalized groups.[272]

c. *Enforcement mechanisms for access to medicines under the African Charter*

The African Charter and the African Court Protocol provide protection mechanisms for access to medicines. They include a non-judicial mechanism performed by the African Commission[273] and the African Court's judicial mechanism.[274]

aa) Non-judicial enforcement mechanisms before the African Commission

Non-judicial enforcement mechanisms under the African Charter include inter-State and other communications[275] and the state reporting procedure.[276]

(1) Inter-state communications

The African Charter entitles every State party to look after the Charter's implementation by other State parties. To this end, each State that considers that another State party has violated the Charter's provisions can either draw the attention of the latter to the matter[277] or refer the matter directly to the African Commission.[278]

---

270 General Comment 14, para 45.

271 African Commission's Guidelines on ESCR, para 17.

272 Ibid. para 67.

273 See Part II of the African Charter on measures of safeguard.

274 African Court Protocol.

275 African Charter, arts 47 and 55.

276 Ibid. art 62.

277 Ibid, art 47.

278 Ibid. art 49.

In the first situation, State parties concerned are involved in reaching an amicable settlement of the issue. The respondent State party has the obligation to give the enquiring State within three months of the receipt of the communication, written explanation or statement elucidating the matter, including information relating to the redress already given or course of action available.[279] When the amicable settlement is not successful, either State can submit the matter to the African Commission. In the second situation, the African Commission may also help reach an amicable solution based on human and peoples' rights. Once achieved, such an amicable agreement may close the inter-state communication procedure. In the absence of any agreement, the Commission prepares a report containing the facts and its findings, which it sends to the State parties concerned and the Assembly of Heads of State and Government.[280] It may also make any recommendations deemed beneficial to the Assembly of Heads of State and Government.[281] However, the African Commision has never received an inter-State communication against the DRC or URT regarding the violation of access to medicines.

(2) Other communications

Article 55 of the African Charter empowers the Commission to consider communications other than those submitted by State parties without expressly mentioning their authors. To fill in this gap, the African Commission has adopted the actio popularis approach that allows everyone, including non-victim individuals, NGOs, and pressure groups with interest, to file a communication for its consideration.[282] These communications must relate to the violation of the Charter's provision, including access to medicines.[283] In examining a complaint, the African Commission may offer its good offices for facilitating an amicable settlement between the parties in compliance with the human rights and fundamental freedoms enshrined in the African Charter.[284] The African Commission can decide on the merits and request the respondent State to take specific measures.[285]

As the oldest Charter supervisory body in Africa,[286] the African Commission has already dealt with communications on the violation of article 16 of the African

279 Ibid. art 47.

280 Ibid, art 52.

281 Ibid. art 53.

282 African Commission on Human and Peoples' Rights, Communication 321/2006: Law Society of Zimbabwe et ali. vs. Zimbabwe, paras 58-59.

283 African Charter, art 56.

284 The amicable settlement procedure shall be initiated, and may only continue, with the consent of the parties. African Commission Rule of Procedure, Rule 123.

285 Ibid. Rule 125.

286 Manisuli Ssenyonjo, "The protection of economic, social and cultural rights under the African Charter," in *The protection of economic, social and cultural rights in*

Charter. It has elucidated the content of article 16 and the nature of the State's obligations. Through the examination of these communications, the African Commission refuted the view that ESCRs protected under the African Charter, including the right to health, are not justiciable.[287] It is worth noting that the African Commission's interpretation of the Charter's provisions is evolving progressively with its strengths and weaknesses.[288]

The present section discusses five selected communications examined by the African Commission following their thematic and connection to the present study. The first communication against Zaïre[289] relates to access to medicines in general. The second and third communications against Nigeria[290] and Mauritania[291] deal with detainees' access to medicines. The fourth communication that involves Gambia[292] deals with access to medicine for mental health, and the fifth communication against Nigeria[293] deals mainly with the nature of the State's obligations and the confirmation of the justiciable nature of all Charter's rights, including the right to health.

(a) Zaïre case

The African Commission examined the Zaïre Case against the Republic of Zaïre (the current DRC) in 1993. Allegations of violation of the right to health include

---

Africa: international, regional and national perspectives, eds. Danwood Mzikenge Chirwa and Lilian Chenwi (Cambridge: Cambridge University Press, 2016), 97.

287 Some authors argue that ESCRs under the Charter, including the right to health, are purely exhortatory, merely promotional and not protective. Obinna Okere, "The protection of human rights in Africa and the African Charter on Human and Peoples' Rights: a comparative analysis with the European and American system," *Human Rights Quarterly* 6, no. 2, (1984): 147. See also Gittleman, "The African Charter," 687.

288 For instance, the Commission's decisions issued from or after 2001 are relatively more elaborated than those issued before 2001. See Manisuli, "Protection of ESCRs," 97-98, Sisay Alemahu Yeshanew, "Approaches to the justiciability of economic, social and cultural rights in the jurisprudence of the African Commission on Human and Peoples' Rights: progress and perspectives," *African Human Rights Law Journal*, (2011): 331.

289 Zaïre Case.

290 Saro Case.

291 African Commission on Human and Peoples' Rights, Communication: 54/91-61/91-96/93-98/93-164/97_196/97-210/98: Malawi African Association and others vs. Mauritania, 2000 (henceforth Mauritania Case).

292 The Gambia Case.

293 African Commission on Human and Peoples' Rights, Communication 155/96: Social and Economic Rights Action Center (SERAC) and Center for Economic and Social Rights (CESR) vs. Nigeria, 1996 (hereinafter Ogoni case).

mismanagement of public finances and the government's failure to provide basic services, including medical services, which resulted in the shortage of medicines in hospitals.[294] One of the particularities of this communication lies in that it brings to the scrutiny of the African Commission questions of mismanagement of public finances. This aspect of the communication reveals that resource issues in the least developed countries such as DRC and URT arise in mismanagement and shortage. The respondent State Zaïre refused to collaborate with the African Commission. Consequently, the Commission based its ruling on the facts of the communication.[295] Accordingly, it ruled that "the failure of the government to provide basic services necessary for a minimum standard of health, such as safe drinking water and electricity and the shortage of medicine constitutes a violation of article 16 of the African Charter."[296] The African Commission's ruling explicitly clarifies that the availability of medicines constitutes an essential service for a minimum standard of health. The African Commission's findings mean that Zaïre, one of the country studies, failed to comply with its Charter's obligations to allow individuals to enjoy the right to health following articles 1 and 16 of the African Charter. Furthermore, the shortage of medicines also meant that the Republic of Zaïre failed to comply with its duty to take the necessary measures to ensure that people receive medical attention when they are sick.

However, the African Commission neither defines the entire content of article 16 nor determines the nature of the State's obligations regarding the right to health. The Commission left unsaid the mismanagement of public finances, which negatively impacted the State's failure to make medicines available within public hospitals. The African Commission would have considered such maladministration a violation of the State's obligation to take other measures, including budgetary, to provide medicines. The question of mismanagement of public funds shows that limited financial resources should not in all circumstances justify the incapacity of a least developed country, such as the DRC, to fulfil its Charter's obligations regarding access to medicines.

Another shortfall to mention in this case is the lack of recommendations and remedies due to the weaknesses of the African Charter regarding the Commission's power in examining individual communications.[297] The absence of recommendations could have harmed both the victims and the respondent

294 Communication 100/93 was submitted by the Union Interafricaine des droits de l'Homme and dated 20th March 1993. Ibid. para 4.

295 Zaïre Case, para 40.

296 Ibid. para 47.

297 The African Charter does not provide a mandate for the African Commission to afford remedies expressly. See Gina Bekker, "The African Commission on Human and Peoples' Rights and remedies for human rights violations," *Human Rights Law Review 13*, no. 3, (2013): 503.

State. Regarding the victims or complainants, they could not have the right to any remedy, discouraging them from submitting other communications to the African Commission in the future. Concerning the respondent State, the absence of these recommendations does not help avoid the repetition of such violations.

(b) The Saro case and the Mauritania case

The Saro Case and the Mauritania Case dealt with the violation of the right to health of detainees by Nigeria in 1998[298] and Mauritania in 2000.[299] The primary approach used by the African Commission in these communications consisted of emphasizing the binding nature of article 1 of the African Charter, by stating that once legally bound, a State must abide by the law in the same way an individual must.[300] Regarding article 16, the African Commission in the Saro case argued that

> The responsibility of the government is heightened in cases where an individual is in its custody and therefore someone whose integrity and well-being is completely dependent on the actions of the authorities. The State has a direct responsibility in this case. Despite requests for hospital treatment made by a qualified prison doctor, these were denied to Ken Saro-Wiwa, causing his health to suffer to the point where his life was endangered. This is a violation of article 16.[301]

In the Mauritania case, the African Commission went on by ruling that

> The state's responsibility in the event of detention is even more evident to the extent that detention centres are its exclusive preserve, hence the physical integrity and welfare of detainees is the responsibility of the competent public authorities. Some prisoners died as a result of the lack of medical attention. The general state of health of the prisoners deteriorated due to the lack of enough food, lack of blankets and adequate hygiene. Consequently, there was a violation of article 16.[302]

From the above, detainees' integrity, welfare and well-being, hospital treatment, food, medical attention, blankets, and adequate hygiene form part of the right to health and fall within the government's responsibility. Regarding access to medicines, in particular, it forms part of hospital treatment and medical attention. The State is responsible for detained persons' health because detention places belong to the only State's authority and it is the State´s exclusive power to deprive

---

298 The communication was submitted by International PEN, Constitutional Rights Project, Civil Liberties Organization and Interights on behalf of Ken Saro-Wiwa Jnr. Ibid. para 80.

299 The Mauritania Case was addressed against the government of Mauritania by the Malawi African Association and others. See Mauritania case, para 12.

300 Saro case, paras 113 and 116. See also the Mauritania case, para 84.

301 Saro case, paras 111-112.

302 Mauritania case, para 122.

individuals of liberty.[303] However, the African Commission does not clearly distinguish between the enjoyment of the right to health by people in detention and those in freedom.[304] Furthermore, in its conclusion under the Mauritania case, the African Commission found only a violation of article 16 (1) of the African Charter, excluding, without convincing justification the violation of article 16 (2).[305] Such a holding seems problematic, as it appears to sustain the view that the Respondent State complied with its obligations under article 16 (2) of the Charter. Simultaneously, the African Commission recognizes that some prisoners died from lack of medical attention. Finally, unlike in the Saro case, the Commission recommended to the Respondent government to carry out an assessment of the status of degrading practices in the country with a view to inter alia, implementing a strategy aimed at their total and definitive eradication.[306] However, the African Commission did not clearly determine in a specific way the nature of the measures to be adopted to facilitate prisoners' access to health-related rights.

(c) The Gambia Case

The African Commission examined the Gambia Case in 2001[307] that dealt with the Gambian mental health Act. The concerns were that the mental health Act was outdated,[308] and did not provide for consent to treatment.[309] The mental health Act also lacked provisions to review medical decisions in case of wrong certification or diagnosis.[310] The risk was that even healthy persons could have been administered medicines for mental disability. The mental treatment for healthy people can be more harmful to their health. The African Commission examined the complaint and addressed issues of general and specific nature.

General issues include the African Commission's mandate to examine domestic laws' compliance with the African Charter,[311] and the reaffirmation of the principle of universality, indivisibility, and interrelation of all the Charter's rights.[312]

---

303 African Commission General Comment N°3, para 36.

304 Ibid. paras 36, 41, and 42.

305 Mauritania Case, para 142.

306 See the African Commission's recommendations.

307 The complainants are mental health advocates, submitting the communication on behalf of patients detained at campama, a psychiatric unit of the royal victoria hospital. See the Gambia Case, para 1.

308 The legislation in dispute in the present communication was enacted in 1917, and was amended for the last time in 1964. Ibid. para 42.

309 Ibid. paras 3, 4, 5, 6 and 8.

310 Ibid. para 30.

311 Ibid. para 43.

312 Ibid. paras 47 and 48.

They further extend to the non-derogable nature of articles 2 and 3 of the African Charter.[313]

Regarding specific issues on the right to health, the African Commission addressed them through the reading of both articles 16 and 18 (4) of the African Charter. It interpreted article 16 to include the right to enjoy health facilities and access to goods, and services without discrimination.[314] Article 18(4) includes, among other things, analysis, and diagnosis of a person's mental condition and treatment, care, and rehabilitation for a mental illness.[315]It was the Commission's view that the mental health Act failed to comply with articles 16 and 18 (4) of the African Charter, to the extent that its scheme was lacking in terms of therapeutic objectives as well as provision of matching resources and programmes of treatment of persons with mental disability.[316]

The African Commission also addressed article 16 in isolation from article 18 (4). The Commission ruled that

> millions of people in Africa are not enjoying the right to health maximally because African countries are generally faced with the problem of poverty which renders them incapable to provide the necessary amenities, infrastructure, and resources that facilitate the full enjoyment of this right. Therefore, it reads article 16 as entailing the state's obligation to take concrete and targeted steps, while taking full advantage of its available resources, to ensure that the right to health is fully realized in all its aspects.[317]

The African Commission identifies challenges faced by African countries, including the DRC and URT, in implementing the right to health. Its ruling suggests that the implementation of article 16 under review is subject to both the clause of available resources and progressive realization.[318] The African Commission's interpretation of the State's obligations under article 16 of the African Charter considers the country's developmental level. However, such interpretation gives rise to some concerns. The respondent State in this communication did not invoke the lack of resources or poverty issues[319] to justify its failure to meet the State's obligations under article 16 at hand. Moreover, in applying only to the right to

313 Ibid. para 49.

314 Ibid.

315 Ibid. para 81-82.

316 Ibid. paras 83 and 85.

317 Ibid. para 84.

318 Bahar Jibriel, "The justiciability and enforcement of the right to health under the African Human Rights system." *Haramaya Law Review*, (2012): 42-44.

319 Elangi Botoy, *Propriété intellectuelle et droits de l'homme: l'impact des brevets pharmaceutiques sur le droit à la santé dans le contexte du VIH/SIDA en Afrique* (Genève: Schulthess Médias Juridiques SA, 2007), 259-260.

health, the African Commission's statement seems to conflict with the letter and spirit of the African Charter itself, which does protect all the rights on the same legal footing without limitation. It is worth recalling that ten years after the examination of the Gambia case, the African Commission acknowledged the general application of the principle of progressive realization to all the Charter's ESCRs.[320]

The African Commission recommended that the Respondent State Gambia repeals the mental health Act and replace it with a new legislative regime for mental health, which is compatible with the African Charter norms for the protection of mentally ill or disabled persons.[321] It further recommended the creation of an expert body to review the cases of all persons detained under the mental health law, and the provision of adequate medical and material care for persons suffering from mental health problems.[322] The Commission's recommendations, in this case, have the potential to benefit and cover other disabled or mentally ill people than the victims under the present communication.

(d) The Ogoni Case

The examination of the Ogoni Case against the government of Nigeria took place in 1996.[323] It alleged the exploitation of oil reserves by the oil consortium in Ogoni land without regard to the local communities' health, resulting in the contamination of water, soil, and air with its serious short and long-term health impacts, including skin infections, gastrointestinal and respiratory ailments.[324]The Commission's ruling in this complaint is relatively revolutionary from several perspectives.[325] The African Commission unequivocally argued that each Charter's right, including the right to health, gives rise to the obligations to respect, protect, promote, and fulfil.[326] It further ruled that all the Charter's rights are effective and justiciable.[327] This Commission's interpretation counters the

---

320 African Commission's Guidelines on ESCRs), para 13.

321 Gambia case, paras 85 (1) (2)(3).

322 Ibid.

323 The communication was submitted by the Social and Economic Rights Action Center (SERAC) and Center for Economic and Social Rights (CESR).

324 Ibid. para 2.

325 Nwobike, C. "The African Commission on Human and Peoples' Rights and the demystification of second and third generation rights under the African Charter: Social and Economic Rights Action Center (SERAC) and the Center for Economic and Social Rights (CESR) vs. Nigeria," *1 Afr. J. Legal Stud. 2*, (2005): 130.

326 Ogoni case, paras 44-47.

327 Ibid. para 69.

traditional view that ESCRs cannot be enforceable through judicial or quasi-judicial review.[328]

Regarding the right to health, the African Commission ruled that

> Article 16(1) of the African Charter obligates governments to desist from directly threatening the health of their citizens. The state is under an obligation to respect the just noted rights and this entails largely non-interventionist conduct from the state for example, not from carrying out, sponsoring or tolerating any practice, policy or legal measures violating the integrity of the individual. Government compliance with the spirit of article 16 of the African Charter must also include ordering or at least permitting independent scientific monitoring of threatened environments, requiring and publicising environmental and social impact studies prior to any major industrial development, undertaking appropriate monitoring and providing information to those communities exposed to hazardous materials and activities and providing meaningful opportunities for individuals to be heard and to participate in the development decisions affecting their communities.[329]

A close and in-depth analysis of this Commission's ruling reveals that the African Commission focuses more on the State's obligations than the content of the right. The lack of care, which would have protected the victims' rights of the violations complained of, amounted to the violation of article 16.[330] Therefore, the African Commission enjoined the respondent State to ensure adequate compensation to victims of the human rights violations, undertake a comprehensive clean-up of lands and rivers damaged by oil operations; and provide information on health and environmental risks. Thus, contrary to its earlier decisions, the Commission provides a more relatively detailed understanding of reparation, including non-monetary remedies for rights violations. However, the African Commission falls short of illustrating the impact of contamination of water, air, and soil on the right to health, including their connection with various diseases. It further did not apply the four levels of State's duties herein developed on the right to health.

In sum, the analysis of the above communications shows that everyone's access to medicine, including detainees and people with mental disability, constitutes a basic service necessary for a minimum standard of the right to health protected under article 16 of the African Charter, which State parties have to ensure within public hospitals. The communications also reveal that several factors can amount to the violation of access to medicines, namely the State's failure to make medicines available within public health facilities, and the implementation of domestic laws

---

328 Fons Coomans, "The Ogoni case before the African Commission on Human and Peoples' Rights," *International and Comparative Law Quarterly 52,* (2003): 8, and Nwobike, "The African Commission," 145.

329 Ogoni case, paras 52-53.

330 Ibid. para 54.

that are inconsistent with the African Charter. More importantly, under the principle of the exhaustion of domestic remedies, the facts that violate the right to health in these communications can also be brought before the national protection mechanisms in the DRC and URT.

(3) State reporting procedure

The underlying idea about the state reporting procedure is that the ratification of human rights instruments, such as the African Charter by State parties, is as important as their word and deed implementation.[331] Regular submission of State reports on the adopted implementation measures provides evidence of the State's compliance with their Charter's duties.[332] To this end, article 62 of the Charter urges each State party to submit every two years, from the coming into force of the Charter, a report on the adopted legislative and other measures on implementing the Charter's rights and freedoms. These reports shall also indicate challenges affecting the implementation of the Charter.[333] The state reporting procedure allows identifying the already adopted implemented measures for each Charter's right and encountered challenges affecting the said implementation. Soboka points out that

> unlike the complaints system that cannot give a true picture of the human rights record of a given state, the state reporting procedure can be used to gauge general compliance with the whole gamut of rights, freedoms and duties guaranteed under the Charter. Furthermore, the main objective underlying the reporting mechanism is to produce state compliance with their obligations under the instrument in question. Since the Charter derives its binding force, inter alia, from article 1 of the African Charter, the state reporting procedure under article 62 of the Charter is a mechanism for monitoring state compliance with their article 1 obligation.[334]

The state reporting procedure provides information about the implementation of each Charter's right, such as the right to health. It is worth recalling that the African Commission has adopted recommendations,[335] Rules of Procedure,[336] and

---

331 African Commission, Guidelines for national periodic reports, 1989 (Guidelines for national periodic reports), para 1.

332 Frans Viljoen, "State reporting under the African Charter on Human and Peoples' Rights: a boost from the south," *Journal of African Law*, (2000):110.

333 African Commission on Human and Peoples' Rights, Rules of Procedure of the African Commission on Human and Peoples' Rights, 2020 (hereinafter African Commission Rules of Procedure), Rule 78.

334 Soboka Bulto, "Beyond the promises: resuscitating state reporting procedure under the African Charter on Human and Peoples' Rights," *Buffalo Human Rights Law Review* 12, (2006): 57-60.

335 African Commission's Recommendation on Periodic Reports, 1988.

336 African Commission Rules of Procedure.

Guidelines for national periodic reports,[337] to supplement some shortcomings relating to modalities and details about the application of article 62.[338]

(a) Examination of State reports by the African Commission

The African Commission considers the State reports in the presence of a representative of the State party concerned who is expected to respond to its questions.[339] During the consideration of the State report, the African Commission explores all the pertinent information relating to the human rights situation in the State concerned, including reports from international, regional, and national human rights organs.[340] After consideration of the State report, the African Commission formulates concluding observations that specify the issues that require particular attention on the part of the State party concerned, and the date of the following periodic report's submission.[341] According to Bulto,

> concluding observations are considered as yardsticks by which the Commission can measure the progress between past and present compliance of a State party in that concerns and recommendations that emerged from the previous reports are to be addressed in subsequent reports, thereby forming the basis for a continuing dialogue and follow up.[342]

The African Commission is under the obligation to transmit issued concluding observations to the State party concerned within thirty days following the session at which they were adopted.[343]

In the absence of a representative of the State party concerned, Rule 81 of the African Commission Rules of Procedure deals with non-submission of reports, but does not prescribe the Commission's power in that regard. The lack of State's reports should not prevent the African Commission from relying on various sources of information to examine the human rights situation within the jurisdiction of

---

337 Guidelines for national periodic reports. See also African Commission on Human and Peoples' Rights, State party reporting guidelines for economic, social and cultural rights in the African Charter on Human and Peoples' Rights, 2012 (Guidelines for ESCRs).

338 See Mutua, "African human rights system", 20, Heyns, "African regional human rights system," 164, and Viljoen, "State reporting," 110.

339 The African Commission can also consider the report if the concerned State party fails to send a representative. African Commission Rules of Procedure, Rule 80.

340 Ibid.

341 Ibid. Rules 82 and 83.

342 Bulto, "Beyond the promise," 84.

343 African Commission Rules of Procedure, Rule 82.

State parties concerned.[344] This recommendation would serve as an alternative to the State parties' failure, such as the URT, to regularly submit their reports.[345]

(b) DRC's report and the African Commission's concluding observations

The submission of the DRC's initial report to the African Commission was expected in 1989. However, it was submitted only in 2002.[346] The DRC submitted its subsequent reports respectively in 2007[347] and 2017.[348] Unlike the 2002 report, which does not refer to article 16 of the African Charter,[349] the DRC's 2007 and 2017 reports do. According to the 2007 report, the DRC commits to protect the life of the population through the organization of a health system, which is accessible to all by developing, among others, 536 health zones for primary health care.[350] For its part, the 2017 report mentions some government efforts to facilitate access to health care by Congolese citizens. These include the equipment and rehabilitation of some public hospitals and other health facilities,[351] and the distribution of insecticide mosquito nets, Vitamin A vaccination, and medical kits to people living with HIV/AIDS.[352] Read together, the above efforts cover some aspects of access to medicines.

However, all these reports do not provide concrete information on adopted laws and other measures that makes medicines of good quality available and accessible.

Following the 2002 and 2017 reports, armed conflicts' recurrence constitutes the main obstacle in implementing the Charter's rights, including access to medicines. The government invests more significant budget allocation in the peace-building

---

344 Viljoen, "State reporting," 117-18, Bulto, "Beyond the promise," 87. See also African Charter, arts 60 and 61.

345 As of November 2017, the URT was among the 19 countries with more than three reports overdue. See African Commission on Human and Peoples' Rights, 41st Activity Report, 2016 (hereinafter African Commission 41st Report), para 15.

346 The report also contains the country's combined 2nd to 7th reports. See Initial Report of the Democratic Republic of Congo under the provisions of the African Charter on Human and Peoples' Rights, 2002 (hereinafter the DRC's 2002 Report to the African Commission).

347 The Democratic Republic of the Congo, Combined 8th to 10th periodic reports to the African Commission on Human and Peoples Rights, 2007 (hereinafter DRC's Report to the African Commission, 2007), para 1.

348 Combined 11th to 13th periodic reports submitted by DRC to the African Commission, 2017 (hereinafter the DRC's 2017 Report to the African Commission).

349 Ibid. See Chapter VI on the right to health.

350 Ibid. paras 160-163.

351 Ibid. para 47.

352 Ibid. para 48.

process to the detriment of social and human rights sectors such as the health sector.[353]

The African Commission's concluding observations to the DRC's 2007 and 2017 reports do not exist. In contrast, the African Commission issued concluding observations to the DRC's 2002 report.[354] It commended the setting up of legislation for the protection of human rights in line with the country's obligations under article 1 of the Charter without mentioning them.[355] However, the African Commission regrets that the report does not strictly comply with the Commission's guidelines set out in that regard. Illustration includes the lack of information about the implementation of article 16 of the African Charter. As Soboka points out,[356] while minimal information may be enough to determine that the report is present, it does not necessarily guarantee the report's quality. In other words, the information's completeness is as essential as the submission of the report.

The African Commission also stated that the government's challenge in protecting its citizens in areas under conflict and the collapsed economy with no meaningful economic infrastructure such as roads and bridges are among the factors that inhibit the enjoyment of the Charter's rights. Lack of roads and bridges can constitute an obstacle to the physical accessibility of medicines when needed.

Finally, the African Commission recommended the promulgation of a new Constitution and other laws for an appropriate implementation of the Charter's rights. However, the concluding observations failed to condemn the fact that there was lack of information on the right to health, including access to medicines, nor did they make specific recommendations in that regard.

(c) URT's report and the African Commission's concluding observations

The present section discusses the Tanzanian 2nd to 10th periodic reports submitted in 2006.[357] Information on the implementation of article 16 of the African Charter includes the adoption of programmes, policies and laws, such as the National Health Policy on primary health care, the review of the laws affecting HIV, and the Traditional and Alternative Medicine Act. The government introduced a community health insurance scheme, which exempted some vulnerable groups of the society, namely disabled, senior citizens and children under five years old. The report referred to the government's efforts to curb the shortage of health workers

---

353 Ibid. para 74.

354 These Concluding observations were issued at the Commission's 34th Ordinary Session held in Banjul, from 6th to 20th November 2003 (hereinafter the Commission 2003 Concluding observations).

355 Ibid. paras 3-6.

356 Bulto, "Beyond the promise," 64 and 72.

357 The United Republic of Tanzania, consolidated 2nd to 10th periodic reports to the African Commission on Human and Peoples' Rights, 2006.

by paying for medical practitioners, nurses, medical assistants, and clinical officers at both public and private universities.

Regarding challenges in implementing the Charter's provisions, the URT has identified difficulties in disseminating reports throughout the country and the short period of two years for submitting its reports to the African Commission.[358] Surprisingly, these challenges did not relate to poverty or lack of resources.

In its concluding observations issued in 2008,[359] the African Commission commended, among others, the inclusion of a Bill of Rights in the 1985 Constitution, the enactment of the 1994 Basic Rights and Duties Enforcement Act, and the provision of free antiretroviral drugs (ARVs) to people living with HIV/AIDS. These measures can directly or indirectly be relevant to access to medicines. However, the African Commission is concerned about the lack of the domestication of most ratified treaties in the URT, which has a dualist legal system. Therefore, it urged the URT to domesticate the African Charter to allow Tanzanians to enjoy the full range of rights herein guaranteed.[360] The domestication of ratified treaties, including the African Charter, should allow people to make access to medicines enforceable before the courts. However, the African Commission's recommendations did not address the issue of access to medicine within the framework of the right to health.

(d) Some general observations about the reporting procedure

The state reporting mechanism under the African Charter seems relatively unproductive to some extent. Its inefficiency is attributable to both State parties and the African Commission. As far as State parties are concerned, in addition to the failure to regularly and timely submit their reports, they have often provided incomplete or even scant information.[361] The issue of insufficient information regarding access to medicine is critical and undermines an essential component of the right to health. The above analysed reports reveal that there is a lacuna concerning measures undertaken to make medicines of good quality available and accessible.

For its part, the African Commission issued only concluding observations in its 29th Session of 2001. The lack of concluding observations in that period can be due to the gaps in the African Charter, which did not determine the ways the African Commission had to handle State's reports. The Charter's gap in this regard may have partly contributed to the lack of seriousness on States' part towards

358 Ibid.

359 African Commission on Human and Peoples' Rights, Concluding observations and recommendations on the consolidated 2nd to 10th periodic report of the United Republic of Tanzania, 2008 (hereinafter African Commission concluding observations to URT, 2008).

360 African Commission concluding observations to URT, 2008, paras 27-42.

361 Bulto, "Beyond the promise," 69-71, and Viljeon, "State reporting," 111.

their reporting obligations under the Charter.[362] Consequently, State parties could not receive feedback from the African Commission regarding areas of concern, breaking down therefore the dialogue with the African Commission. Moreover, the lack of concluding observations could have led to the loss of motivation to submit further periodic reports. It is worth noting that concluding observations passed by the African Commission did not appropriately address access to medicine in all its aspects of availability, accessibility, acceptability, and quality.

(4) Execution and follow-up of the African Commission's decisions

The State parties have the duty to execute the African Commission's concluding observations and decisions on communications. In contrast, the African Commission should ensure the follow-up on the implementation of its issued decisions.[363] Regarding the concluding observations, the Commission Rule of Procedure vests the Commission's members with the mission to ensure the follow-up on the implementation of the recommendations contained herein.[364] However, the Rule under discussion does not prescribe any period for implementation of the Commission's concluding observations by the State party concerned. Instead, the African Commission has developed a practice that consists of inviting the concerned State party to provide information about concluding observations within its next periodic reports.[365] However, both the Charter and the Rules of Procedure do not provide further details in the case of non-compliance with the Commission's concluding observations. This legal gap can partly justify why State parties do not take the reporting seriously and why the Commission's recommendations do not have any discernible effect on States.[366] Moreover, follow-up through the state reporting procedure can become unproductive since State parties do not appropriately report to the African Commission.[367]

In the event of a decision on the merits requesting the respondent State to take specific measures, the parties have 180 days to inform the African Commission of all action taken by the State Party concerned to implement the Commission's decision.[368] The African Commission may send a reminder to the State party concerned

---

362 Viljeon, "State reporting," 111, Bulto, "Beyond the promise," 83-84.

363 Rachel Murray and Elizabeth Mottershaw, "Mechanisms for the implementation of decisions of the African Commission on Human and Peoples' Rights," *Human Rights Quarterly 36*, no. 2, (2014): 350.

364 African Commission Rules of Procedure, Rule 83.

365 African Commission concluding observations, 2008.

366 Mutua, "African human rights system," 21.

367 Sabelo Gumedze, "Bringing communications before the African Commission on Human and Peoples' Rights," *African Human Rights Law Journal 3*, (2003): 145-146. See also, Bekker, "The African Commission," 520-521.

368 African Commission Rules of Procedure, Rule 125.

to submit its information within 90 days from the date of their communication.[369] Indeed, recommendations made by the African Commission are binding and the adherence to these recommendations by the respondent State is consistent with the obligations to give effect to the Charter's provisions under article 1 of the same.[370] However, the African Commission has no power to compel the respondent State to implement its decisions. The only available legal option at the African Commission's disposal consists of referring all cases of non-compliance with its decisions to the competent policy organs of the African Union.[371]

(5) Enforcement of the African Commission's decisions by the AU Assembly

The African Commission submits its activity report to the competent policy organs of the African Union for each Conference.[372] The activity report indicates the status of the implementation of the African Commission's decisions, including issues of non-compliance by State parties.[373] Two reasons justify the inclusion of cases of non-compliance with the African Commission's decisions in its report. First, the African Commission can request the AU's competent organs to take the necessary measures to implement its decisions.[374] Secondly, the AU Assembly is competent to take decisions on reports and recommendations from the other organs of the AU, and determine the appropriate sanctions against a member that fails to comply with the decisions and policies of the Union.[375] Other organs of the Union shall include organs other than those foreseen in the AU Constitutive Act,[376] such as the African Commission,[377] and the African Court.[378]

In practical terms, on behalf of the Assembly, the Executive Council adopts a decision on the African Commission's activity report calling for implementation of the Commission's decisions.[379]The Executive Council's decision transforms the African Commission's decisions, views or recommendations into the AU decisions,

369 Ibid.

370 Gumedze, "Bringing communications," 143-4.

371 African Commission Rules of Procedure, Rule 125, and African Charter, art 54.

372 African Commission Rules of Procedure, Rule 138.

373 Ibid. Rule 125.

374 Ibid. Rule 138.

375 AU Act, arts 9 and 23 (2).

376 Ibid. art 5.

377 African Charter, art 30. See also African Commission 41st Report, para 7.

378 African Court Protocol, art 1.

379 Executive Council, decision on the activities of the African Commission on Human and People's Rights, 2017. See also AU Act, arts 6, 9 and 13 (2).

which become binding and enforceable on Member States.[380] Failure to comply with this Executive Council's decision entitles it to recommend the Assembly to adopt sanctions.[381]

Before taking any sanction, the Assembly stipulates the time frame for compliance failure to which then sanctions are adopted. Applicable sanctions include the denial of transport and communication links with the other Member States and other measures of a political and economic nature to be determined.[382]

In brief, the Assembly's power to take sanctions gives teeth to the Commission's decisions and constitutes a qualified hope for the protection of human rights in Africa.[383] Commentators consider these AU Act's provisions as progress over the former OAU legal framework, by arguing that the degree of applicability and the fear it will engender are yet to be seen in practice.[384] However, the AU Assembly has never taken sanctions to enforce the African Commission's decisions, including its concluding observations.

(6) Practical constraints on the implementation of the sanction regime

The procedure for the sanctions against State parties that do not comply with the Commission's decisions is subject to some practical constraints related to the role of the African Commission, the Executive Council, and the AU Assembly.

Concerning the African Commission, its activity report mentions only some cases of non-submission of State reports and non-compliance with other communications procedures. It fails to report non-compliance with its concluding observations.[385] The Commission's activity report fails to expressly request the Assembly to take necessary measures to implement its decisions.[386]

Like the African Commission's report, the Executive Council's decision does not exclusively deal with the States that fail to comply with the Commission's decisions. Besides, the Executive Council has never recommended the adoption of sanctions by the Assembly against State parties concerned. The absence of recommendations for sanctions weakens the AU enforcement mechanism on the

380 Chairman Okoloise "Circumventing obstacles to the implementation of recommendations by the African Commission on Human and Peoples' Rights," *African Human Rights Law Journal 1*, (2018): 47-48.

381 AU General Assembly Rule of Procedure 36 (1).

382 Ibid. Rule 36 (2) and (3).

383 Bekker, "The African Commission," 526, Murray and Mottershaw, "Mechanisms for the implementation," 368-9, and Gumedze, "Bringing communications," 145-8.

384 Bulto, "Beyond the promise," 89 – 91, AU Act, arts 9 and 23 (2).

385 African Commission on Human and Peoples' Rights, 42nd Activity Report covering the period of January to May 2017, 2017 (hereinafter African Commission 42nd Report), paras 29 and 58. See also African Commission 41st Report, paras 15 and 42.

386 Murray, *Human rights in Africa*, 60.

decisions of the African Commission. Instead, the Executive Council has developed a practice that consists of repeating its findings on reminding the involved State parties to implement the Commission's decisions.[387] Since the Assembly has a tied competence, it cannot undertake any sanctions against the State parties concerned without explicit recommendations from the Executive Council. The lack of the AU General Assembly's reactions weakens the African Commission's commitment to the protection of human rights under the African human rights follow-up mechanism. The absence of sanctions from the General Assembly can partly justify States' failure to implement the African Commission's decisions.[388]

bb) Judicial enforcement mechanism

The African Court Protocol establishes an African Court as the only judicial protection mechanism for Africa's human rights. Both the DRC and URT are parties to the African Court Protocol. The African Court's jurisdiction covers all human and peoples' rights argued under the African Charter, including access to medicine.[389] In that regard, it complements the protective mandate of the African Commission conferred upon it by the African Charter.[390] It is important to note that the Court's protective mandate is broader[391] than the one of African Commission under the African Charter since it extends to other ratified relevant human rights instruments by the State party to the African Court Protocol.[392] While making an opinion on the African Court's jurisdiction over other human rights instruments besides the African Charter, Heyns[393] argues that it would be highly unusual for an institution from the AU to enforce the treaties of another system such as the UN, while the latter does not enforce the said treaties through a court of law. Therefore, the author urges the African Court to make it explicit that it does not exercise jurisdiction over the entire corpus of human rights treaties ratified by African States.[394] Other critics suggest that entitled entities should prioritize human

---

387 Executive Council decision 2017, Paras 2, 3, 4, Executive Council, decision on the 42nd Commission report, paras 3-4. See also African Commission 41st Report, paras 24-26.

388 Bekker, "The African Commission," 523-4.

389 African Court Protocol, art 3 (1).

390 Ibid. art 2.

391 Frans Viljoen, "Regional institutional and remedial arrangements for the judicial enforcement of economic, social and cultural rights in Africa," in *The protection of economic, social and cultural rights in Africa: international, regional and national perspectives*, eds. Danwood Mzikenge Chirwa and Lilian Chenwi (Cambridge: Cambridge University Press, 2016), 250.

392 African Court Protocol.

393 Heyns, "African regional human rights," 167.

394 Ibid. 168.

rights protected under the AU's human rights treaties in suing cases to the African Court.[395] Indeed, logic would dictate that the African court, which supplements the African Commission's protective mandate conferred upon it by the African Charter, has limited jurisdiction over the African Charter and its protocols. However, the African States that have drafted, negotiated, adopted and ratified the African Court Protocol within the African continent have freely decided to extend the Court's jurisdiction to other relevant human rights instruments ratified by the State party. Therefore, one cannot, from a strictly legal point of view, restrict the expression "any other relevant human rights instruments" to the only human rights instruments adopted within the framework of the AU. Such restriction is irrelevant in that the African Court has confirmed and reaffirmed its jurisdiction over all ratified treaties by State parties.[396] In other words, such a suggestion seems to restrict the freedom of qualified entities, which have the latitude to base their complaints on any relevant ratified human rights treaty of their choice.

In sum, unlike the CESCR, which issues views and recommendations, the African Court's unique competence to apply other treaties allows it to enforce access to medicines protected in the ICESCR through binding judgments. Therefore, it constitutes an appropriate alternative, especially, for both the DRC and URT, which are not parties to the Optional Protocol to the ICESCR.

(1) Access to the African Court and its practical constraints

The African Court has both advisory[397] and contentious[398] jurisdictions. The present section focuses on the Court's contentious jurisdiction. According to article 5 of the Court Protocol, the following entities qualify to bring cases before the African Court: the African Commission, State parties, African Intergovernmental Organizations, NGOs, and individuals.

(a) Access to the African Court by the African Commission

The African Commission may, before deciding on the admissibility of a communication submitted under Articles 48, 49 or 55 of the Charter, transfer received communication to the Court, provided that the respondent State has ratified the African Court Protocol.[399] The use of the verb "may" suggests that the African Commission

---

395 Viljoen, "Regional institutional and remedial arrangements," 252-253.

396 The Court has reaffirmed its jurisdiction to consider the violation of the ICCPR ratified by the Republic of Mali. African Court, Application 009/2016: Diakite Couple vs. Republic of Mali, 2017, paras 22-23.

397 African Court Protocol, art 4.

398 Ibid. art 5.

399 African Commission Rules of Procedure, Rule 130 (1).

has a discretionary[400] power to seize or not the African Court. Moreover, the African Commission's latitude in that regard is limited. Firstly, the respondent State before the African Commission must be a party to the African Court Protocol.[401] Secondly, the African Commission shall obtain the complainant's consent to any referral to the Court.[402] The Rule under discussion allows the African Commission to seize the African Court for any violation of access to medicines by State parties to the African Court Protocol, such as the DRC and URT. In seizing the Court, the African Commission becomes the applicant before the African Court.[403]

(b) Access to the African Court by State parties

Three kinds of States may seize the Court, namely the complainant State to the African Commission, the respondent State before the African Commission, and the State party whose citizen is a victim of human rights violation.[404]

The complainant State before the African Commission can only be a State party that has submitted an inter-state communication under article 47 of the African Charter. To avoid any case of lis pendens, the complainant State concerned must formally withdraw its application before the African Commission.[405]

For its part, the respondent State before the African Commission is involved either in an inter-state communication procedure or other communications. However, neither the African Court Protocol nor the African Court Rules nor the African Commission Rules of Procedure provide for the withdrawal of an application by a respondent State before the African Commission. Further, it is not clear how a respondent State before the African Commission can become an applicant to the African Court. The provision under discussion can become a dead letter considering that the said State is not likely to initiate a case against itself at an international court such as the African Court.[406]

Finally, regarding the State party whose citizen is a victim of a violation of human rights, the application relates exclusively to its citizens. The State's action

400 Dan Juma, "Access to the African Court on Human and Peoples' Rights: A case of the poacher turned gamekeeper," *Essex Human Rights Review* 4, no. 2 (2007): 8.

401 African Commission Rules of Procedure, Rule 130(1).

402 Ibid. Rule 130(2).

403 Ibid. Rule 130(3).

404 When a State party has an interest in a case, it may also be allowed to join. Art 5 of the African Court Protocol.

405 African Court on Human and Peoples' Rights, Rules of Court, 2020 (hereinafter African Court Rules), Rule 37. See also African Commission Rules of Procedure, Rule 124.

406 Juma, "Access to the African Court," 4 and 12.

in that regard constitutes a form of diplomatic protection of its citizens,[407] which technically works as a variant of the inter-state complaints mechanism.[408] However, unlike the inter-state communication that is general and covers all the inhabitants within the respondent State irrespective of their citizenship, the procedure under discussion applies only to the complainant State's citizens.

(c) Access to the African Court by African intergovernmental organizations

Access to the Court by African intergovernmental organizations constitutes one of the African Court's specificities compared to the other regional courts.[409] However, the Protocol to the African Court and its Rules of Procedure remain silent on whether the State party involved should be a Member State of the said intergovernmental organization. Moreover, they do not prescribe the procedure to follow between the victims and these African intergovernmental organizations. Given that these organizations are State parties' alter ego, they will be reluctant, if not unwilling, to submit applications to the Court.[410] The African Court has never received complaints from African intergovernmental organizations that involve the DRC or URT regarding access to medicines.

(d) Access to the African Court by individuals and NGOs

According to article 5 (3) of the Court Protocol, the Court may entitle relevant NGOs with observer status before the Commission, and individuals to institute cases directly before it when the respondent State has acknowledged the Court's competence following article 34 (6) of the Protocol at hand. A combined reading of articles 5 (3) and 34 (6) suggests that the use of the verb "may" and the respondent State's express acknowledgement of the Court's competence constitute significant limitations for individuals and NGOs' access to the Court.[411] Moreover, following article 6 (3) of the Court Protocol, the African Court has the latitude to consider the filed cases or transfer them to the African Commission. However, the provision at hand does not determine the circumstances under which the African Court can decide to transfer to the African Commission cases submitted by NGOs and individuals.

---

407 Gino Naldi, "Observations on the Rules of the African Court on Human and Peoples' Rights," *AHRLJ 14*, (2014): 375, and Juma, "Access to the African Court," 13.

408 Juma, "Access to the African Court," 13.

409 International Federation for Human Rights, Practical guide: The African Court on Human and Peoples' Rights, towards the African Court of Justice and Human Rights, 2010 (hereinafter International Federation for Human Rights): 73.

410 Juma, "Access to the African Court," 8 and 14.

411 Mutua, "African human rights system," 28, and Juma, "Access to the African Court," 2.

Individuals and NGOs' ability to access the African Court is limited by the absence of the State's declaration recognizing the African Court's jurisdiction and the State's right to withdraw such declaration. Regarding the absence of State's declaration, it is due to the optional nature of article 34 (6) of the African Court Protocol. State parties have a free hand in that regard. As of December 2021, only eight (8) out the 32 State parties to the African Court Protocol, namely: Burkina Faso, Gambia, Ghana, Malawi, Mali, Guinea-Bissau, Niger and Tunisia, have deposited the declaration provided under article 34(6) of the Protocol.[412] It is worth recalling that the African Court Protocol does not explicitly provide for the withdrawal of the deposited declaration under article 34 (6). However, the African Court granted the Republic of Rwanda's request to withdraw its declaration.[413] Other State parties, which have withdrawn their declarations, comprise the URT, Benin, and Côte d'Ivoire.[414] Although there is no obligation to provide reasons for such withdrawal, the reality shows that only State parties against which the African Court has already issued one or more judgment (s) have withdrawn their declarations.[415]

Regarding the URT, the host State, the African Court has rendered more than twenty judgments, including provisory orders against it.[416] However, none of these Court's decisions dealt with access to medicines as argued under the African Charter or the ICESCR. Thus, upon the withdrawal of their declaration, individuals and NGOs in these countries, like those in countries with no declaration under article 34 (6) of the African Court Protocol, cannot enforce access to medicines before the African Court.

(2) Execution of the Court's judgment

At first glance, the African Court has not yet dealt with any case concerning the right to health or access to medicine against the DRC or URT. Nonetheless, both the DRC and URT are still parties to the African Court Protocol. The African Court can deal with a case on the violation of access to medicines that involve URT or

412 Activity Report of the African Court on Human and Peoples' Rights: 1 January-31 December 2021.

413 African Court Report 2016, para 7, African Court on Human and Peoples' Rights, Application 003/2014 Ingabine Victoire Umuhoza vs. Republic of Rwanda, 2016, paras 53- 69.

414 Coalition for an Effective African Court on Human and Peoples' Rights, "African Court Coalition discussions: States withdrawals from article 34 (6) of the African Court Protocol," *Official Bulletin 1*, (2020) 1.

415 A worrying trend which seems to be emerging is for States against which the Court has rendered a judgment to withdraw or threaten to withdraw their article 34(6) declaration. African Court Activity report 2021, para 39.

416 Ibid. Paras 18-36.

DRC. Therefore, it appears necessary to discuss the nature of the Court's decision and the applicable law on its execution and enforcement.

Accordingly, article 27 (1) of the Court Protocol empowers the African Court to make appropriate orders to remedy the violation of human or peoples' rights, including fair compensation or reparation. Payment of fair compensation or reparation in this provision is merely illustrative. The African Court can order other reparation measures, including rehabilitation, satisfaction, and guarantees of non-repetition.[417]

Article 30 of the Court Protocol governs the execution of the Court's decisions. It reads as follows, "the states parties to the Court Protocol undertake to comply with the judgment in any case to which they are parties within the time stipulated by the Court and to guarantee its execution." A close look at this provision suggests that the State parties are bound to twofold obligations. First, they shall voluntarily comply with the judgment within the time stipulated by the Court. Secondly, upon ratification of the Court Protocol, they guarantee the execution of the Court's ruling in any case that involves them. Though article 30 does not make it explicit, the underlying idea behind this obligation is the binding nature of the Court's judgments on the parties.[418] Indeed, since the Court Protocol does not foresee measures of constraint to force States to comply with the Court's judgments, the implementation or execution of the latter by States parties is obligatory but voluntary.[419]

In practice, however, non-compliance with the Court's decisions constitutes one of the Court's main challenges. For instance, some State parties concerned either do not take the required measures to remedy the violations of rights as ordered by the Court or decide not to report on the implementation measures.[420] Others, including the URT expressly report on their inability to implement the Court's order without justification.[421] One cannot tell whether the same State parties would have behaved differently if the Court's orders had to deal with issues relating to access to medicines. In case of non-compliance with its orders or decisions, the African Court is required to report to the AU Assembly, which is responsible for its enforcement.

417 African Commission on Human and Peoples' Rights, General Comment N° 4 on the African Charter on Human and Peoples' Rights: the right to redress for victims of torture and other cruel, inhuman or degrading punishment or treatment, 2017 (hereinafter African Commission General Comment 4), para 10.

418 African Court Rules, Rule 72. See also Naldi, "Observations on the rules," 385.

419 International Federation of Human Rights, 128.

420 African Court Report, 2016.

421 Ibid.

(3) *Follow-up and enforcement of the African Court's judgments*

Articles 29 (2) and 31 of the Court Protocol govern the African Court's judgment's follow-up and enforcement. To this end, article 31 obligates the African Court to submit to the Assembly in its work report any cases of non-compliance with its judgment. It is worth recalling that the "Court's judgments" include interim measures.[422] Under article 29 (2), the Council of Ministers monitors the execution of the Court's judgment on behalf of the Assembly. In practice, the Executive Council adopts a decision on the African Court's report, which also urges State parties concerned to implement the Court's rulings.[423] Failure to comply with this Executive Council's decision enables the latter to recommend the adoption of sanctions by the Assembly.[424] The undertaking of sanctions by the Assembly is not automatic. Indeed, the Assembly gives State parties concerned a second chance by adopting a decision. It stipulates the time frame for the compliance, before it undertakes any sanctions following article 23 (2) of the AU Constitutive Act.[425] Unlike under the OAU Charter,[426] the AU Act is very progressive regarding the monitoring of the Court's decisions by the Assembly. However, despite reported cases of non-compliance with the Court's decisions, the AU Assembly has never taken sanctions provided under article 23 (2) of the AU Act.[427]

(4) *Practical constraints in the enforcement of the African Court's judgments by the AU Assembly*

Factors that hinder an appropriate implementation of the Assembly's follow-up procedure relate to the African Court, the Executive Council and the Assembly. Regarding the African Court, it submits the cases of non-compliance with its judgments to the Assembly as part of its annual report together with all its activities for the previous year.[428] It cannot, for instance, submit before the end of the year issues of non-compliance with the Court's interim measures, which are urgent.

---

422 African Court Rules of Procedure, Rule 51 (4).

423 Executive Council, decision on the 2016 Activity Report of the African Court, 2017.

424 AU Act, art 23 (2), and AU General Assembly Rule of Procedure 36 (1).

425 AU General Assembly Rule of Procedure 36 (3).

426 Due to the lack of explicit sanctions, reporting on non-compliance with the Court's judgments under the OAU has been described as a shaming tactic that marks the violator. See Mutua, "African human rights system," 30.

427 As of December 2018, the Court has rendered 28 judgments on the merits. However, apart from Burkina Faso that has fully complied with the judgments of the Court, the other countries concerned did not. African Court's annual report 2018, paras 48-49.

428 African Court 2016 Report.

Like the Court's report, the Executive Council's decision on the Court's report does not deal exclusively with the issues of non-compliance with the Court's judgments.[429] Therefore, the Council's decision dealing with all the Court's activities raises concerns about its notification to the States that fail to implement the Court's judgments. Indeed, unlike the Court's report that mentions all cases of non-compliance with its decisions, the Executive Council decided not to mention anymore the names of State parties that refuse to implement the Court's judgments in its decision on the Court's annual report.[430] This decision of the Executive Council is contrary to the spirit and letter of article 31 of the Court Protocol. It undermines the effectiveness of the Court in particular, and the African human rights protection system as a whole.[431] Consequently, the Assembly can no longer inquire about the execution by the Council of its office for this purpose.[432] The situation worsens with the Executive Council's permanent failure to expressly recommend adoption of sanctions against those State parties that fail to comply with its decisions calling for the implementation of the Court's judgment.[433] The Assembly cannot adopt sanctions without recommendations from the Council. Thus, instead of prioritizing justice, African heads of States and governments involved in protecting human rights as members of the Executive Council and General Assembly are more concerned with favouring their ideological solidarity, and political considerations.[434]

C. Protection of access to medicines under the SADC human rights law

African countries started in the 1970s to create sub-regional organizations to supplement the AU's deficit in economic and political domains.[435] The same claim also applies to the AU's deficit in human rights, including access to medicines. With the ratification of the African Charter and the African Court's existence, AU Member States of some Regional Economic Communities (RECs),[436] such as the Economic

---

429 Executive Council, decision on the 2016 Activity report of the African Court on Human and Peoples' Rights, 2017.

430 African Court's Activity Report 2018, para 51.

431 Ibid.

432 Ibid. para 52.

433 Despite over four decisions of the Executive Council, Libya did not comply with the Court's orders for provisional measures. African Court 2016 Report, para 56.

434 Okere, "Protection of human rights," 158, and International Federation of Human Rights, 128-9.

435 Christine Meyer, *Menschenrechte in Afrika: Regionaler Menschenrechtsschutz als Herausforderung an menschenrechtliches Universalitätsdenken*, (Baden-Baden: Nomos, 2013), 64.

436 Some of the RECs recognized by the AU include the Common Market for Eastern and Southern Africa, East African Community, Economic Community of Central

Community of West African, and the East African Community, are committed to promote, protect and fulfil human rights, including through the establishment of sub-regional courts or tribunals.[437] The section focuses only on the protection of the right to health under the SADC human rights law for three main reasons. Firstly, SADC is the only REC to which belong the DRC and URT.[438] Secondly, SADC's legal instruments contain various provisions on the right to health.[439] Thirdly, unlike the ICESCR and the African Charter, SADC Health Protocol expressly mentions pharmaceuticals and TM.[440]

Initially, Member States established in 1980 the Southern Africa Development Co-ordination Conference (SADCC).[441] In 1992, they founded the SADC as an organization for economic integration by adopting both the Declaration[442] and the SADC Treaty.[443]At first glance, it might appear that the promotion and protection of human rights are not the SADC's top priority.[444] Nonetheless, an in-depth analysis of the SADC legal framework[445]reveals that envisaged economic integration

---

African States, Economic Community of West African States and Southern African Development Community.

437 Examples include articles 4 (g) of the 1975 Treaty establishing the Economic Community of West African States (ECOWAS) as revised, 6 (d) of the 2000 Treaty for the Establishment of the East African Community as amended in 2006, and 4 (c) of the SADC Treaty.

438 Others SADC Member States are Angola, Botswana, Comoros, Eswatini, Lesotho, Madagascar, Malawi, Mauritius, Mozambique, Namibia, Seychelles, South Africa, Zambia and Zimbabwe.

439 SADC Treaty, arts 4 and 5, SADC Gender Protocol, arts 11 and 26, and SADC Health Protocol, arts 2 and 29.

440 SADC Health Protocol, arts 20 and 29.

441 Southern Africa Toward Economic Liberation: A Declaration by the Governments of Independent States of Southern Africa, 1980. The Declaration does not make any explicit reference to human rights. However, it makes some references to the fight against the spread of moth disease in some member States.

442 Towards a Southern African Development Community. A Declaration made by the Heads of State or Government of Southern Africa at Windhoek, 1992.

443 SADC Treaty, arts 1 (1) and 2 (1).

444 Oliver, Ruppel, "Regional economic communities and human rights in East and Southern Africa," in *Human rights law in Africa: Legal perspectives on their Protection and Promotion*, eds. Bösl, A. and Diescho, J. (Windhoek: McMillan Education, 2009): 291.

445 SADC Treaty's principles, objectives, and general undertakings, relate to human rights issues in one way or another. Another category of legal documents that is either directly or indirectly relevant to human rights consists of SADC Protocols. Ibid. 292-293.

goes hand in hand with human rights in general and health-related rights in particular.

Indeed, in addition to erecting human rights into one of the principles of SADC and making the fight against HIV/AIDS and other diseases one of its objectives,[446] subsequently adopted SADC instruments, including protocols,[447] declarations,[448] and charters,[449] explicitly cover health-related rights. The present subsection starts by looking at human rights and the right to health under the SADC Treaty, the SADC Health Protocol, and the SADC Gender Protocol. In addition, it discusses the protection mechanisms for access to medicine under the SADC human rights law.

1. Protection of human rights under the SADC Treaty

Unlike the ICESCR and the African Charter, the SADC Treaty does not exclusively deal with human rights. However, it contains various provisions, which directly or indirectly cover both human rights and health-related issues.[450] For instance, human rights, democracy, and the rule of law constitute the main principles, according to which SADC and its Member States shall act.[451] Furthermore, the SADC Treaty expressly proscribes all discrimination against any person based on, among others, the grounds of ill health and disability.[452] The principle of non-discrimination is one of the pillars of human rights. It is worth acknowledging that SADC Treaty's reference to human rights is opaque and framed in overarching general terms.[453] However, two main arguments can help to elucidate the SADC Treaty's protection of human rights. First, subsequently adopted instruments within the SADC framework can fill in and specify the content of the SADC Treaty's human rights.[454] These include, among others, the SADC Declaration on Gender and Development,

---

446 SADC Treaty, arts 4 and 5.

447 SADC Protocol on Employment and Labour, 2014, arts 2 (b), 5 and 13, SADC Health Protocol, arts 20 and 29, and SADC Gender Protocol, arts 11 and 26.

448 SADC Declaration on Gender and Development, 1997, and SADC Declaration on the fight against HIV and AIDS, 2003.

449 SADC Charter of the Fundamental Social Rights, 2003.

450 Jonas Obonye, "Neutering the SADC Tribunal by blocking individuals' access to the Tribunal," *International Human Rights Law Review 2*, (2013): 316-17.

451 SADC Treaty, art 4 (c).

452 Ibid. art 6 (2).

453 Solomon Ebobrah, "Human rights developments in African sub-regional economic communities during 2009," *African Human Rights Law Journal 10*, (2010): 259, Frederick Cowell, "The death of the Southern African Development Community Tribunal's human rights jurisdiction," *Human Rights Law Review*, (2013): 155-56.

454 SADC Member States are under the legal obligation to implement human rights protected under the SADC Charter of Fundamental Social Rights, and SADC

the SADC Declaration on the fight against HIV and AIDS, the SADC Charter of the Fundamental Social Rights, the SADC Protocol on employment and labour, and the SADC Protocol on Gender, the provisions of which protect specific human rights following the principles of SADC Treaty. Secondly, human rights under the SADC Treaty also include those rights protected under various instruments to which SADC Member States have subscribed at regional and international levels, such as the UDHR, ICESCR, the African Charter, CEDAW, and the Convention to the Rights of the Child.[455] In the Campbell Case,[456] for instance, the SADC Tribunal used the provisions of, among others, the African Charter, the UDHR, the ICCPR, and ICESCR to determine the content of the right of access to the courts and the right not to be discriminated against on the basis of race as part of article 4 (c) of the SADC Treaty.

a. Protection of access to medicines under the SADC Treaty

At first glance, it is worth recalling that the SADC Treaty does not expressly provide a human right of access to medicines. Instead, it deals with the protection of the said right impliedly in articles 4 (c) and 5 (1) (i) of the SADC Treaty. Article 4 (c) of the SADC Treaty provides that SADC and its Member States shall act following the principle of human rights, democracy, and the rule of law. Although the SADC Treaty does not mention human rights, one can broadly interpret the treaty provision under discussion to protect access to medicines in three ways. First, the expression of "human rights" is broad enough to include access to medicines as part of the right to health. Secondly, democracy is another name for respecting human rights,[457]including the right to health. Thirdly, full compliance with the principle of the rule of law[458] implies respect for human rights, including the right to health.

Access to medicine under the SADC Treaty may be implied from various SADC instruments dealing with access to medicines through health care,[459] universal

Declaration on Gender and Development. See SADC Protocol on Employment and Labour, art 5 (1), and SADC Gender Protocol, art 3 (b).

455 SADC Protocol on Employment and Labour, art 5 (1) and (3), SADC Protocol on Gender, arts 3 (b) and 9.

456 SADC Tribunal, Case N° 2/2007 Mike Campbell (Pvt) Ltd and 78 Others vs. The Republic of Zimbabwe (henceforth Campbell Case), paras 30,46 and 48.

457 A society that recognizes, and respects human rights is a democracy. See Limburg Principles on the implementation of the International Covenant on Economic, Social and Cultural Rights, 1987, para 55.

458 According to the SADC Tribunal, the right of access to the courts and the right to a fair hearing are essential elements of the rule of law. Campbell Case.

459 SADC Protocol on Employment and Labour, 2014, art 13, SADC Gender Protocol, art 11

access to HIV and AIDS treatment,[460] health services,[461] affordable essential medicines,[462]and protection of health.[463] Furthermore, like in the Campbell Case, in which the SADC Tribunal relied on human rights instruments other than those adopted within the auspice of SADC, access to medicines under the UDHR, the ICESCR, the African Charter, and CEDAW can also form part of the SADC Treaty provision under discussion. This assertion is consistent with the SADC Gender Protocol, which urges SADC Member States parties, including DRC and URT, to fulfil their human rights obligations under ratified human rights treaties at international and regional levels.[464]

According to article 5 (1) (i) of the SADC Treaty, the fight against HIV/AIDS, and communicable disease, constitutes the SADC's objectives. Although they do not explicitly mention the human right to health, these SADC's objectives cannot be entirely successful without the contribution of medicines necessary to prevent and treat diseases. Once read in conjunction with article 4 (c) of the SADC Treaty, the implementation of these SADC's objectives will follow the human rights approach towards access to medicines. According to the SADC Declaration on the fight against HIV and AIDS, upholding human rights,[465] including the right to health care, constitutes a necessary element in the SADC's regional response to HIV/AIDS pandemic.

b. State's obligations to access to medicines

All the SADC Treaty provisions are subject to the general obligations of article 6, which urges Member States to

> adopt adequate measures to promote the achievement of the objectives of SADC, refrain from taking any measure likely to jeopardize the sustenance of its principles, the achievement of its objectives and the implementation of the provisions of this treaty, not discriminate against any person or any member state, take all steps necessary to ensure the uniform application of this treaty, take all necessary steps to accord this treaty the force of national law, and cooperate with and assist institutions of SADC in the performance of their duties.

In concrete terms, article 6 talks about "adequate measures" without listing them. These can include legal, budgetary, judicial, social or other measures to implement

460 SADC Gender Protocol, art 27 (3)(b).

461 SADC Declaration on Gender and Development, para h(vi).

462 SADC Declaration on the fight against HIV and AIDS, para 2(h).

463 SADC Charter of the Fundamental Social Rights, art 12.

464 SADC Gender Protocol, art 3.

465 Human rights form an essential component of SADC economic integration. Ebobrah, "Human rights developments," 259.

access to medicines without discrimination. According to the SADC Treaty, health and HIV/AIDS constitute one of the core areas of integration, subject to the co-operation between all Member States.[466] Cooperation under the SADC Treaty extends to other stakeholders, other States, and international organizations.[467] Regarding cooperation with other stakeholders, it takes the form of support of people's initiatives that contribute to the SADC Treaty's objectives in health to foster closer relations among the communities, and people of the Region.[468] This provision is crucial in the health sector, where the State and non-state entities concurrently provide health care services. It suggests that in addition to the State's regulatory power, the government has a further obligation to support people's initiatives in the health sector through subvention.

Another important aspect of cooperation relates to the availability of resources in articles 25 and 26[469] of the SADC Treaty.[470] According to article 25, SADC makes its resources available to the Member States to pursue the Treaty's objectives, including fighting diseases, on terms and conditions mutually agreed between SADC and the Member States involved. The same also provides that Member States shall use SADC's resources most efficiently and equitably. In their efforts to implement the SADC Treaty provisions on access to medicine, for instance, both the DRC and the URT can benefit from the Community's resources.

In sum, as the SADC Tribunal points out, all human rights argued under the SADC Treaty, including access to medicines, give rise to the obligations to respect, protect and fulfil.[471]

To further give full effect to the SADC Treaty provisions, Member States adopt Protocols, including in the area of cooperation.[472] In this context, they have adopted the SADC Health Protocol and the SADC Gender Protocol.

2. Protection of the right to health under the SADC Health Protocol

The SADC Health Protocol came into force on 18 August 2004. It is binding on all State parties,[473] including the DRC and the URT. Being legally based on article 22

466 SADC Treaty, art 12 (1)(2).

467 Ibid. arts 23 and 24.

468 Ibid. art 23 (1) and (2).

469 Article 26 establishes the Regional Development Fund.

470 Admark Moyo, "Defending human rights and the rule of law by the SADC Tribunal: Campbell and beyond," African *Human Rights Law Journal* 9, (2009): 599-600.

471 In the Campbell Case, the applicants challenged the compulsory acquisition of their agricultural lands by Zimbabwe's government.

472 SADC Treaty, arts 10 (3) and 22.

473 Ibid. art 22 (9).

of the SADC Treaty, it deals with one of the SADC's areas of integration, namely health, HIV, and AIDS.[474] Three main reasons explain the consideration of the SADC Health Protocol as a human rights instrument. The first reason is that the SADC Health Protocol's objectives to provide health services are subject to the principles of human rights, democracy, and rule of laws contained in article 4 of the SADC Treaty.[475] This provision maintains an umbilical cord with the SADC Treaty's principle of human rights. As the SADC Tribunal pointed out, human rights under article 4 of the SADC Treaty entail the State's obligations to respect, protect and fulfil.

The Tribunal further showed that one could rely on human rights instruments subscribed to by SADC countries at international and regional levels to fill in the content of human rights provided in article 4 of the SADC Treaty. Read in conjunction with article 4 of the SADC Treaty, the SADC Health Protocol can be interpreted and applied as a human right instrument regarding the State's duty to protect access to medicines as part of health services. Similarly, individuals become rights-bearers and can claim access to medicines based on the SADC Health Protocol's provisions under review in conjunction with the SADC Treaty's principle of human rights. The second reason is that scholars[476] consider the SADC Health Protocol one of the essential instruments regarding access to medicines and human rights. The third reason is that other human rights instruments adopted within the SADC framework expressly refer to the right to health under the SADC Health Protocol. For instance, the SADC Protocol on Employment and Labour urges State parties to ensure that adequate health care is available to all following the relevant provisions of the SADC Health Protocol.[477] For its part, the SADC Gender Protocol obligates State parties to adopt, by the SADC Health Protocol, legislation and related measures to protect people with disabilities in considering their vulnerabilities,[478]including their health needs such as access to medicines. Therefore, the present subsection focuses on protecting access to medicines and implementing measures under the SADC Health Protocol.

474 SADC Treaty, art 12 (2)(iv).

475 SADC Health Protocol, art 2 (a)(d).

476 The SADC Health Protocol is one of the most important SADC instruments regarding access to medicines and human rights. See Lonias Ndlovu, Access to medicines under the WTO Trips agreement: a comparative study of select SADC countries, Thesis, University of South Africa, 2014, 102-103, Ferdinand Temba, "Right to health with focus on people with HIV and AIDS in Tanzania," *The Eastern African Law Review* 42, no. 2 (2015): 34.

477 SADC Protocol on Employment and Labour, art 13.

478 SADC Gender Protocol, art 9.

a. *Access to medicines under the SADC Health Protocol*

Several provisions of the SADC Health Protocol, including its objectives and principles, can be interpreted to cover access to medicines. As regards the SADC Health Protocol's objectives, they consist of, among others, addressing the health needs of women, children and other vulnerable groups, and achieving harmonization in the provision of health services.[479] From these objectives one can deduce that access to medicines can be part of both health needs of these identified categories of persons and the provision of health services. Moreover, the promotion of health care through better access to health services constitutes one of the SADC Health Protocol's principles.[480] Although the Protocol's principle does not mention the right to health directly, access to medicines is regarded as subsumed in better access to health care.[481] It is worth recalling that the objectives to provide health services and satisfy children's, women's and other vulnerable's health needs are implemented in accordance with the principle of human rights provided in article 4 of the SADC Treaty.

Unlike the African Charter and the ICESCR, the SADC Health Protocol expressly mentions within its body those specific diseases which threaten African people's health, namely HIV/AIDS, malaria, tuberculosis, chronic diseases, reproductive and mental health-related issues.[482] To tackle these diseases, the SADC Health Protocol, unlike other treaties, makes explicit provisions for harmonizing pharmaceuticals, quality assurance, registration, production, procurement, and distribution of affordable essential drugs, and their rational use.[483] These provisions aim to make medicines of good quality available, accessible and acceptable. Also, reference to "affordable essential drugs"' implies that State parties should consider the above-mentioned diseases as a matter of priority in the elaboration of their national list of essential drugs.

b. *Implementation measures*

Article 31 of the SADC Health Protocol imposes sanctions against any State party that fails to fulfil the obligations assumed under this Protocol, or implements policies that undermine its objectives and principles.[484] In other words, State parties are under the legal obligation to fulfil all obligations assumed under this Protocol through the adoption and implementation of policies that are consistent with both the principles and objectives of the SADC Health Protocol. Express mention of

479 SADC Health Protocol, art 3 (g), (h).
480 Ibid. art 2 (d).
481 Ndlovu, "Access to medicines under the WTO Trips agreement," 102-103.
482 SADC Health Protocol, arts 8-17, 21-25.
483 Ibid. art 29.
484 SADC Health Protocol, art 31.

policies does not exclude the adoption of other measures. For instance, the SADC Health Protocol's objectives call for the development of common strategies for epidemic preparedness, mapping, prevention, control and the eradication of communicable and non-communicable diseases.[485] For their part, the Protocol's principles expressly mention the adoption of both policies and strategies in the implementation of health care for all.[486]

In implementing the SADC Health Protocol, State parties act individually and collectively.[487] As far as the collective action is concerned, the SADC Health Protocol stresses the relevance of close cooperation in controlling diseases and addressing common health concerns in the region.[488] Reference to "close cooperation" under the SADC Health Protocol means cooperation within the SADC region as opposed to international cooperation argued in the ICESCR.[489]

More importantly, the SADC Health Protocol provides a combined use of both human and non-human resources to give effect to both its principles and objectives relating to access to health services. Accordingly, human resources consist of modern health practitioners (MHPs)[490] and traditional health practitioners (THPs).[491] For their part, non-human resources include health care resources,[492] health laboratory services, health technology, and equipment,[493] and pharmaceuticals. The singularity of the SADC Health Protocol lies in that it expressly extends within its body the notion of resources to human personnel, health facilities, and services, and financial aids. Such a holistic approach towards resources,[494] suggests that financial resources are not the only issue that affects an appropriate implementation of access to medicines in the least developed countries, such as the DRC and the URT. In sum, implementing the SADC Health's objective of providing health services in accordance with the SADC Treaty's principle of human rights entails the State's obligations to respect, protect and fulfil.

---

485 Ibid. art 3.

486 Ibid, art 2.

487 Ibid. art 2 (b).

488 Preamble to the SADC Health Protocol.

489 ICESCR, arts 2 (1) and 23.

490 SADC Health Protocol, art 18.

491 Ibid. art 20.

492 Ibid. art 19.

493 Ibid. art 27.

494 Resources necessary to implement ESCRs must be broadly understood to include natural and human resources. See Committee on the Rights of the Child, "Day of general discussion on resources for the rights of the child- Responsibility of states", 2007, para 24.

3. Protection of the right to health under the SADC Gender Protocol

The SADC Gender Protocol came into force in February 2013. It was amended in 2016. Like all SADC protocols, it is binding on State parties that have ratified it, including DRC and URT. The SADC Gender Protocol is founded on the rights-based approach to development.[495] Its legal basis is twofold. Firstly, it is based on article 6 (2) of the SADC Treaty, which prohibits discrimination against any person on the grounds of, among others, sex or gender. Secondly, the SADC Gender Protocol refers to other human rights instruments to which SADC Member States have subscribed, or ratified, namely the CEDAW, CRC, the African Women Protocol, and the UN Convention on the Rights of People with Disabilities.[496] It is worth recalling that all these human rights instruments protect the right to health. The present subsection discusses the protection of health-related rights and the State's obligations to it under the SADC Gender Protocol.

a. Access to medicines under the SADC Gender Protocol

The SADC Gender Protocol explicitly provides health-related rights. For instance, under article 9, State parties protect people with disabilities by considering their particular vulnerabilities. Moreover, article 11 guarantees the girl and boy child's right to equal healthcare access. Furthermore, under article 26, State parties enhance appropriate and affordable quality health care to eliminate maternal mortality and address women's and men's mental, sexual and reproductive health. Finally, under article 27 (3) (b), State parties ensure universal access to HIV and AIDS treatment for infected women, men, girls and boys. All these health-related rights cannot be appropriately implemented without adequate access to medicines. Moreover, the SADC Gender Protocol applies to everyone, including women, men, girls and boys. The Protocol's provisions on universal access to HIV and AIDs treatment constitute a very positive improvement on the African Women Protocol because sub-Saharan Africa is the region hardest hit by the HIV and AIDS pandemic, of which most affected people are women.[497]

---

495 This approach requires the mainstreaming of human rights in the development process. It means embracing human rights in policies and the implementation of programmes. See Mulela Mulela Margaret Munalula, "SADC Protocol on Gender and Development: Road map to equality?" *SADC Law Journal 1*, (2011): 189.

496 See preamble to SADC Gender Protocol, and article 3.

497 Malebakeng Forere and Lee Stone, "The SADC Protocol on Gender and Development: duplication or complementarity of the African Union Protocol on Women's Rights?" *African Human Rights Law Journal*, (2009): 451.

b. State's obligations

The protection of health-related rights under the SADC Gender Protocol entails both specific and general obligations. Specific duties are inherent to each protected health-related right, as discussed in the previous section. They mainly consist of the adoption of legislation and related measures, policies, programs, and services.[498]

General duties relate to the harmonization of national laws, policies and strategies with relevant regional and international human rights instruments, and the implementation of domestic legislation and policies that eliminate all practices which negatively affect fundamental rights, including the right to health.[499] Further general obligations include implementation of the SADC Gender Protocol at the national level[500]through the provision by the competent judicial, administrative or legislative authority of appropriate remedies to any person whose rights are violated based on gender.[501] Reference to the provision for remedies in case of violation of human rights reinforces and confirms the human rights character of the SADC Gender Protocol.

In its original version, most of the SADC Gender Protocol provisions,[502] including those relating to reducing maternal mortality and universal access to HIV and AIDS treatment, imposed a kind of "implementation deadline obligation" that all State parties should have met in 2015.[503] As Malebakeng and Stone[504] point out, in its previous version, the SADC Gender Protocol was framed in a way that did not give the respective member States the discretion to implement it considering their individual economic, political, and social situations. Conscious that they failed to meet the 2015 targeted goals, Member States have decided to revise the SADC Gender Protocol in selectively removing or deleting the 2015 deadline, especially for all the provisions dealing with health-related rights.[505]

4. Enforcement mechanisms

A close look at the SADC Treaty, SADC Health Protocol, and SADC Gender Protocol reveals that they distinguish three kinds of enforcement mechanisms, namely the procedure before the Summit of Heads of State and Government, the state reporting procedure and the judicial procedure. Except the judicial procedure that applies to the SADC Treaty and its two Protocols, the procedure before the Summit

---

498 SADC Gender Protocol, arts 9, 11, 26 and 27.
499 Ibid. arts 2, 3, 4 (2), and 32.
500 Ibid. art 35 (1) and (2).
501 Ibid. art 32.
502 Ibid. arts 6, 12, 14, 15, 17, 18, 19, 22, and 25.
503 Ibid. arts 26 and 27 (3) b.
504 Forere and Stone, "SADC Protocol on Gender and Development," 457.
505 See amendments brought to, among others, arts 26 and 27.

concerns only the SADC Treaty and SADC Health Protocol. For its part, the state reporting procedure applies only to the SADC Gender Protocol.

a. The procedure before the Summit of Heads of State and Government

The SADC Summit is the supreme policy-making institution of SADC.[506] Both the SADC Treaty and SADC Health Protocol explicitly vest the Summit with the power to sanction any Member State that persistently fails, without good reason, to fulfil obligations assumed under these two instruments, or implements policies that undermine their principles and objectives.[507] Put differently, State parties' failure to give effect to the principle of human rights, the fight against HIV, and other deadly diseases, and the provision of pharmaceuticals as argued in the SADC Treaty and the SADC Health Protocol is subject to sanctions. Equally, State parties that implement inconsistent policies with both the principles and objectives of these two instruments are subject to the Summit's sanctions. The provisions under discussion also suggest that such sanctions shall not apply to a State party that has acted with good reason. However, both the SADC Treaty and the SADC Health Protocol do not define the word "good reasons," nor do they set up the assessment criteria. Moreover, it is not clear whether the State party concerned should justify its good reasons before the SADC Summit.

In practical terms, it is up to the Summit to decide, on a case-by-case basis, to give a decision on the appropriate sanction.[508] However, unlike the SADC Treaty, which remains silent, the SADC Health Protocol states that the SADC Council shall make a recommendation to the Summit if it decides that a sanction is called for.[509] While these sanctions are not expressly listed, the provisions under consideration do not clarify how and by whom the Council and the SADC Summit shall receive information about a State's non-compliance with the SADC Treaty and the SADC Health Protocol.

b. State reporting procedure under the SADC Gender Protocol

According to article 35 (4) and (5) of the SADC Gender Protocol, States Parties shall submit reports to the Executive Secretary of SADC once every two years, indicating the progress achieved in the implementation of the measures agreed to in this Protocol. The same provision states that the Executive Secretary of SADC shall submit the progress reports to the SADC Council and Summit for consideration. Unlike under the African Charter and the ICESCR, State parties are not

506 SADC Treaty, arts 9 and 10.

507 Ibid. art 33. See also SADC Health Protocol, art 31.

508 SADC Treaty, art 33 (2), and SADC Health Protocol, art 31 (2).

509 SADC Health Protocol, art 31 (2).

expressly required to report on challenges in implementing the SADC Gender Protocol. Moreover, the provision under discussion does not spell out details on both the Council and Summit's functions concerning the consideration of State reports. For instance, it remains silent whether these two organs, like the African Commission and the CESCR, can issue concluding observations to the State reports.

Some critics argue that by falling short of providing other enforcement mechanisms, such as individual complaint procedure, the Gender Protocol has settled for less than what the African Union provides in terms of implementation mechanisms.[510] These critics go further by concluding that

> the all-important implementation of rights is undermined in the Gender Protocol, with the result that victims of infringements of their rights in the SADC sub-region would have to circumvent the sub-regional mechanisms as they are clearly inadequate and rely on the AU mechanisms to vindicate their rights. The institution of the only reporting procedure under the Gender Protocol amounts to unnecessary duplication of efforts, because multiple reporting by member states can be unduly onerous and is not cost-effective.[511]

From this quote, the SADC Gender Protocol does not institute any individual complaints procedure. However, the SADC Tribunal, whose competence extends to the SADC Treaty and its Protocols, can still enforce all the rights argued under the SADC Gender Protocol, including access to medicines. Moreover, the SADC Gender Protocol is a sub-regional instrument, the content of which differs from other human rights instruments in many respects. In addition to covering human rights protected in other human rights treaties, SADC Gender Protocol deals with specific SADC region issues, such as widower's rights, multiple roles of women, economic empowerment, HIV and AIDS. Therefore, State reports under the SADC Gender Protocol can emphasize these specific issues and make appropriate reference to their previously submitted information to other treaty bodies for commonly protected rights.[512]

c. Complaints procedure before the SADC Tribunal

The present subsection deals with the SADC Tribunal human rights jurisdiction, the implementation, and enforcement of its judgments.

aa) SADC Tribunal human rights jurisdiction

Article 9 (g) of the SADC Treaty establishes the SADC Tribunal. Its jurisdiction under the SADC Treaty consists of ensuring adherence to and the proper

510 Forere and Stone, "SADC Protocol on Gender and Development," 452-53.
511 Ibid. 452.
512 ICESCR, article 17 (3).

interpretation and application of the Treaty provisions, its protocols, and subsidiary instruments and adjudicating upon any disputes.[513] Treaty provision under discussion remains unclear regarding the Tribunal's human rights jurisdiction since it does not expressly mention the involved parties in the above disputes.

Article 15 (1) of the SADC Tribunal Protocol fills in the Treaty's gap by providing that the Tribunal is competent for disputes between, among others, natural or legal persons and States. Moreover, articles 17, 18 and 19 of the SADC Tribunal Protocol extend the Tribunal's jurisdiction[514] to disputes between States and Community, between natural or legal persons and Community, and between community and staff.

Like the SADC Treaty, the SADC Tribunal Protocol does not determine the nature of the disputes it mentions. For instance, regarding disputes between natural persons and States, neither the SADC Treaty nor the SADC Tribunal Protocol expressly says that the Tribunal has jurisdiction to consider human rights violations.[515] However, as long as the violation of human rights constitutes a legal dispute between the State and individuals,[516] then the lack of any explicit reference to the Tribunal's jurisdiction on human rights should not mean depriving it of such a power. Instead, the above provisions impliedly[517] recognize the Tribunal human rights jurisdiction by making it competent to deal with applying the SADC Treaty and its Protocols' provisions on human rights in any dispute between natural persons and States. Article 15 (2) of the SADC Tribunal Protocol reinforces this assertion. It urges individuals who want to bring action against a State party before the SADC Tribunal to first exhaust the domestic remedies or prove that they were unable to proceed under the domestic jurisdiction of the State party concerned. The SADC Tribunal confirmed its human rights jurisdiction in the Campbell case against Zimbabwe.

bb) Confirmation of the SADC Tribunal human rights jurisdiction in the Campbell case

In the Campbell Case, applicants challenged the acquisition of agricultural land by the Republic of Zimbabwe while alleging the violation of their rights of access to the courts and not to be discriminated against based on racial discrimination.[518]

513 SADC Treaty, arts 16 (1) and 32.

514 Henok Birhanu Asmelash, "Southern African Development Community (SADC) Tribunal," *MPILux Working Paper 10*, (2017): 6.

515 Moses Phooko, "No longer in suspense: clarifying the human rights jurisdiction of the SADC Tribunal," *PER / PELJ 18*, no. 3, (2015): 546, and Ebobrah, "Human rights developments," 261.

516 Obonye, "Neutering the SADC Tribunal," 297.

517 Phooko, "No longer in suspense," 553.

518 Campbell Case.

Along with this primary application, the applicants have applied to an interim measure restraining the respondent from removing them from the agricultural land mentioned above until the dispute's adjudication.[519] The Republic of Zimbabwe did not question the SADC Tribunal's competence. Instead, it submitted that the applicants had first to exhaust local remedies.[520]

Surprisingly, in the main application, the respondent State refuted the SADC Tribunal's human rights jurisdiction. It submitted that the SADC Treaty only sets out the principles and objectives of SADC without setting the standards against which one should assess member States' actions. Zimbabwe further submitted that there should first be a Protocol on human rights and agrarian reform to implement the principles set out in the Treaty.[521] The SADC Tribunal rebutted the respondent's submissions. It confirmed its human rights jurisdiction through a combined reading of articles 4 (c) and 6 (1)[522] of the SADC Treaty, and 21 (b) of the Tribunal Protocol.[523] To begin with, the SADC Tribunal held that article 4 (c) of the SADC Treaty recognizes its competence to deal with any dispute concerning human rights, democracy and the rule of law, which are the very issues raised in the Campbell case.[524] This Tribunal's reasoning considers the view that treaty´s principles providing the overall framework relating to the understanding of States' obligations are justiciable.[525] Therefore, the SADC Tribunal interpreted article 4 (c) to entail the State's obligations to respect, protect and promote[526] human rights under the SADC Treaty.

For its part, article 21 (b) of the SADC Tribunal Protocol allowed the SADC Tribunal to use, among others, the African Charter, the ICESCR, and the Vienna Convention on the Law of Treaties[527] to either emphasize the State's obligations or to fill in the content of human rights referred to in article 4 (c) of the SADC Treaty. The SADC Tribunal found the Republic of Zimbabwe in violation of articles 4 (c) and 6 (2) of the SADC Treaty.[528]

---

519 Case N° SADCT: 2/07, Mike Campbell (PVT) limited and William Michael Campbell vs. the Republic of Zimbabwe, 2007.

520 Ibid.

521 Campbell Case.

522 Article 6 (1) of the SADC Treaty obligates member States to refrain from taking any measure likely to jeopardize the sustenance of its principles, the achievement of its objectives and the implementation of the provisions of the Treaty.

523 Article 21 (b) of the SADC Treaty allows the Tribunal to develop its own community jurisprudence having regard to applicable treaties, general principles, and rules of public international law.

524 Campbell Case.

525 Moyo, "Defending human rights," 599.

526 Campbell case.

527 Ibid.

528 Ibid.

In sum, as long as the exercise of the implied power of the SADC Tribunal to deal with human rights violation is necessary for the organization and its Member States to achieve its object and purpose as specified in the constituent treaty, the SADC Tribunal did not do anything that the SADC Treaty prohibited.[529] The Campbell Case is an indication that residents of SADC Member States, such as Congolese and Tanzanians, can bring to the SADC Tribunal, any cases of violation of access to medicines according to article 4 (c) of the SADC Treaty.

cc) Enforcement of the SADC Tribunal's judgments

According to article 32 (1) of the SADC Tribunal Protocol, every State party involved ensures the enforcement of the Tribunal's decisions following its law and civil procedure rules relating to the registration and enforcement of foreign judgments. This provision considers the Tribunal's decisions tantamount to foreign States' judgments as far as their implementation is concerned. Though the Tribunal's judgments are binding upon the parties to the dispute,[530] the voluntary execution of the Tribunal's ruling by the State party concerned can give rise to some concerns. These may include, among others, the lack of the law and rules of civil procedure for the registration and enforcement of foreigner judgments within a Member State,[531] the failure of such law and rules to expressly contain provisions on the registration of SADC Tribunal's judgments,[532] and the express refusal of the State party concerned to execute the Tribunal's decision. In the Campbell case, for instance, the government of Zimbabwe expressly refused to implement the Tribunal's judgment for two reasons. Firstly, it argued that the SADC Tribunal lacked jurisdiction to hear the Campbell case and that the Tribunal's decision was "nonsense" and "of no consequence."[533] Secondly, the High Court of Zimbabwe has rejected requests to register and enforce the Tribunal's decision in the Campbell case, on the ground that such registration and consequent

529 Phooko, "No longer in suspense," 536 and 555.

530 SADC Tribunal Protocol, art 32 (1)(3).

531 Frimpong, Oppong, "Enforcing judgements of the SADC Tribunal in the domestic courts of member states, Monitoring regional integration in Southern Africa Yearbook 2010, *Trade Law Centre for Southern Africa*, (2011): 116 and 123, Laurie Nathan, "The disbanding of the SADC Tribunal: A cautionary tale," *Human Rights Quarterly 35*, no. 4, (2013): 874 and 877. See also Case N° SADC (T) 01/2010.

532 The relevant laws dealing with foreign judgments in the DRC and the URT do not make provisions for the enforcement of the SADC Tribunal judgments. See Tanzanian Reciprocal Enforcement of Foreign Judgements Act, 2002, and Loi Organique N° 13/011-B du 11 Avril 2013 portant organisation, fonctionnement et compétences des juridictions de l'ordre judiciaire, art 119.

533 Case N° SADC (T) 01/2010.

enforcement of the judgment were fundamentally contrary to the public policy of the country.[534] However, the SADC Tribunal has no legal means at its disposal to force the succumbed party to execute its decision. Such competence rests with other SADC's institutions.

dd) *Role of the SADC Summit in the case of non-compliance with the SADC tribunal's judgment*

Article 32 (4) of the SADC Tribunal Protocol entitles any party concerned to refer to the SADC Tribunal any failure by a State party to comply with the SADC Tribunal's decision. If the Tribunal establishes the existence of such failure, it submits its findings to the SADC Summit for appropriate action.[535] Although the Tribunal Protocol does not define the expression "appropriate action," it means to include any Summit's decision that aims to enforce the SADC Tribunal's decision. The Campbell Case constituted the first time the Summit had to enforce the SADC Tribunal's judgment. However, the Summit turned its back on both the Tribunal and the SADC Treaty.[536] In other words, the Summit did not take any appropriate action to give effect to the findings of the SADC Tribunal relating to Zimbabwe's refusal to implement its judgments.[537] The SADC Summit's attitude in the Campbell case contradicts its jurisprudence. Although it did not relate to the execution of the Tribunal's decisions, the Summit had already undertaken sanctions against Madagascar by suspending it from all the Community's institutions and organs until the country's return to constitutional normalcy.[538] It went further to state that, in the event of non-compliance with the SADC's decisions, SADC was mandated in collaboration with the AU and the UN, to consider other options to restore constitutional normalcy.[539] The question is whether the Summit will force Zimbabwe to comply with the Tribunal's judgment,[540] or whether its silence or inertia is akin to any of its decisions, which are binding and without appeal.

---

534 The Minister of Justice and Legal Affairs of Zimbabwe also informed the Tribunal that any decisions that the Tribunal may have made against the Republic of Zimbabwe are null and void. See SADC Case N° (T) 03/2009 and SADC Case N° (T) 01/ 2010.

535 Ibid. art 32 (5).

536 Laurie, "Disbanding of SADC Tribunal," 874 and 877.

537 Case N° SADC (T) 03/2009, 2009, and Case N° SADC (T) 01/2010.

538 Extraordinary SADC Summit of Heads of State and Government, Communiqué, Kingdom of Swaziland, 2009, para 16.

539 Ibid. para 18.

540 The SADC Summit is still bound to the Treaty's obligation to take appropriate action against Zimbabwe. See Ariranga G. Pillay et al., "Three illegal and arbitrary decisions taken in bad faith by the SADC Council of Ministers and Summit of Heads of State and Government. Letter to the Executive Secretary of SADC," 2011, https://

Meanwhile, the SADC Summit highly influenced by Zimbabwe's political pressure[541] decided through a communiqué not to reappoint members of the Tribunal whose term of office had expired. SADC Summit further reiterated the moratorium on receiving any new cases or hearings of any cases by the Tribunal pending the amending SADC Tribunal Protocol.[542]

Accordingly, the SADC Summit signed in Zimbabwe a new Protocol to repeal the existing Tribunal Protocol.[543] Its primary reform consists of removing the Tribunal's jurisdiction on disputes between natural persons and States, including on human rights.[544] From the above, it follows that by putting the tribunal's human rights jurisdiction in its death throes,[545] the Summit's decision or communiqué is contrary[546] to both the SADC Treaty and the SADC Tribunal Protocol. It is worth noting that the coming into force of the amending Protocol seems uncertain. For instance, while South Africa has withdrawn its signature from this Protocol,[547] the High Court in URT has urged the government to reconsider its position regarding the signing and ratification of the said.[548]

All in all, as long as the amending SADC Tribunal Protocol has not yet come into force,[549] the SADC Tribunal Protocol remains binding on all the SADC Member

---

www.politicsweb.co.za/documents/three-illegal-and-ultra-vires-decisions (accessed July 12, 2019).

541 In South Africa, the High Court ruled that the signature by the President of South Africa of the Amending Protocol on the SADC Tribunal signalled South Africa's participation in a conspiracy initiated by the President Mugabe regime in Zimbabwe. See Law Society of South Africa and Others vs. President of the Republic of South Africa and Others, 20382/2015, 2018 (hereinafter Law Society Case), para 64.

542 Extraordinary SADC Summit Heads of State and Government of the Southern Africa Development Community, Communiqué, Windhoek, 2011 (SADC Summit Communiqué, 2011), para 6-8.

543 SADC Summit of SADC Heads of State and Government, Communiqué, Victoria Falls, 2014 (hereinafter the SADC Summit Communiqué, 2014).

544 SADC amending Tribunal Protocol, arts 33 and 35.

545 Cowell talks about the "death of the SADC Tribunal's human rights jurisdiction". See Cowell, "Death of the SADC Tribunal," 401.

546 Following the South African High Court, the President's participation in suspending the SADC Tribunal and his subsequent signing of the 2014 Protocol on SADC Tribunal were unlawful, irrational and unconstitutional. See Law Society Case, para 72 (1).

547 The SADC Summit noted the withdrawal of South Africa's signature from the amending SADC Tribunal Protocol. See SADC Summit of Heads of State and Government, Communiqué, United Republic of Tanzania, 2019, para 20.

548 Tanganyika Law Society vs. Ministry of foreign affairs and international cooperation of the URT and the Attorney General of the URT, 2019.

549 SADC Tribunal Protocol, art 37.

States and organs. Therefore, SADC Summit is urged to return to normality in lifting the decision suspending the SADC Tribunal's work. It is worth recalling that after the country had a new president, South Africa withdrew its signature from the amending SADC Tribunal Protocol. Therefore, one possible way to achieve this might be the reconfiguration of the current composition of the SADC Summit, which must involve the change of Heads of state and Government in the SADC Member States.

D. Chapter summary

The ICESCR, the African Charter, the SADC Treaty, and its two Protocols protect access to medicines, spell out the State's obligations and establish various enforcement mechanisms.

Regarding access to medicines, it is a derivative right of the right to health protected under the examined human rights treaties, despite their language differences. Accordingly, article 12 of the ICESCR covers everyone's right to enjoy the highest attainable standard of physical and mental health, including creating conditions that would assure medical services and medical attention in the event of sickness. Influenced by the ICESCR, article 16 of the African Charter protects everyone's right to enjoy the best attainable state of physical and mental health. Furthermore, like article 12 of the ICESCR, article 16 talks about medical attention individuals should receive when they are sick. Under the SADC human rights law, the SADC Treaty urges the SADC and the Member States to follow human rights principles. Therefore, the provisions of articles 12 of the ICESCR and 16 of the African Charter can fill in the content of the right to health as part of the SADC human rights principle. Unlike the ICESCR, which talks about medical services, the SADC Health Protocol promotes health care through access to health services. Like the SADC Health Protocol, the SADC Gender Protocol protects equal access to health care for boys and girls. Moreover, unlike other human rights treaties, the SADC Gender Protocol covers universal access to HIV and AIDS treatment for infected people. This right is a concrete component of providing medical service and attention in the event of sickness, as argued under articles 12 of the ICESCR and 16 of the African Charter.

Regarding the State's obligations, the ICESCR subjects the adoption of implementation measures, including legislation, to the clause of progressive realization and available resources, including international assistance and cooperation. Like the ICESCR, implementation measures under the African Charter expressly mention legislative measures. However, unlike the ICESCR, the African Charter compels each State party to immediately implement the right to health within its available resources. As can be seen, the State's obligations under the African Charter conflict with those in the ICESCR. To bring these two instruments into harmony, the African Commission states that State's obligations towards ESCRs under the African Charter are similar to those under the ICESCR. For its part, the SADC Treaty requires the Member States to take adequate measures without listing them. Reference to adequate measures is broad enough to include expressly and non-expressly implementation measures under the ICESCR, the African Charter, the SADC Health Protocol, and the SADC Gender Protocol, such as laws, policies, strategies, programs, and programs budgets.

Moreover, like under the ICESCR, the SADC human rights regime considers international cooperation in implementing the right to health. However, it is essential to note that the SADC human rights law does not expressly provide for the progressive realization of the right to health. Therefore, it conflicts with the nature of the State's obligations under the ICESCR, endorsed by the African Commission regarding the implementation of the African Charter.

Given that the right to health in the SADC Treaty also encompasses articles 12 of the ICESCR and 16 of the African Charter, one can argue that progressive realization also applies to the right to health within the framework of the SADC human rights regime. Moreover, the fact that State parties to the SADC Health Protocol implement access to health services according to the SADC Treaty's principle of human rights reinforces such interpretation. Also, under the SADC Gender Protocol, State parties consider their obligations in other human rights treaties, such as the ICESCR and the African Charter.

Despite the language differences in their formulation, the provisions under discussion are complementary. They all aim to ensure that people get access to medicines within the domestic jurisdictions of State parties. In other words, appropriate domestic implementation of access to drugs by DRC or URT is sufficient enough to justify the State's compliance with its treaty's obligations under the above ratified human rights instruments.

The enforcement mechanisms include the state reporting procedure, the interstate and individual communications, and the procedure before the SADC Summit. In respect of the state reporting, unlike under the SADC human rights law, both the DRC and URT have submitted some reports to the CESCR and African Commission on the implementation of the right to health. However, in addition to the delay in their submission, the State's reports do not address all the aspects of access to medicines. Concerning inter-state and individual communications, unlike the African Court and SADC Tribunal, which have never dealt with any application on the violation of access to medicines by DRC or URT, the African Commission has already examined a communication on the right to health against Zaïre (DRC) in 1996.

Although the existing enforcement mechanisms have not been of any practical relevance for the protection of access to medicines in DRC and URT, treaty provisions that provide them are still binding on these two countries. For instance, in reporting on the implementation of the right to health, including access to medicines under the ICESCR and the African Charter, both the DRC and URT reiterate the view that domestically adopted measures in that regard are consistent with their human treaty's obligations. Regarding the implementation of the SADC human rights law, the High Court ruled that the URT is bound to give effect to the SADC law in good faith and confirmed its inherent powers to entertain all adjudicative disputes between individual and legal persons against the URT in matters arising out of the SADC Treaty.[550] In the DRC, the Women Law expressly claims to implement the SADC Gender Protocol.[551] For its part, the Decree on the registration of pharmaceutical products is legally based on the SADC Health Protocol's provision on the harmonization of registration procedures for medicines within SADC Member States.

In sum, the chapter illustrates the potential for simultaneous protection of access to medicines through a multilevel human rights regime. It also points at some difficulties associated with such a multilevel regime of protecting human rights, namely different formulations of the right to health, which affect its content, and different nature of the State's obligations regarding the same right.

550 Tanganyika Law Society vs. Ministry of foreign affairs and international cooperation of the URT and the Attorney General of the URT, 2019.

551 Loi N° 15/013 portant modalités d'application des droits de la femme et de la parité, 2015 (Women Law).

III. Protection of access to medicines under the domestic law of the DRC and URT

The present chapter discusses the protection of access to medicines under the domestic laws of the DRC and URT, using two main approaches. Firstly, it focuses on the constitutional protection of access to medicines as the most effective means of protecting human rights in the domestic law.[552] Indeed, as the country's supreme law in DRC and URT,[553]the Constitution governs the domestic protection of all human rights,[554]including access to medicines. Furthermore, the Constitution recognizes ratified human rights treaties as part of the domestic law in these two countries.[555] Secondly, due to the complexity and diversity of implementation measures on access to medicines, the chapter discusses the measures following their goals to make good quality medicines available, accessible, acceptable,[556] and justiciable.

A. Domestic laws and their implementation in respect to access to medicines in the DRC

The present section discusses the protection of human rights under the DRC Constitution focusing on access to medicines. It further examines adopted implementation measures, and the justiciability of access to medicines.

1. Protection of human rights under the DRC Constitution

The DRC Constitution dedicates its Title II to "human rights, fundamental freedoms, and duties of citizens and State." Protected rights comprise CPRs, ESCRs and collective rights. Chapter I dealing with CPRs covers articles 11 to 33. Protected CPRs include, among others, the rights to human dignity, equality before the law, and the right to life. It is worth recalling that Title I of the DRC Constitution relating to general provisions on the sovereignty also protects some CPRs, namely, the rights to vote, to be voted, to create a political party and to nationality.[557]

552 Manisuli Ssenyonjo, "The influence of the International Covenant on Economic, Social and Cultural Rights in Africa," *Neth Int Law Rev*, (2017): 262.

553 DRC Constitution, art 221, and URT Constitution, art 64 (5).

554 ICCPR, art 2 (2).

555 DRC Constitution, art 215, and URT Constitution, art 63 (3).

556 General Comment 14.

557 DRC Constitution, arts 5, 6 and 10.

Chapter II on ESCRs include articles 34 to 49. Protected ESCRs cover, among others, the rights to property, work, education, culture, health, and housing.[558] Chapter III protects collective rights,[559] such as the rights to peace and security, the right to a healthy and conducive environment, and the right to enjoy the natural resources.

Theoretically, all these categories of human rights enjoy the same legal status.[560] They are subject to article 60 of the Constitution, which provides that "respect for human rights and fundamental freedoms enshrined in the Constitution is compulsory for both the State and individuals."

a. Constitutional protection of the right of access to medicines

The DRC Constitution does not expressly protect the right of access to medicines as an independent and autonomous right. Instead, a close look at its provisions reveals that it deals with access to medicine in four ways. Firstly, article 47 of the DRC Constitution expressly provides that "the right to health and food security is guaranteed. The law sets the fundamental principles and rules regulating public health and food security." Unlike ratified treaties, which talk about the right to the enjoyment of the highest attainable physical and mental health, the DRC Constitution provides a human right to health. The Courts of law in DRC have not yet determined the contents of the constitutional right to health,[561] nor have they determined the nature of the State's obligations to it. Nonetheless, one can argue that, in using the concept of the right to health, article 47 opts for broad and holistic protection of the right to health, which includes among others, appropriate health care, access to medicines and other underlying determinants of health.[562] Implementing the constitutional right to health, article 17 of the Public Health Law provides for everyone's right to quality health care, which covers medicines. Secondly, other constitutional provisions are relevant to the enjoyment of the right to health. They relate[563] to parents' duty to ensure their children's health care with the State's support and the special protection of old persons and people with disabilities following their physical, intellectual, and moral needs. A

558 For a detailed list of protected ESCRs, read title I, chapter 2 of the DRC Constitution.

559 See title I, chap 3 of the DRC Constitution.

560 Lumbu Ngoy, "Contrôle et protection des droits sociaux fondamentaux en droit congolais: portée et état de la question, " *Presse de l'Université Internationale du Congo*, (2014): 303.

561 Garry Sakata, *Introduction au droit économique: droit de l'OHADA, transformation des entreprises publiques, état entrepreneur, établissements publics, sociétés du portefeuille, nationalisation, rétrocession, libéralisation et politique des prix, protection des consommateurs, droits de l'homme*, (Kinshasa: Presse Universitaire de Kinshasa, 2013), 147.

562 General Comment 14, para 11.

563 DRC Constitution, arts 40, 42, and 49.

successful implementation of these constitutional rights should include right of access to medicines. Thirdly, according to article 215 of the DRC Constitution, ratified human rights treaties form part of the country's domestic law. They have precedence over national laws other than the Constitution. Therefore, the right to health in the ICESCR, the African Charter, and SADC human rights instruments becomes incorporated into the DRC's domestic legal system.

In protecting the right to health under the constitution, the Public Health Law, and ratified human rights treaties as part of the domestic law, the DRC provides for the three main routes through which the State can recognize the right to health in national legal frameworks.[564] Finally, the constitutional right to life[565] also constitutes indirect protection of some components of the right to health, such as provision of life-saving medicines.[566]

b. Relationship between treaty and constitutional right of access to medicines

Article 215 of the DRC Constitution regulates the relationship between ratified treaties and the domestic laws by stating that "treaties and international agreements duly ratified, have, upon their publication, primacy over national laws, on the condition of the application of each treaty or agreement by other states." This provision institutes the monist legal approach and subjects the application of ratified treaties to two conditions, namely their publication in the official gazette and reciprocity. It is worth recalling that the DRC has already published its main ratified human rights treaties in the gazette.[567] As far as the reciprocity clause is concerned, it does not enjoy an absolute character since it does not apply to ratified human rights instruments.[568] Nevertheless, article 215 under discussion has some implications on the extent of the right to health, the relationship between treaty's right and constitutional right to health, and the nature of the State's

---

564 SK. Perehudoff, Ro. Laing, and HV. Hogerzeil, "Access to medicines in national constitutions," *Bulletin of the World Health Organization 88*, (2010): 800.

565 DRC Constitution, art 16.

566 Improving access to medicines can save millions of lives. Human Rights Council Resolution 12/24.

567 Makengo Mazyambo, "Introduction aux droits de l'homme: théorie générale, instruments, mécanismes de protection," in *Mandats, rôles et fonctions des pouvoirs constitués dans le nouveau système politique de la République Démocratique du Congo. Journées d'information et de formation organisées à l'intention des parlementaires, députés provinciaux et des Hauts Cadres de l'administration*, ed. Programme des Nations Unies pour le Développement (Kinshasa: PNUD, 2007), 243.

568 Ibid, 243-244. See also Mpiana Kazadi, *La position du droit international dans l'ordre juridique congolais et l'application de ses normes* (Paris: EPU, 2013), 449.

obligations. To begin with, article 215 implies that the DRC's domestic law protects the right to health as argued simultaneously in the ICESCR, the African Charter, the SADC human rights instruments, and the DRC Constitution. At first glance, it may seem like a duplication. However, an in-depth analysis of the country's legal system provides explanations that lead one to the conclusion that these rights supplement each other. For instance, the right to health under the ICESCR and the African Charter is anterior to the constitutional right to health. Moreover, due to the lack of a judicial interpretation of the constitutional right to health, elements of the right to health under ratified human rights treaties can fill the gap.

In incorporating duly ratified human rights treaties into the domestic legal system, article 215 assigns to human rights herein protected a superior status over human rights protected under the national laws other than the Constitution.[569] The supremacy of international human rights treaties over domestic laws opens to natural persons new legal possibilities of recourse against the abuses of the laws and regulations that violate their rights.[570] Regarding human rights protected in both the Constitution and ratified treaties, such as the right to health, people have the option to challenge laws and regulations that violate them based either on the Constitution or ratified human rights treaties. If the claim relates to the violation of both the Constitution and ratified treaties, the Courts should give priority to the Constitution.[571] In contrast, violation of treaty rights which the Constitution does not expressly protect, such as the rights to an adequate standard of living, social security, and social insurance,[572]are assessed only in the light of ratified treaties, which provide them. Direct assessment of these rights by the Court is further possible by the provision of article 153 of the Constitution, which entitles civil and military courts and tribunals to apply duly ratified international treaties.

Regarding the State's obligations, contrary to the ICESCR and similar to the African Charter and SADC human rights treaties, article 47 of the DRC does not subject its implementation to the clause of progressive realization within the country's available resources. The priority of the constitutional right to health over treaty rights implies that the Congolese government should immediately implement right of access to medicines regardless of its developmental level. Though legally logical, such interpretation remains unrealistic since it does not consider the country's socioeconomic realities. As discussed earlier, the African Commission has endorsed the progressive realization of the Charter's ESCRs within domestic, international, and regional resources. To be consistent with its treaty's obligations, the DRC should adopt the progressive approach in implementing the treaty and constitutional right to health.

---

569 The Constitution has primacy over ratified treaties and nationally adopted laws.

570 Mazyambo, "Introduction aux droits de l'homme," 244.

571 Kazadi, *La position du droit international*, 449.

572 ICESCR, arts 9 and 11.

From a theoretical point of view, the DRC Constitution is one of the rare Constitutions in the world, especially in Africa,[573] which provides for broad protection of the right to health.

c. *Nature of the State's obligations*

For the reason of convenience, the present subsection divides the State's duties into specific and general obligations.

aa) Specific State's obligations from article 47 of the Constitution

Article 47 of the DRC Constitution guarantees the rights to health and food security and calls for adopting the law on the fundamental principles and rules regulating public health and food security. Article 47 talks only about the obligation to guarantee, without further details. Neither the courts and tribunals nor the National Commission of Human Rights (NCHR) has interpreted the State's obligation to guarantee the right to health. Instead, in one of its decisions on the right to be elected to a political mandate,[574] the constitutional court expressly ruled that, as part of the judicial power, it is competent to adjudicate the violation of any constitutionally protected rights. From this constitutional court's ruling, one can argue that the duty to guarantee the constitutional right to health implies, among others, the State's responsibility to provide judicial remedies in case of its violation. It is, therefore, recommendable to broadly interpret the obligation to guarantee to cover measures and actions that other branches of the government, namely the government and the parliament, shall take within their competences.

To this end, article 47 expressly calls for adoption of the framework law on public health's fundamental principles and rules. Explicit reference to public health law does not prevent the State from taking other measures and actions, including laws, budgets, policies, or programs, to make access to medicines of good quality available, accessible, and acceptable. Moreover, though the Constitution does not define the word public health, the Public Health Law refers to it as a set of benefits that enable every citizen to benefit from the right to health and from longevity that confers his birth.[575] From this definition, one may argue that access to medicines

573 Le Roux-Kemp identifies the DRC Constitution as providing for a comprehensive exposition of a right to health and health-related rights. However, he falls short by arguing that it does not offer measures to ensure the enforceability of the right to health. Le Roux-Kemp, "Recognition of health rights," 150.

574 The case involved two substitutes of a Senator who was simultaneously elected as a member of the National Assembly. It was submitted by the second substitute against the first one. See Affaire R. Const. 0038 RH 010/CC 28, 2015.

575 Public Health Law, art 3 (34).

forms part of that set of benefits since it contributes to the enjoyment of both the rights to health and long life.

Furthermore, like the African Charter, the DRC Constitution does not subject the implementation of the right to health to the qualification of progressive realization or resource availability. Some critics describe such unqualified State's obligations as unrealistic. For instance, Kumbu, Kabamba, and Esambo[576] commend the protection of ESCRs, CPRs, and collective rights into the Constitution's body through substantive provisions. However, they express concerns about the lack of financial resources at the DRC disposal to ensure their full enjoyment by people.[577] Therefore, they conclude that ESCRs under the DRC Constitution are merely conceived as guidelines for the State's action and do not entail the obligations of result.[578] The fact that DRC is one of the world's poorest nations despite its wealth in human and natural resources cannot be overlooked.[579] Nonetheless, the implementation of ESCRs, just like that of CPRs entails financial implications and calls for the adoption of implementation laws.[580] Therefore, interpreting constitutionally protected ESCRs, including the right to health, as mere guidelines for the State's action contradicts both the letter and the spirit of the Constitution itself,[581]which subjects all human rights herein protected to the same legal status. Such interpretation may negatively influence the government's commitment towards constitutional ESCRs, including right of access to medicines. Therefore, instead of qualifying the constitutional ESCRs as programmatic, the government should implement them following the progressive realization principle provided in the ICESCR and endorsed by the African Commission.

576 Jean M., Kumbu, Bob Kabamba et Jean L., Esambo, "La constitution de la République Démocratique du Congo," in *Mandats, rôles et fonctions des pouvoirs constitués dans le nouveau système politique de la République Démocratique du Congo. Journées d'information et de formation organisées à l'intention des parlementaires, députés provinciaux et des Hauts Cadres de l'administration*, ed. Programme des Nations Unies pour le Développement (Kinshasa: PNUD, 2007), 24-25.

577 Ibid.

578 Ibid.

579 Jacques Bahati, *Evaluating peace and stability in the Democratic Republic of Congo and the United States policy in the Great Lakes Region* (Washington: Africa Faith and Justice Network, 2009), 5.

580 DRC Constitution, arts 14, 22, 24, and 26.

581 The DRC Constitution does not belong to the category of African constitutions that restrict the right to health to state policy's principles and objectives. See Le Roux-Kemp, Recognition of health rights, 145.

bb) General State's obligations

All protected rights under the DRC Constitution are subject to the general obligation of article 60, which states that "respect for all human rights and freedoms protected under the DRC Constitution is compulsory for the government and every person." This provision calls for the following comments. First, in addition to the State's specific obligation to guarantee the right of access to medicines, the State is under the obligation to respect this right. The lack of a constitutional definition of this obligation coupled with the absence of its interpretation by the courts and tribunals may legitimate one to interpret the duty to respect to extend to the duties to protect and fulfil.

Secondly, the concept of "government" must include the national, provincial and local institutions.[582] The national government consists of the President of the Republic, the government, the parliament, and the judiciary.[583] The Constitution explicitly empowers the national or central government[584] to take legislation on the practice of medicine, including preventive medicine, public health, profession of pharmacist, and pharmaceutical trade. Concerning the judiciary, article 150 of the DRC Constitution explicitly states that "the judicial power is the guarantor of individual freedoms and fundamental rights of citizens." All these provisions suggest that each organ of the national government shall implement the right to access medicines following its functions and power.

Regarding provincial governments, the Constitution vests them with both shared and exclusive competencies regarding health matters. Shared competencies between provincial and central governments[585] include the creation of medical institutions, recruitment of medical professionals, and prevention of epidemics. In contrast, exclusive competencies comprise[586] the appointment of the medical professional, the application, and control of medical and pharmaceutical legislation, and the organization of pharmaceutical services, and promotion of primary health care.

Finally, unlike the constitutional competencies of the central and provincial governments on health-related issues, the 2008 Decentralization Law[587]determines the competencies of local government regarding health matters. These include, among others, the promotion of the fight against HIV/AIDS and endemic diseases and the vaccination campaign of the population.[588]

582 DRC Constitution, arts 3 and 68.

583 Ibid. art 68.

584 Ibid. art 202.

585 Ibid. art 203.

586 Ibid. art 204.

587 Loi Organique N°08/016 Portant composition, organisation et fonctionnement des entités territoriales décentralisées et leurs rapports avec l'Etat et les Provinces, 2008 (hereinafter the 2008 Decentralization Law).

588 Ibid. arts 11, 50, 73 and 91.

2. Existing implementation measures relevant for access to medicines

The DRC government is under the constitutional and treaty obligation to implement access to medicines through various implementation measures. The present section analyses those adopted measures by the DRC, aiming to make medicines of good quality available, accessible, and acceptable. It also examines the question of judicial enforcement of access to medicines.

a. Quality medicines and the regulation of the pharmaceutical sector

Medicines are a two-edged sword that can do good or harm. Therefore, pharmaceutical regulation is one of the main ways to ensure medicines' quality. In the DRC, several laws and regulations deal with pharmaceutical activities. To begin with, the 1972 Ordinance-law vests the pharmaceutical regulatory authority in the President of the Republic,[589] in charge of regulating the establishment of pharmacies, the sell, import and export of medicines, and the culture of medicinal plants.[590] The Decree on the trade of pharmaceuticals also recognizes the role of competent organs to set up rules that regulate the creation of pharmaceutical establishments, detention, manufacturing, offer, import and purchase of medicines, and issues of counterfeit medicines.[591] Adopted in 2018, the Public Health Law establishes a public institution responsible for pharmaceutical regulation vested with the power to, among others, grant marketing approvals for medicines, inspect pharmaceutical establishments, control the quality of medicines, and monitor the medicine market.[592] The problem with this provision is that it overlooks the already existing pharmaceutical regulatory authorities, namely the President of the Republic and the Direction de la Pharmacie et du Médicament (DPM), a direction within the national health ministry vested with the same attributions and powers as those provided in the Public Health Law.[593] Implementing the Public Health Law, the prime

589 1972 Ordinance-law, art 12.

590 Ibid.

591 Arrêté Ministériel 1250/CAB/MIN/SP/008/CPH/OBF/2015 portant réglementation du commerce des produits pharmaceutiques en RDC, 2015 (hereinafter Decree on the trade of pharmaceuticals), 1972 Ordinance Law, art 12.

592 Public Health Law, art 53.

593 Arrêté ministériel 1250/CAB/MIN/SP/011/CPH/OBF/2015 modifiant et complétant l'arrêté ministériel N°1250/CAB/MIN/S/AJ/MS/013/2001 portant dispositions relatives à l'enregistrement et à l'autorisation de mise sur le marché des produits pharmaceutiques, 2015, art 1 (8) (henceforth Decree on the registration of pharmaceutical products), and Decree on the trade of pharmaceuticals, art 1 (2).

minister took a decree[594] establishing the "Autorité Congolaise de Règlementation Pharmaceutique," (ACOREP) in substitution of the DPM. As a result, the pharmaceutical regulatory authority in the DRC is carried out concurrently by the President of the Republic and ACOREP.

As can be seen, a panoply of regulations and laws adopted during pre- and post-colonial periods govern the pharmaceutical sector. However, some of these provisions are to some extent scattered, uncoordinated, older, sparse, and inconsistent with both ratified human rights treaties and the DRC Constitution.[595]As an illustration, during the colonial period, the government adopted two main regulations concerning pharmacy practice, namely the 1933 Ordinance[596] and the 1952 Decree.[597] In 1972, while the 1972 Ordinance[598] abrogated the 1933 Ordinance, the 1972 Ordinance-law abrogated[599] articles 9 and 10 of the 1952 Decree on the profession of pharmacists. However, subsequently adopted measures in the pharmaceutical sector, including ordinance-law,[600] ministerial Decrees,[601] and national health policies[602] are still legally based on the 1933 Ordinance and articles 9 and 10 of the 1952 Decree. They neither refer to the 1972 Ordinance-Law nor to the 1972 Ordinance. The above explicit reference to abrogated regulations also influenced some scientific works on the subject, which do not consider the legal change in 1972.[603] The present thesis fills in this gap.

594 Décret N°20/002 du 05 mars 2020 portant création, organisation et fonctionnement d'un Etablissement public dénommé Autorité Congolaise de Règlementation Pharmaceutique, en sigle " ACOREP » (henceforth Decree establishing ACOREP), arts 1 et 4.

595 Public Health Law.

596 The 1933 Ordinance deals with the exercise of pharmacy.

597 The 1952 Decree deals with all the medical professionals, including pharmacists.

598 Article 171 (1) of the 1972 Ordinance expressly abrogates the 1933 Ordinance.

599 Article 19 of the 1972 Ordinance Law abrogates articles 9 and 10 of the 1952 Decree.

600 1991 Ordinance Law, arts 43 and 73.

601 Decree on the trade of pharmaceuticals, art 49, Arrêté ministériel 1250/CAB/MIN/SP/007/CPH/OBF/2015 portant création de la commission d'homologation des produits pharmaceutiques et autres produits de santé, 2015 (hereinafter Ministerial Decree on the homologation of pharmaceuticals), Arrêté ministériel 1250/CAB/MIN/SP/009/CPH/OBF/2015 portant des lignes directrices dans le domaine pharmaceutique en RDC, 2015, Decree on the registration of pharmaceutical products, art 45, et Arrêté ministériel n°1250/CAB/MIN/SP/010/ CPH/OMP/2015 modifiant et complétant l'Arrêté ministériel n°1250/CAB/MIN/ S/AJ/01 du 14 mars 2000 portant conditions d'octroi des autorisations d'ouverture et de fonctionnement des établissements pharmaceutiques, 2015, art 25.

602 PNDS 2016-2020.

603 Starmans Bofoe Lokangu, *La criminalité pharmaceutique en République Démocratique du Congo. Une véritable menace au droit à la santé*, (Paris: L'Harmatan, 2019), 51

The section focuses on the regulation of the profession of pharmacists, creation of pharmaceutical establishments, the control quality, and sanctions to that.

aa) The monopoly of pharmacists in the pharmaceutical business

Article 202 (36) (h) of the DRC Constitution provides for the law on the exercise of pharmacist's profession. However, the Public Health Law, which implements this constitutional provision, is silent on the pharmacist profession's practice. Meanwhile, the 1972 Ordinance law and the 1991 Ordinance law on the national board of pharmacists constitute the primary legal texts that regulate this profession, the provisions of which conflict with each other to some extent. Accordingly, a pharmacist under the 1972 Ordinance law offers a guarantee of professional morality, holds a pharmacy degree, and obtains a pharmacy license from the national public health adviser.[604] In contrast, under the 1991 Ordinance law, a pharmacist should have an enrolment into the board of pharmacists, hold a degree in pharmacy, and comply with the reciprocity clause in case of foreigner pharmacists.[605] As a result, the condition relating to a pharmacy license's obtention under the 1972 Ordinance law conflicts with the relevant provisions of the 1991 Ordinance law, which do not prescribe such requirements.

The pharmaceutical law recognizes the pharmacist's monopoly in all the activities relating to pharmacy and medicines.[606] It is the pharmacist's exclusive responsibility to manage a pharmaceutical establishment, be responsible for the quality of the medicines, including their possession, preservation, and delivery, execute all medical prescriptions, and ensure supervision of all the pharmaceutical services within both public and private health facilities.[607] It is worth recalling that other health professionals, namely pharmacy graduates,[608] medical doctors,[609] surgeons, nurses, dentists, colonial nursing assistants, birth attendants, health agents, midwife, and midwife assistant, can also deal with some pharmaceutical activities.[610] All these health professionals must meet education or training conditions prescribed by the existing law.[611]

---

and 218, Wikha Tshibinda, "Guarantee mechanisms of "rights-claims" recognized by the constitution: right to health, state obligation," *African Law Study Library 4*, (2010): 14 and 18, and Masikini Bazu, "République Démocratique du Congo: droits et défis pharmaceutiques," *Université de Neuchâtel*, (2013): 20, 21, and 58.

604 1972 Ordinance law, arts 1 and 2.

605 1991 Ordinance law, arts 3 and 40.

606 1972 Ordinance, art 4.

607 Ibid, arts, 6, 20 and 28.

608 1972 Ordinance law, arts 4 and 6.

609 1972 Ordinance, arts 27 and 30.

610 See titles II-IV of the 1952 Decree.

611 1958 Ordinance, arts 3 and 5.

To ensure that medicines are produced and kept in good conditions, all the pharmaceutical's activities occur within the established pharmaceutical establishments, namely pharmacies, pharmaceutical services of health institutions, and pharmaceutical manufacturing laboratories.[612] Moreover, pharmaceutical establishments must have suitable premises and facilities to preserve medicines.[613] The law proscribes any pharmaceutical activities outside the above- prescribed premises.[614]

Concerning medicines, their marketing is subject to a previous authorization granted by the health minister, aiming to ensure the quality of medicines.[615] To further guarantee medicines' quality, the existing regulations prohibit any business with altered, falsified, or counterfeit medicines.[616] Article 3 (26) of the Public Health Law provides a broad definition of counterfeit, medicine, which covers, among others, medicines with no active substance, deteriorated and contaminated medicines, and any medicines imported without prior authorization from the national health ministry. By proscribing the sale of medicines of doubtful quality and punishing anybody involved in such business, the legislator protects the consumers and their human rights.[617]

However, on the ground, especially in the private health sector, individuals without a medical background own and manage pharmacies, flouting the existing legislation on this area.[618] Consequently, they can misinform patients or consumers about the use of medicines. Thus, the government's failure to enforce and implement the existing legislation in this area amounts to the State's violation of the obligation to protect people's health from third parties.[619]

bb) Control quality of medicines

The ACOREP's missions in contoling medicines' quality are twofold. First, it contributes to the universal access of the Congolese population to the offer of health services by ensuring the marketing of quality and effective medical products.[620] Secondly, ACOREP protects public health by setting up a control

---

612 1972 Ordinance, art 1.

613 Ibid. art 3.

614 Ibid. art 26.

615 Bazu, "Droits et défis," 25.

616 1972 ordinance, art 69, and Decree on the trade of pharmaceuticals, art 21.

617 Sakata, *Introduction au droit économique*, 148.

618 Commission Nationale des Droits de l'Homme de la République Démocratique du Congo, Troisième rapport annuel d'activités de la Commission Nationale des Droits de l'Homme (Janvier à Décembre 2018), Kinshasa, 2019 (hereinafter CNDH Annual Report 2019), 60.

619 The illegal running of pharmacies is a violation of the right to health. Ibid.

620 Decree establishing ACOREP.

system for pharmaceutical products.[621] An in-depth analysis of the pharmaceutical legislation reveals that control quality of medicines occurs before (an a priori control) and after (an a posteriori control) the marketing of medicines.

(1) An a priori control

An a priori control occurs by regulating the manufacturing conditions of locally produced medicines and the import of medicines. Accordingly, pharmaceutical manufacturing laboratories should have adequate premises, installations, industrial and scientific equipment, and qualified personnel.[622] Moreover, raw materials and manufactured medicines are subject to a checkup to conclude their compliance with the required specifications. This requirement implies that the Congolese regulatory authority is well equipped in terms of both human and material resources to ensure that quality requirements, including the appropriate quantity of active substance of produced medicines, are met. Otherwise, the pharmacy inspectors' role in controlling pharmaceutical manufacturing laboratories[623] would remain unproductive.

For its part, the import can only concern medicines with a product license, which then are subject to a prior analysis following the relevant prescribed procedures.[624] It is worth stressing that such import is subject to prior authorization.[625] Furthermore, all pharmaceuticals, whether imported or locally produced, cannot be marketed without being previously approved and without a licensed product issued by the competent regulatory authority.[626] The regulatory authority may grant or not such a product license.[627] It further means that the regulatory authority carries out some laboratory's analysis of the medicines concerned, including medicines with product license from the exporting country. Such a counter-expertise is necessary for the quality of medicines manufactured abroad before their distribution or marketing. Following articles 42 and 28 of the ministerial decree on the product license, the competent regulatory authority can suspend or withdraw an already issued product license.[628]

Exceptionally, individuals can import medicines for personal use.[629] Further, donations on medicines must comply with the established relevant

---

621 Ibid.

622 1972 Ordinance, arts 37 and 39.

623 Ibid. art 49. See also Decree on the trade of pharmaceuticals, art 46.

624 1972 Ordinance, arts 9, 102 and 107, Decree on the trade of pharmaceuticals, art 2.

625 Decree establishing ACOREP, art 4, and Decree on the trade of pharmaceuticals, art 6.

626 Ministerial Decree on product licence, arts 2-3, and Decree establishing ACOREP, art 4.

627 Ministerial Decree on product licence, art 27.

628 Ibid, arts 27 and 42.

629 1972 Ordinance, art 103, and Decree on the trade of pharmaceuticals, art 35.

procedure.[630] For instance, potential donors cannot send medicines to DRC without prior contact with the latter.[631] Besides, they can only donate registered medicines in the country of origin, which were produced following the good manufacturing practices guidelines.[632] To avoid that medicines object of a donation reach the population after their expiry, received medicines must have upon their arrival, a duration of life of at least one year.[633] However, the import procedure under discussion does not apply when imported medicines aim to respond to emergencies.[634] Unless these exceptions comply with the prescribed import procedure, they may open the door to importing medicines of lousy quality.

To sum up, if appropriately applied, an a priori control can nip in the bud medicines of poor quality, preventing them from reaching the population.

(2) Postmarketing control of medicines

The postmarketing control concerns medicines that are already available to the market. ACOREP is competent to inspect pharmaceutical establishments and control the quality of medicines in collaboration with the ministry responsible for trade.[635] However, the Decree establishing ACOREP does not determine how the ACOREP should conduct these inspection and control. The 1972 Ordinance fills in the gap in that regard. It vests the power to carry out the post-marketing control with pharmacy inspectors appointed among pharmacists and university professors in medicine and pharmacy.[636] In their tasks to ensure the pharmaceutical legislation's application,[637] these inspectors have the power to, among others,[638] enter any pharmaceutical establishment, take any samples deemed necessary, and send them to the designed laboratory for analysis. Moreover, they can seal products that seem altered, defrauded, or falsified until the outcome of the laboratory analysis.[639] Pharmacy inspectors also seize medicines distributed or manufactured without consideration to the prescribed conditions. Once appropriately applied, the postmarketing control can supplement and fill in the gap of the

630 Decree on the trade of pharmaceuticals, art 33, and Ministerial Decree on product licence, art 4. See also Ministère de la santé publique, Lignes directrices relatives aux dons de médicaments, 2015 (hereinafter Guidelines for medicines donation).

631 It is the beneficiary State's responsibility to specify its needs in pharmaceuticals or to refuse gifts. See Guidelines for medicines donation, art 1.

632 Ibid. art 3.

633 Ibid.

634 Decree on the trade of pharmaceuticals, art 34.

635 Decree establishing ACOREP, art 4.

636 1972 ordinance, art 46.

637 1972 ordinance, art 48.

638 Ibid. art 49, 51-52.

639 Ibid. art 51.

a priori control by discouraging any pharmaceutical activity contrary to the pharmaceutical legislation.

However, the shortage of pharmacists, including university professors in pharmacy and in medicine, does not allow for an appropriate discharge of this control in every village, town, or city, which is supposed to have at least one pharmaceutical establishment. Despite the above legislation, substandard[640] and falsified[641] medicines are still available in public and private health institutions.[642] Indeed, the pharmaceutical inspection is not carried out expertly because of the lack of appropriate laboratory devices for drugs' quality control.[643] For instance, with the support of Quality Medicine for All (QUAMED) and Institut de Médecine Tropicale (IMT) of Antwerp, the health ministry conducted a control quality on three pediatric patients' drugs available in Kinshasa. The result revealed that in addition to lacking the standards of quality, the above-analysed medicines were sold without product license.[644] Further studies conducted in 2018[645] and 2020[646] revealed the circulation and consummation of substandard and falsified medicines. It is worth recalling that quality control materials used to analyse these medicines belonged to the government's foreign partners in Germany and Belgium. These

---

640 Also called "out of specification", substandard medical products are authorized medical products that fail to meet either their quality standards or their specifications, or both. See World Health Organization, Member State mechanism on substandard/spurious/falsely-labelled/falsified/ counterfeit medical products, Seventieth World Health Assembly, A70/23 Provisional agenda item 13.6, 2017.

641 Falsified medicines are medical products that deliberately/fraudulently misrepresent their identity, composition, or source. Ibid.

642 PNDS 2016-2020.

643 Bofoe, *La criminalité pharmaceutique*, 51.

644 PNDS 2016-2020.

645 Mufusama Jean Pierre et ali, "Quality of the antimalarial medicine artemether–lumefantrine in 8 cities of the Democratic Republic of the Congo," *Drug Testing and Analysis 10* (2018): 1601-1603. Schiavetti B et al., "The quality of medicines used in children and supplied by private pharmaceutical wholesalers in Kinshasa, Democratic Republic of Congo: a prospective survey," *American Journal of Tropical Medicine & Hygiene 98*, (2018):898-900.

646 WHO Medical Product Alert N°4/2020: Falsified Chloroquine products circulating in the WHO region of Africa (Update of 9 June), 2020. See also Schäfermann S et ali, "Substandard and falsified antibiotics and medicines against noncommunicable diseases in western Cameroon and north-eastern Democratic Republic of Congo," *American Journal of Tropical Medicine & Hygiene 103*, no. 2, (2020): 12, and Gnegel G et ali, "Identification of falsified chloroquine tablets in Africa at the time of the COVID-19 pandemic," *American Journal of Tropical Medicine & Hygiene 103*, no. 1 (2020): 73, and 75.

studies indicate that ensuring the postmarketing control of medicines in the least developed countries such as the DRC remains a challenge. Unless the government provides pharmaceutical inspection with appropriate quality control materials, the fight against doubtful drugs remains a big challenge.

Moreover, the above analysis took place only in some areas of the country and dealt with only some selected medicines, leaving aside the country's other provinces and the rest of the drugs in circulation throughout the country. One can legitimately deduce that if such an analysis were general, one would have found other drugs of poor quality in the rest of the country. The national health ministry was aware of all these reported cases. However, it did not provide detailed information on whether these medicines were seized, destroyed, or are a subject before the competent tribunals. The absence of information in that regard may be dangerous for people's health since it does not deter medicines dealers from selling medicines of bad quality or the reported drug dealers from committing subsequent offences.

cc) Sanctions for non-compliance with pharmaceutical regulation

Non-compliance with the pharmaceutical regulation gives rise to penal and disciplinary sanctions. Concerning punitive sanctions, legal texts seem uncoordinated to some extent. For instance, under the 1972 Ordinance law penal sanctions comprise three months to 2 years of prison and a fine of 10 to 100 Zaïres or one of these sanctions.[647] The same sanction regime applies to the violation of the 1972 ordinance, including the selling of falsified, altered or counterfeit medicines.[648] In contrast, the 1991 Ordinance Law refers to the sanctions regime of article 17 of the 1952 Decree.[649] Finally, the Ministerial Decree on marketing authorization of medicines and the Decree on the trade of pharmaceuticals refer to the sanctions regime of article 64 of the 1933 Ordinance.

All these provisions call the following observations. First, the 1972 ordinance law and 1972 ordinance provisions have already repealed the sanctions regime of the 1952 Decree and the 1933 Ordinance. Regarding the 1952 Decree, it only applies to other health personnel than pharmacists.[650] Secondly, the currency used to determine the fine in all these legal texts is outdated.[651] Article 131 of the Public Health Law has partly filled in this gap. The sanctions include imprisonment for two to five years and a fine of one million Congolese francs, for anyone who voluntarily sells, delivers or administers pharmaceutical products for which

647 1972 Ordinance-law, art 13.

648 1972 ordinance, art 169.

649 1991 Ordinance-Law, art 73.

650 For instance, physicians who exercise medical profession without being members of the physicians' board shall be sanctioned according to articles 17 to 20 of the 1952 decree. See Ordonnance-Loi 68-070 créant l'ordre des médecins, 1968, art 53.

651 Bazu, "Droits et défis," 44.

he is found guilty of counterfeiting, forgery, alteration or expiry. The Public Health Law considers the current Congolese currency. Therefore, it partly repeals any previous legal provision, such as the sanctions applied to medicines of doubtful quality under the 1972 ordinance-law and 1972 ordinance.[652] However, it does not apply to the illegal practice of the profession of pharmacist. It is worth recalling that the intellectual property law provides sanctions such as imprisonment for one to six months and a fine to be fixed by enabling measures.[653]

Along with the penal sanctions, the tribunal can further order the temporary or definitive closing down of the establishment, which served to commit the offence, the profession's prohibition by the author, and the seizure of the used pharmaceutical products, including their destruction.[654] In addition, some health personnel such as pharmacists, physicians and nurses can be subject to disciplinary sanctions.[655]

In sum, by discouraging any person who deals with pharmaceutical activities in flouting the existing legislation, these provisions ensure the protection of people's life and health. However, the existence of reported unauthorized pharmaceutical establishments and the overall circulation of both unregistered medicines and medicines of poor qualities[656]without any judicial sanctions calls into question an appropriate enforcement of the existing laws and regulations. The health ministry attributes this alarming situation to the obsoleteness and inconsistency of both the 1933 Ordinance and the 1952 Decree.[657] Such a justification seems debatable for two main reasons. First, as mentioned above, both the 1933 Ordinance and 1952 Decree's pharmacy provisions no longer legally exist. Secondly, except for their obsoleteness concerning the fine, existing pharmaceutical legislation does not condone the marketing of both unregistered medicines and medicines of bad quality and neither does it allow unauthorized exploitation of pharmaceutical activities. The justification based on the obsoleteness of legislation is an indication that most legal texts in the pharmaceutical field, such as 1972 Ordinance-Law and 1972 Ordinance, are not well known by the competent authorities for their enforcement.[658]

---

652 Public Health Law, art 143.

653 Loi N°82-001 sur la propriété industrielle, 1982, arts 88 and 93.

654 1972 ordinance-law, art 17, and Decree on the trade of pharmaceuticals, art 21.

655 1991 Ordinance-Law, art 47.

656 PNDS 2016-2020.

657 Ibid.

658 Existing legislation and regulation on pharmacy in the DRC are inadequately implemented and even unknown by the competent authorities. Bofoe, *La criminalité pharmaceutique*, 51.

b. Ensuring the availability and accessibility of medicines

The present subsection looks at where medicines come from in the DRC and where people can access them. To make medicines available and accessible, the government mainly resorts to both its traditional function to protect its citizens's health and its regulatory role.

aa) The State's traditional function to protect people's health

The State's traditional function to protect its citizens's health in the DRC is older than existing human rights instruments providing for the right to health.[659] The State fulfils this role through the national health system, a coordinated set of structures, people, and activities that aims to prevent disabilities, illnesses, and early mortality, promote better health of the population, and ensure coverage, quality, and efficiency of services.[660] The national health system consists of three stages, namely the central, provincial, and peripheral levels[661] headed by the national health ministry.[662]

About medicines, the government establishes a national drug supply system responsible for promoting local production and rational use of medicines, ensuring the availability of medicines of good quality, and making them accessible to the entire population.[663] Pending the adoption of the decree of the prime minister, which shall set out the organization and operation of the above national drug supply system,[664] the national health ministry discharges the above tasks. For instance, it has adopted a National Pharmaceutical Policy[665]and set up a National List of Essential Medicines with about 487 identified products deemed essential for managing priority diseases.[666] To supply these essential medicines, the government resorts to both the Système National d'Approvisionnement en Médicaments Essentiels (SNAME), which provides the national system of supply of essential medicines,[667] and the public subsystem of the National Health Ministry run by the Ministry of

659 See, for instance the 1952 Decree regulating the health sector in the DRC.

660 Public Health Law, art 4.

661 Ibid. art 6.

662 Ordonnance N° 20/017 du 27 mars 2020 fixant les attributions des Ministères, art 24.

663 Public Health Law, art 54.

664 Ibid.

665 Politique Nationale Pharmaceutique, 2008 (hereinafter the National Pharmaceutical Policy)

666 Ministère de la santé publique de la RDC: Cartographie des systèmes d'approvisionnement et de distribution des médicaments et autres produits de santé, 2010 (henceforth Cartographie des systèmes d'approvisionnement et de distribution des médicaments et autres produits de santé), 33.

667 Ibid. 25-26.

Health.[668] The SNAME's strategy consists of a centralized process in the procurement of medicines done through two central procurement co-ordination offices, and a decentralized process of their distribution done through regional drug distribution centres (CDRs).[669] The National Health Ministry's subsystem has a central storage depot for medicines, the distribution of which is ensured by politicians, namely the members of the national Assembly.[670] However, unlike the SNAME's procedure of distributing medicines within established public health facilities,[671] the distribution of medicines by the 500 members of the national Assembly in the form of gifts raises some concerns about its traceability.[672] It is not clear whether members of the national Assembly distribute these medicines through public health facilities or they give them directly to the population.

bb) The regulatory function of the State and access to medicines

The State´s regulatory function enables the government to regulate and authorize non-state actors, such as the State's partners, programs, owners of pharmaceutical industries, and both natural and legal persons to carry out pharmaceutical activities. Three main reasons may justify such regulation. First, in dealing with health-related issues such as medicines, these non-state actors intervene within the traditional functions of the State. Second, the State should protect access to medicines provided by third parties. Third, quite often, the State's efforts to ensure access to medicines in both developed and least developed countries are supplemented by those of non-state actors. These non-state actors' activities include local manufacturing of medicines, and purchase of medicine, including import, donations and distribution, and selling of medicines. All these processes supplement each other. For instance, while local production of medicines contributes only to 10% of the national needs,[673]import of medicines, including donations, may fill in this gap.

Moreover, programs, such as Programme Elargi de Vaccination (PEV),[674] Programme National Multisectoriel de Lutte Contre le Sida (PNMLS)[675] and

668 Ibid. 28.
669 Ibid. 25-6.
670 Ibid. 28.
671 Ibid, 26.
672 Bofoe, *La criminalité pharmaceutique*, 38.
673 PNDS 2016-2020.
674 PEV procurement strategy is based on a centralized supply of vaccines at the program level in Kinshasa and distribution through provincial depots and PEV relay antennas.
675 PNMLS acts as a procurement agency to purchase or import HIV / AIDS pharmaceuticals.

Programme National de Transfusion Sanguine[676] provide respectively vaccines, HIV/AIDS drugs and reagents for blood safety. In contrast, donations from State's partners,[677] including multilateral donors, bilateral donors and private or NGOs,[678] cover all kinds of pharmaceuticals. Finally, some of these non-state actors, including religious confessions,[679] NGOs and individuals are legally authorized upon some conditions to directly supply medicines to the people within their health institutions, including private pharmacies.

In sum, an appropriate and simultaneous fulfilment of both the State's functions to protect the health of its populations and regulate pharmaceutical activities of non-state actors makes medicines of good quality available and accessible. However, to prioritize and favour local production, the DRC government suspended the import of 15 prescribed medicines.[680] For a country with the lowest local production of medicines, such a prohibition measure seems inopportune as it can affect both the availability and accessibility of medicines.[681] Further information on whether the prohibition measure has achieved its goal is lacking.

cc) Some constraints on the availability and accessibility of medicines of good quality

The DRC government's efforts to ensure the accessibility and availability of medicine give rise to some concerns. For instance, health institutions, both public and private, face various challenges regarding availability, accessibility, quality, and rational use of medicines. Factors that justify this alarming situation include, among others, the low availability of essential medicines, vaccines and necessary inputs,[682] and the dilapidation of health infrastructures and equipment.[683] Other challenges include unequal distribution of health professionals, the shortage of

676 It acts as a procurement agency for the purchase / import of reagents for blood safety.

677 Decree on the trade of pharmaceuticals, art 33, and Guidelines for medicines donation.

678 These include inter alia, French Cooperation, World Fund, World Bank, WHO, and European Union. See Cartographie des systèmes d'approvisionnement et de distribution des médicaments et autres produits de santé, 28-30.

679 Faith-based health structures represent approximately 40% of the supply of care.

680 Arrêté ministériel N°1250/CAB/MIN/SP/069/CJ/OMK/2010 Portant renouvellement de la suspension des importations de certains médicaments, 2010.

681 Bazu, "Droits et défis," 53-54.

682 PNDS 2016-2020.

683 Ibid.

pharmacists,[684] and the worst work conditions of health personnel.[685] These issues negatively impact both the geographical accessibility and acceptability of medicines in rural areas, where people have to walk beyond 5 kilometres to reach a nearby health facility.[686] Finally, thousands of unauthorized pharmacies open randomly in Kinshasa, the capital of the country.[687] This situation indicates that throughout the country, other unofficial health establishments may also open to the public with a probability of being managed by non-pharmacists supplying medicines of doubtful quality.

dd) Financial accessibility

Financial accessibility to medicines implies the affordability of medicines. It is underlined by the idea that access to medicines is not free of charge. The government's responsibility is to ensure that its people have financial accessibility to medicines through, among others, adequate funding of the health system, price regulation, and the universal health care coverage system.

(1) Funding the national health system

To support the national health system, the Public Health Law establishes a Health Promotion Fund. However, the prime minister has not yet taken the implementation decree on the organization and operation of the said Fund.[688] Meanwhile, the State´s budget and external assistance constitute the primary sources of financing of the national health system.

As part of the health field, the pharmaceutical sector is covered by the national health system's budget portion. Since 2001, the unit of measurement for State´s financing of the national health system in African countries, including DRC, remains African governments expressed intent and commitment to allocating at the minimum 15% of their national budgets to the health sector.[689] However, the Congolese government has never met this budget percentage. For instance, in 2017 and 2018, the government has allocated respectively 7,84% and 7,64% of its general

684 Public health institutions experience a shortage of health professionals, especially pharmacists. Most of them are performing in the capital Kinshasa and the main towns of the country. Ibid.

685 In 2014, for instance, out of 127. 716 health professionals, only 40.626 were receiving a salary. See PNDS 2016-2020.

686 About 48% of women living in rural areas are facing challenges to reach health facilities. Ibid.

687 Ibid.

688 Public Health Law, art 128.

689 OAU Heads of State and Government, Abuja declaration on HIV/AIDS, tuberculosis and other related infectious diseases, 2001 (hereinafter Abuja Declaration), para 26.

budgets to the health sector.[690] This budget percentage negatively impacts the pharmaceutical sector's portion. External assistance provided by bilateral and multilateral cooperation, NGOs, foundations, and international initiatives, contributes up to about 47%[691] of the health expenditure. However, external funds' main concern is that the State's partners themselves directly manage more than 60% of these funds. Such management of external funds by the partners gives rise to different management units and multiple procedures of management's essential costs.[692] Nevertheless, it constitutes a crucial alternative to the government's misuse of public resources, including international assistance.[693]

(2) Price regulation of medicines

The Organic Law on price regulation and competition is the primary law on price regulation.[694] Economic operators freely set the price of goods and services, including pharmaceuticals.[695] However, the same law states that these economic operators shall submit for a posteriori control by the minister of the national economy, the fixed prices together with the relevant file.[696] Dealing specifically with drugs, article 48 of the Decree on the trade of pharmaceuticals subjects the cost of medicines to the profit margins allowed as fixed by the ministry of the economy and prohibits the practice of illicit price. In regulating the price of medicine, these provisions protect the rights of the consumers or patients.[697] In practice, however, the price regulation lacks standardization. As a result, pharmaceuticals' price differs from one health training to another, and from one place to another.[698] It is worth recalling that illicit prices cover only higher costs than the regulated price.[699] Consequently, patients may prefer cheaper medicines that can be of questionable quality at the expense of too expensive medicines of good quality they cannot afford.

---

690 DRC's report to the CESCR, 2019, para 139.

691 PNDS 2016-2020.

692 Ibid.

693 CESCR's Concluding observations to DRC, 2009, para 16.

694 Loi Organique N° 18-020 Relative à la Liberté des prix et à la concurrence, du 9 Juillet 2018 (hereinafter Organic Law on Price Regulation), art 2.

695 Ibid. art 6.

696 Ibid.

697 Sakata, *Introduction au droit économique*, 148.

698 PNDS 2016-2020.

699 Organic Law on Price Regulation, art 5 (12).

(3) Universal health coverage system

To facilitate people's financial access to medicines, the government should provide for, among others, a public or hybrid health insurance system that is affordable for all.[700] The Public Health Law establishes a universal health coverage system based on the principles of equity, quality of care assurance, and financial protection for all.[701] Focus on the principle of equity aims to ensure that poorer households or vulnerable groups of society are not disproportionately burdened with health expenses than wealthier households.[702] The universal health coverage system's goals consist of guaranteeing the health benefit of all Congolese residing in the country and entitling its beneficiary to the consumption of quality health care, and services at an affordable cost.[703] To fund the established universal health coverage system, the Public Health Law establishes the Health Solidarity Fund to be fed by the State's budget, the insurance of any health scheme or other taxes to be fixed by the government.[704] However, the implementation of both the universal health coverage system and the Health Solidarity Fund is subject to the prime minister's decree, which has never been adopted.[705] As a result, the DRC remains one of the world's countries with no compulsory and universal health insurance.[706]

ee) Access to medicines with financial implication

This subsection deals with some adopted measures providing access to medicines using the source of health care expense as a starting point. It deals with access to medicines at one's own expense, at public expense, and at employer's expense. It also examines access with public financial assistance, and through the social security system.

(1) Access to medicine at one's own expense

As its heading suggests, access to medicines at one´s own expense excludes the idea of any financial assistance from the State or employer. The Public Health Law entitles everybody to quality health care without discrimination.[707] Though it does not address the issue of financial accessibility, health care services herein protected are subject to the direct payment of user fees. Indeed, along with the

700 General Comment 14, para 36.
701 Public Health Law, art 41.
702 General Comment 14, para 12.
703 Public Health Law, arts 42-43.
704 Ibid, art 129.
705 Ibid. arts 42 and 129.
706 CESCR's concluding observations to DRC, 2009, para 24. See also DRC's Report to the CESCR, 2007, para 144.
707 Public Health Law, art 16, 17, 18, and 25.

budget allocated to the health sector and external assistance, user fees for health services constitute one of the significant financing health sources.[708] This direct payment of health user fees without any flat fare is in a clash with the principle of equity.[709] It prevents an essential portion of the population from accessing health care, especially vulnerable groups of society, such as the elderly, people with disabilities, and unemployed persons. For instance, about 39% of Congolese people do not have access to medicines due to financial constraints.[710] At the same time some practice self-medication, others need to borrow money or pledge their property in exchange for health services, and in case of non-payment of the bill, the patients are forced or obliged not to leave the health institution.[711] Thus, financial accessibility conflicts with other fundamental human rights, such as a patient's freedom of movement.

(2) Access to medicines at public expense

Access to medicines at public expense is totally and fully covered by the public treasury on behalf of its beneficiaries. It applies to, among others, members of the national government, public servants, and two categories of vulnerable groups of the society,[712] namely people living with HIV and prisoners.

(a) Access to medicine for members of the national government and other public servants

The public treasury covers health user fees for members of the national government and the staff of their cabinets, members of armed forces, agents of specialized services and their family members.[713] It further covers health user fees for any former elected president, his/her spouse and minor children,[714] magistrates,[715]

---

708 PNDS 2016-2020.

709 Bazu, "Droits et défis," 61-62.

710 PNDS 2016-2020.

711 Ibid.

712 Vulnerable groups under the DRC law include children, women, people with disability, old people, people living with HIV, prisoners, refugees, displaced people for reasons of war, victims of calamity, homosexuals, and prostitutes. DRC Constitution, arts 49, 51 and 123 (16), HIV Law, art 2 (5).

713 Circulaire N°001 /CAB/MIN/BUDGET/2012 Contenant les instructions relatives à l'exécution de la Loi de Finances N°12/002 du 20 Juillet 2012, 2012, Para IV.1.4.10.1 (hereinafter 2012 Circular).

714 Loi N° 18/021 du Portant statut des anciens Présidents de la République élus et fixant les avantages accordés aux anciens chefs de corps constitués, 2018, art 15.

715 Loi Organique N° 06/020 Portant statut des magistrats, 2006, art 25 (2) (hereinafter the Magistrates Law).

public physicians,[716]traditional leaders,[717] members of the Congolese national police,[718] public servants,[719] and their spouses and children. These health care services form part of social benefits. Their beneficiaries can receive them in the DRC or abroad.[720] Furthermore, family members include spouses and all children. Concerning spouses, unlike other legal texts that use a neutral language such as "spouse/conjoint" or "family member,"[721] the 2006 Public Physicians Decree talks about the "physician's wife" only.[722] Such a language formulation seems discriminatory since it suggests that only men can perform as physicians. It indicates that, even though women can also serve as physicians, their husbands further cannot benefit from the above health services as part of social advantages.

Practically speaking, upon request, the public treasury can either refund on receipts[723] or directly pay to medical institutions[724] that provided for health care services. While refund on receipts implies that, the beneficiary pays for medical services and gets a refund from the public treasury,[725] direct payment requires the public treasury to pay directly to the health institution that provided health services.[726] Concerning health care services abroad, the beneficiary receives the needed fund upon request before travelling. However, due to the established procedure's burdensome,[727] the request may or not be granted.

In sum, since the above social protection measures do not apply to the rest of the population, they are described as discriminatory.[728] However, in practice, the government does not adequately implement these social benefits measures due to economic difficulties and lack of financial resources.[729]

716 Décret N° 06/130 Portant statut spécifique des médecins des services publics de l'Etat, 2006, art 30 (hereinafter Public Physicians Decree).
717 Loi N° 15/015 fixant le statut des chefs coutumiers, 2015, art 20 (2) (hereinafter the Traditional Leaders Act).
718 Loi N°13/013 portant statut du personnel de carrière de la police nationale, 2013, art 240 (3) (5). See also the 2012 Circular.
719 Loi N° 16/013 Portant statut des agents de carrière des services publics de l'Etat, 2016, arts 2 and 55 (hereinafter the Public Servants Act).
720 The 2012 Circular.
721 Illustrations include Public Servant Act, and the Traditional Leaders Act.
722 Public Physicians Decree, art 30.
723 2012 Circular.
724 Ibid.
725 Ibid.
726 Ibid.
727 Documents to be sent to the Minister of the budget shall include a medical certificate signed by three doctors working in public hospitals, a confidential medical report, and a release for shipment signed by the Minister of Health.
728 Bazu, "Droits et défis," 61.
729 DRC's Report to the CESCR, 2007, paras 146 and 148.

(b) Access to medicines for People with HIV

In implementing the right to health, States are urged to tackle newly identified obstacles for health, including HIV/AIDS.[730] It is for this reason that the DRC has adopted the HIV Law in 2008. The HIV Law implements article 123 (16) of the DRC Constitution, which calls for adopting the law protecting vulnerable persons.[731] The Constitution does not expressly enumerate vulnerable persons. In contrast, under article 2 (5) of the HIV Law, vulnerable persons include women, young persons, prostitutes, drug addicts, homosexuals, displaced people, refugees, street children, and adults. Articles 11 and 12 of the HIV Law deal with the right to health. Accordingly, article 11 obligates the government to ensure free access to preventive and curative care of people living with HIV/AIDS within both public and affiliated private health institutions.[732] For its part, article 12 emphasizes the obligation to make accessible, economically, socially, and geographically antiretroviral and drugs against opportunistic infections and cancers associated with HIV.[733]

These provisions justify the following comments. First, compared to ratified human rights treaties and the DRC Constitution, the HIV Law seems theoretically revolutionary by providing free access to preventive and curative care for people living with HIV. Secondly, the State's obligation to make antiretroviral and other drugs economically accessible seems antithetical to the State's responsibility to ensure free access to preventive and curative care of people living with HIV. Indeed, preventive and curative care is broad enough to cover antiretrovirals and drugs against opportunistic infections and cancer associated with HIV. Thirdly, it is plausible to commend free access to preventive and curative care for people with HIV. However, it seems quite surprising that the DRC government, which does not have State's pharmaceutical industries, grants free access to more expensive medicines such as antiretrovirals.

In implementing the HIV Law, a presidential ordinance has established the PNMLS as the primary national program in charge of the fight against HIV and related diseases.[734]In practice, however, the supply of antiretrovirals is mainly ensured by State's partners within their health facilities,[735]or indirectly through both public and affiliated health institutions.

---

730 General Comment 14, para 10.

731 HIV Law, art 1.

732 Ibid. art 11.

733 Ibid. art 12.

734 Ordonnance N° 11/023 modifiant et complétant le Décret N° 04/029 du 17 Mars 2004 portant création et organisation du Programme National Multisectoriel de Lutte Contre le Sida, 2011.

735 Cartographie des systèmes d'approvisionnement et de distribution des médicaments et autres produits de santé.

However, significant dependence on the State´s external partners in that regard, coupled with the permanent shortage of medicines within the public and affiliated health institutions, hinders the government´s good intent to ensure free access to preventive and curative care for people with HIV. As a result, the DRC remains one of the world's countries with a higher prevalence of HIV/AIDS, especially for women and born babies.[736]

(c) Access to medicines for prisoners

In addition to their right to access medicines under article 47 of the DRC Constitution and ratified treaties, prisoners have a right to a treatment that preserves their life and physical and mental health.[737] From a human rights perspective, the State has a positive obligation to provide prisoners with adequate healthcare, including maternal healthcare and antiretroviral drugs.[738] Both the Public Health Law and the Prison Ordinance[739] subscribe to this principle. According to article 24 of the Public Health Law, every person in detention or prison has the right to health care at the government expenses. The same article states that the prison medical services or other public health facilities are responsible for the delivery of healthcare. In concrete terms, the Prison Ordinance[740] urges the national health minister and the provincial governor to appoint a physician and nurses to serve prisons, detention camps, and amigos established within each province.[741] This obligation's underlying idea is to ensure that skilled medical personnel, including nurses under the physician's supervision, administer health care to detainees and prisoners.

However, despite the above legal framework, detainees and prisoners live under substandard conditions regarding health care, sanitation, and food, which lead to a significant number of deaths in custody and prisons.[742] Factors that justify the lack of access to proper medical care for persons in detention and prison[743] are manifold. They mainly include the absence or irregular supply of medicines, shortage of

---

736 CEDAW, concluding observations to DRC, 2013, paras 31 and 32.

737 DRC Constitution, art 18.

738 African Commission on Human and Peoples' Rights, General Comment N° 3 on the African Charter on Human and Peoples' Rights: The right to life (Article 4), 2015 (hereinafter African Commission General Comment 3), para 36.

739 Ordonnance N° 344 relative au régime pénitentiaire, 1965 (hereinafter Prison Ordinance), arts 59 and 60.

740 Ibid. arts 54-55.

741 Ibid.

742 Human Rights Committee, concluding observations to the DRC, 2017, para 33, and CESCR's concluding observations to DRC, 2009, para 32.

743 CESCR's concluding observations to DRC, 2009, para 34.

medical personnel, and lack of an appropriate transfer system from prison medical services to other public health institutions.[744]

(3) Access to medicines at the employer's expenses

The present subsection considers access to medicines at a higher education institution expense and access to medicines at the employer's expense under the labour law.

(a) Access to medicine for members of the higher education institutions

According to article 139 of the law regulating the status of members of higher education institutions,[745] health care and pharmaceuticals necessitated by the health state of any higher education school member are at the institution's charge. This provision also applies to the family members entitled to the familial allowance, namely children under 19 years old.[746] However, article 136 of the law under discussion does not expressly mention spouses of a member of the higher education institution among entitled persons to familial allowance, excluding them, therefore from benefiting access to medicines herein provided.

In practice, however, the higher education institution member remains the only one responsible for his/her health user fees and that of his/her family members.

(b) Access to medicine at the employer's expenses

Amended in 2016,[747] the labour law obligates every employer, whether the natural or legal person,[748] to provide medical services to his employees.[749] Furthermore, in the event of sickness, accident, or pregnancy, the employer shall give the worker and his family[750] medical, dental, surgical, pharmaceutical, and hospitalization expenses and the necessary travel expenses when the employee or his family is physically unable to move.[751] These provisions consider the close link that exists

744 Commission Nationale des Droits de l'Homme, Rapport synthèse des visites des centres pénitentiaires et de détention effectuées en République Démocratique du Congo, (2018), 11.

745 Loi N° 18/038 portant statut du personnel de l'enseignement supérieur, universitaire et de la recherche scientifique, 2018, art 139 (hereinafter the Higher Education Law).

746 Ibid. art 136.

747 Loi N°015/2002 Portant Code de travail telle que révisée par Loi n° 16/010 du 15 Juillet 2016 modifiant et complétant la Loi N° 015-2002 Portant Code du Travail (hereinafter the Labour Law).

748 Ibid. art 7 (2).

749 Ibid. art 177.

750 The worker's family consists of his/her spouse, and children. Ibid. art 7 (11).

751 Ibid. art 178.

between health workers and productivity at work. Therefore, they facilitate access to medicines of every person under the employment contract[752] and his/her family members. However, the provisions under discussion constitute, at the same time, a substantial financial burden for the employer. To this end, commentators suggest implementing an appropriate social security system, which would protect everybody irrespective of the exercise of any professional activity.[753]

(4) Access to medicines with public financial assistance

As part of the vulnerable Congolese groups, children and women can access to medicines with the public financial support, as discussed in this subsection.

(a) Access to medicines for children

The physical and mental immaturity of the child, vulnerability, and dependence on adults necessitates special care and protection.[754] Despite the DRC's commitment to protecting the child through both the Constitution and ratified treaties,[755] many children still lack access to health care services.[756] To fill in these shortfalls, the DRC adopted the Children Law in 2009. According to article 21, every child has the right to enjoy the best health status possible, including health care, breastfeeding and a healthy, adequate, and balanced diet. The same article urges the State to implement effective strategies that reduce infant morbidity and mortality. Unlike the DRC Constitution, which uses the expression of the right to health, the Children Law provides for the right to enjoy the best health status possible. Besides, the reference to health care and State's efforts to reduce infant morbidity and mortality means that access to medicines is a vital component of children's right to enjoy the best health status possible. It is in this context that the government provides vaccination for children free of charge. However, access to medicines as provided under article 21 at hand is not free of charge. To this end, the Children Law urges the government to assist parents who cannot ensure their children's survival, including children with physical or mental disabilities, with material and financial assistance, and ensure health and food needs of children with one or both parents imprisoned.[757] Neither parents' financial constraints nor parent's imprisonment should impede children from getting access to medicines, which is critical for their survival.

752 Ibid. art 7 (3).
753 Mukadi Bonyi, *Droit du travail*, (Bruxelles: CRDS, 2008), 316.
754 See the preamble to the CRC.
755 ICESCR, art 12 (2 a) and, DRC Constitution, art 41.
756 Committee on the Rights of the Child, concluding observations to DRC, 2009.
757 Children Law, arts 42, 69, and 70.

However, the competent authorities have not yet taken the inter-ministerial decrees to implement these provisions by prescribing their applicability's modalities.[758] The DRC government attributed this inaction to budgetary constraints.[759] As a result, children whose access to health care services depends on the State's assistance and support cannot enjoy their rights under the Children Law. This situation becomes worse with the government's failure to appropriately tackle children health issues in general, such as malaria and HIV/AIDS,[760]and the reduction of the child mortality rate, especially in rural areas.[761]

In sum, if appropriately and sufficiently implemented,[762] the Children Law can cover an essential aspect of the right to health, which is children's access to medicines, and an essential portion of Congolese people, which consists of children.

(b) Access to medicines for women

In addition to the right to health under article 47, the DRC Constitution urges the government to eliminate discrimination against women, protect, and promote their rights.[763] DRC has adopted a law in 2015 to give effect to women's rights, including access to medicine.[764] Various provisions of the Women Law deal with the right to health, namely articles 14, 15[765] and 16.[766] According to article 14 "the State guarantees to the woman, during pregnancy, childbirth and after childbirth, appropriate health care services at a reduced cost, within reasonable distances and, where appropriate, free of charge." Reference to "appropriate health care services" is broad enough to cover access to medicines. Furthermore, the expression "at reduced cost" sustains the view that access to healthcare for women is not free of charge. It also implies that women, especially pregnant women, are affected by the high health care costs. In addition to financial barriers, women in DRC face severe geographical challenges in accessing health services, especially in remote areas. For instance, while some pregnant women give birth without personnel's

---

758 Ibid., art 70.

759 DRC's Report to the CESCR, 2019, para 55.

760 Committee on the Rights of the Child, concluding observations to DRC, 2017, paras 7 and 35.

761 Ibid. para 7.

762 Ibid.

763 DRC Constitution, art 14.

764 Women Law.

765 Article 15 deals with HIV/AIDS- related issues, which are part of the HIV Law as discussed earlier.

766 Article 16 obligates the state to ensure the medical care of women, victims of sexual violence.

assistance in rural areas, about 69% of women have met with a financial barrier to get treatment or receive a medical opinion.[767]

However, the provision under discussion falls short by not providing the way women should enjoy health care services at reduced costs or free of charge, within a reasonable distance. Though the provision at hand seems to equate to article 12 (2) of the CEDAW, it does not indicate its applicability. Instead, the whole implementation of Women Law is subject to the prime minister's decree,[768] and other implementation measures whose authors are not expressly identified,[769] which todate have never been adopted. Therefore, the article under discussion remains ornamental. This is because of higher maternal mortality rate due to women's limited access to basic healthcare services, including essential obstetric care, especially in rural areas.[770] Furthermore, women who cannot afford to pay the maternity costs after delivery, are victims of forced confinement with their babies within the hospitals concerned.[771]

(5) Access to medicines under the Social Security Law

The Social Security Law[772] sets forth the rules for the general social security system.[773] It covers persons with supervisory positions within public enterprises, local employees, company associates, public servants without social benefit under any specific legislation, and voluntary insured persons.[774] It deals with the occupational risk branch for benefits in an accident at work and illness, the family benefits branch covering family, prenatal, maternity benefits, and the pension branch for disability, old age, and survivor benefits.[775]

While voluntary policyholders's contributions are their responsibility, the employer is responsible for his contributions and those of his employees.[776] Covered health-related issues include prenatal allowances for any insured pregnant women or pregnant spouse of an insured member, and the supply of pharmaceuticals for any worker, victim of a work accident, or occupational disease.[777] However, the

767 PNDS 2016-2020.

768 Women Law, art 31.

769 Ibid. art 36.

770 CEDAW concluding observations DRC, para 31.

771 CNDH Annual Report 2019, 66

772 Loi N° 16/009 fixant les règles relatives au régime général de la sécurité sociale, 2016 (hereinafter Social Security Law)

773 Ibid. arts 8 and 9.

774 Ibid. arts 3, 4 and 6.

775 Ibid, art 1.

776 Ibid. arts 14, 16 and 19.

777 Ibid. arts 39, 40, 64 and 67.

provisions under discussion do not expressly cover health care services for an insured member's children or non-pregnant spouse.

Selected health institutions, including public and private, deliver health services under the present law.[778] The public institution in charge of the social security system reimburses incurred costs. These costs can also cover health services provided by a medical facility not preselected in the case of emergency[779] or when health services are provided abroad. However, the law under discussion came to force only in 2018 and its intended reform of the social security system is currently underway.[780] For instance, the prime minister has not yet adopted the decree on the nature of benefits and the contribution of voluntarily insured.[781]

c. *The justiciability of access to medicines*

The present section discusses the justiciability of the right to access medicines through judicial and quasi-judicial procedures before the National Commission of Human Rights (NCHR) and the courts.

aa) Enforcement of access to medicines before the NCHR

Article 222 (3) of the DRC Constitution establishes the NCHR as a supporting democracy institution.[782] As a technical and advisory body responsible for promoting and protecting human rights,[783] the NCHR ensures respect for human rights and mechanisms for guaranteeing fundamental freedoms.[784] Article 6 of the NCHR Law sets out the NCHR's attributions, involving investigating human rights violations, assisting complainants and victims in seizing the courts and settling some instances of human rights violations conciliation. It is worth recalling that violation of human rights under the NCHR Law relates to all human rights, including access to medicines, as argued under the DRC Constitution, ratified human rights treaties, and other domestic laws.[785] In assisting complainants or victims in seizing the courts for violation of human rights, article 6 under discussion reinforces the assertion that all human rights under the DRC Constitution are justiciable. The NCHR does not substitute itself for the courts and tribunals. Finally, the NCHR's power to settle some cases of violation of human rights through

778 Ibid. arts 41, 44, 69 and 70.

779 Ibid. art 69.

780 Ibid. art 134. See also DRC's 2019 Report to the CESCR, para 48.

781 Social Security Law, arts 14 and 15.

782 Title II of the DRC Constitution and its article 222 (3). See also the preamble to the CNDH Law.

783 NCHR Law, art 1.

784 Ibid. art 4.

785 Ibid. art 2.

the conciliation procedure can constitute an appropriate alternative to a judicial remedy, where it effectively meets the victims' interests.[786]

Entitled persons to lodge complaints to the NCHR include natural persons, group of peoples, the victim (s) of human rights violation, and legally constituted organizations defending and promoting human rights.[787] The NCHR also acts motu proprio. Interestingly, the NCHR has already examined several cases on the violation of the right to health, including access to medicines.[788] These cases relate to the illegal running of pharmacies, poor quality control of medicines, the shortage of medicines within public hospitals, and prisoners' lack of access to health care services. Although these cases appear in the NCHR's annual report without further details, they seem necessary to discuss since they are relevant to the present study.

(1) The illegal running of pharmacies

According to the NCHR's report, the illegal running of pharmacies amounts to the violation of the right to health. Though the NCHR does not define the word illegal running of pharmacies, it implies that people open and manage pharmacies without complying with established legal conditions. As discussed, and analysed earlier, the law in DRC regulates the exercise and running of pharmacies. These regulations relate to the pharmacies' owners, medicines, and facilities. Therefore, if involved persons in the illegal opening of pharmacies are subject to sanctions, the Congolese government is responsible for failure to enforce or implement the existing law regulating this sector. In addition, although NCHR does not make it explicit, the illegal opening of pharmacies amounts to the State's violation of the obligation to protect people from third parties involved in the provision of medicines. Following General Comment 14,[789] failure to protect consumers from practices detrimental to health, including manufacturers or dealers of medicines of poor quality constitute a breach of the State's obligation to protect.

As a result of the State's failure, unauthorized persons sell medicines in facilities where the competent authorities do not control. The risk for violating patients' right to health increases with the lack of the State's control over owners of pharmacists, sold medicines, and used facilities. In this case, the complaint should also involve the Autorité Congolaise de Règlementation Pharmaceutique (ACOREP), the State's

786 The African Court ruled that the term local remedy is understood in human rights jurisprudence to refer primarily to judicial remedies as the most effective means of redressing human rights violations. See Applications N° 009/2011 and N° 011/2011, 1, Tanganyika Law Society and The Legal and Human Rights Centre vs. the United Republic of Tanzania, 2013, paras 82 (1), (3).

787 Ibid. art 28.

788 CNDH Annual Report 2019, 60.

789 General Comment 14, para 51.

organ in charge of regulating and implementing the pharmaceutical legislation established under the Public Health Law.

(2) Poor quality control of medicines in circulation

The NCHR identified poor quality control of medicines in circulation as a violation of the right to health. Good quality medicines constitute an essential component of the human right to health. As discussed in previous sections, quality control of drugs in the DRC occurs before and after entering the market. The present case suggests that preventive control did not prevent substandard and falsified medicines from reaching consumers or patients. It also indicates that the Congolese government does not adequately control the quality of available drugs within public and private health facilities, including pharmacies.

Like in the previous case, the State fell short in not fulfilling its duty to protect people from violation of their right to access good quality medicines by third parties. As a result, patients buy and use drugs of poor quality, threatening their health since they are unsafe or ineffective.[790] The present complaint should also involve the State's organs responsible for quality control of medicines, namely the ACOREP and the national minister in charge of trade.[791] Unlike the duty to enforce the existing law on pharmacy exercise, ensuring control quality of available medicines on the market requires adequate human, financial, and equipment resources. Moreover, as the studies on some medicine's quality revealed, the Congolese government cannot adequately fight substandard and falsified drugs without its partners' assistance.

(3) The shortage of medicines in public hospitals

Like the African Commission in the Zaïre Case, the NCHR held that the shortage of medicines within public hospitals violates the right to health. The government should provide public hospitals with drugs. The deficiency of drugs affects their availability in sufficient quantity within the DRC's jurisdiction. It, therefore, results in limited access to needed medicines. Failure to make medicines available and accessible amounts to the violation of the State's duty to fulfil, which consists of taking all necessary positive steps to ensure the realization of the right to health.[792] It is important to recall that the duty to make medicines available depends on numerous factors, including the State party's developmental level.[793] From a least developed county's perspective, limited resources can affect and justify the DRC's

790 World Health Organisation, A study on the public health and socioeconomic impact of substandard and falsified medical products, Geneva, 2017.

791 Decree establishing ACOREP, art 4 (i).

792 General Comment 14, paras 37 and 52.

793 Ibid. para 12 (a).

inability to ensure the availability of medicines. Due to the resource's constraint, priority should consist of providing essential medicines.[794] However, the NCHR does not expressly distinguish between essential and non-essential drugs. The mission to ensure the availability of medicines under the Public Health Law rests with the government through the national medicines supply system.

(4) Lack of prisoners' access to health care services

The fourth human right to health violation issue is related to the government's and prison authorities' failure to provide health care services to 7 critically ill prisoners in the city of Kenge. As above-mentioned, prisoners and detainees in the DRC have the right to health care at the government's expense.[795] These medical services, including medicines, are provided either by prison medical facilities or public health institutions. According to the African Commission,[796] two main reasons justify the State's exclusive responsibility for prisoners' health care. First, prisons and detention places belong to the only State's authority. Secondly, only States are competent to deprive individuals of their liberty. In this case, the government could not reasonably justify prisoners' lack of access to health care for many reasons. Suppose prison's health facilities did not have needed medical care services. The State still was under the legal obligation to transfer sick prisoners to public hospitals. Kenge is a big city with various public health facilities, including hospitals, clinics, and dispensaries. Unlike the violation related to the shortage of medicines within public hospitals, the country's developmental level cannot justify the government's failure to use health services provided by public health facilities in Kenge.

In sum, the Congolese government failed to comply with the duty to protect the right to health, by denying or limiting access for prisoners to health services.[797] Furthermore, it was in violation of the obligation to fulfil (provide), which requires the Congolese government to provide access to medicines to persons, including prisoners, who cannot realize their right to health for reasons beyond their control.[798]

(5) Concluding observations

These cases cover various aspects of the right of access to medicine, namely quality, availability, and accessibility of drugs for all, including prisoners. In qualifying the above acts and omissions from the government as a violation of the right to health,

794 Ibid.

795 Public Health Law, art 24.

796 African Commission General Comment N°3, para 36.

797 General Comment 14, para 34.

798 Ibid. para 37.

the CNHR marked an essential step towards enforcing the right to health under Congolese law. However, the NCHR's report does not provide further details on whether the NCHR has settled these issues through a conciliation procedure or has assisted the victims in bringing them to the courts of law. It is worth stressing that the NCHR identified the State, including its organs and representatives, as the violator of the right to health in all these complaints.[799] These cases also indicate that violating the right to access medicines is a multifaceted issue.

It can relate to the State's obligations to respect, promote, protect, and fulfil. They also reveal that the State's compliance with its legal obligations towards access to medicines does not always entail financial resources implications. Illustration includes the issue of prisoners' denial of access to health care. However, the NHRC's annual report does not provide information on the final decisions the NHRC has taken in that regard.

bb) Enforcement of access to medicines before the courts

Like all the State's organs, courts contribute to the realization of human rights by providing judicial remedies in case of their violation.[800] Everyone has a right to an effective remedy which is to be granted by competent national tribunals for acts violating the fundamental rights conferred by the Constitution or the law.[801]

In addition to article 6 of the NCHR Law discussed in the precedent subsection, the judiciary's jurisdiction to stand for respect for human rights can be derived from a combined reading of articles 60 and 150 (1) of the DRC Constitution. According to article 60 "respect for human rights and fundamental freedoms protected by the Constitution is compulsory for all the State's organs and individuals." For its part, article 150 (1) states that "the judicial power is the guarantor of individual freedoms and fundamental rights of citizens." These two provisions justify the following comments. Firstly, article 60 binds the judiciary to assign adequate protection to all the constitutionally protected ESCRs, which are as justiciable as CPRs and collective rights.[802] Secondly, article 150 (1) vests all the courts and tribunals that constitute the judicial branch with a general human rights jurisdiction.[803] These courts and tribunals comprise the constitutional court, the court of cassation, the council of state, the high military court, and civil and military

799 NHRC Report.
800 General Comment 3, para 6.
801 UDHR, art 8, General Comment 14, para 59.
802 Ngoy, "Contrôle et protection des droits," 299.
803 Roger Mvita Kalubi, "La nouvelle compétence de la cour constitutionnelle fondée sur la protection des droits humains. Une lecture critique de l'Arrêt R. Const. 0038 du 20 Août 2015," *Annuaire Congolais de Justice Constitutionnelle 1*, (2016): 210.

courts and tribunals.[804] As a result, no court or tribunal in the DRC has an exclusive human rights jurisdiction.[805]

Theoretically, in protecting the right to health under the Constitution, acknowledging ratified treaties as part of domestic law, and empowering courts and tribunals to ensure individual freedoms and fundamental rights, the DRC Constitution makes access to medicines justiciable.[806] The possibility to enforce access to medicines by the courts and tribunals increases with the adoption of the Public Health Law, which implements article 47 of the DRC Constitution.

(1) The relevance of the Public Health Law

Both constitutional and treaty human rights provisions expressly refer to adopting appropriate and adequate legislative measures for the full realization of all rights herein guaranteed.

In the health field especially, legislation is an indispensable element for many purposes,[807] including operationalizing the State's right to national health strategy and creating any right of action on behalf of individuals or groups victims of a violation of their right to health.[808]A framework law on ESCRs places a statutory obligation on the executive arm of government to provide the services, programs, human resources, and infrastructure needed to give effect to the right, creating, therefore, a statutory entitlement to the relevant service.[809] It further clarifies the roles and responsibilities of each sphere of government in the delivery of services and provides the regulation of the service or programs to ensure that service is of good quality and is delivered properly.[810]

Within this context, the Public Health Law defines individuals' rights, clarifies, and determines the State's organs responsible for medicines' quality, availability, and accessibility. Individuals' rights cover, among others, access to quality health

---

804 DRC Constitution, art 150.

805 Néhemie Mwilanya, "Mécanismes nationaux de promotion et de protection des droits de l'homme," in *Mandats, rôles et fonctions des pouvoirs constitués dans le nouveau système politique de la République Démocratique du Congo. Journées d'information et de formation organisées à l'intention des parlementaires, députés provinciaux et des Hauts Cadres de l'administration*, ed. Programme des Nations Unies pour le Développement (Kinshasa: PNUD, 2007), 283.

806 Gaspard Ngondankoy, "Droit constitutionnel des droits de l'homme," in *Cours intensifs sur les droits de l'homme et le droit international pénal*, ed. Bakama Bope (Kinshasa: Université Protestante au Congo, 2012), 86-87.

807 General Comment 3, para 3.

808 Ibid. para 6, General Comment 14, para 56.

809 Paula Proudlock, "Children's socio-economic rights," in *Child law in South Africa*, ed. Trynie Boezaart (Cape Town: Juta, 2009), 296-297.

810 Ibid.

care services without discrimination at affordable cost, including through a universal health coverage system and information regarding medical treatments, their advantages, and eventual risks.[811] These rights partly fill in the content of the constitutional right to health.

Regarding medicines quality, the government establishes a public institution in charge of pharmaceutical regulation, including inspecting pharmaceutical establishments, monitoring the quality of medicinal products, and granting authorizations for the marketing of medical products.[812] To give effect to this provision, the prime minister's decree[813] establishes the " Autorité Congolaise de Règlementation Pharmaceutique, (ACOREP). »

As regard medicines's availability and accessibility, the Public Health Law establishes a national medicines supply system, the mission of which consists of making good quality medicines available and accessible to the entire population.[814] Furthermore, the Public Health Law establishes a universal health coverage system.[815] However, the implementation decree does not exist. It is essential to note that the Public Health Law establishes a Health Promotion Fund and a Health Solidarity Fund to respectively fund both the national health system and the universal health coverage.[816] These provisions are subject to the implementation decrees that the prime minister still has to take.

It is worth recalling that the Public Health Law does not expressly entitle individuals to any judicial action regarding the violation of their right to health. Nevertheless, its adoption[817] and content is vital in adjudicating the constitutional right to health. For instance, potential complainants can rely on the Public Health Law to sustain the violation of a specific aspect of access to medicines as part of the constitutional right to health. Also, in suing the government, they can address their complaints against the State's organs responsible for the violated aspect of access to medicines, such as those in charge of quality, availability, or accessibility of drugs as described in the Public Health Law.

(2) The law and human rights jurisdiction for each court and tribunal

This section discusses the extent to which the law organizes the exercise of human rights jurisdiction by each court and tribunal. It also looks at whether the law establishes the rule of procedure on the submission of complaints dealing with human rights violation, including access to medicines.

811 Public Health Law, arts 16, 17, 25, and 43.
812 Ibid. art 53.
813 Decree establishing ACOREP, arts 1 et 4.
814 Ibid. art 54.
815 Public Health Law. arts 41-42.
816 Ibid. arts 128-129.
817 Mazyambo, "Introduction aux droits de l'homme," 259 and 277.

(a) Constitutional court

Article 169 of the DRC Constitution subjects the organization and working of the constitutional court to an organic law. A close look at the organic law on the constitutional court reveals that it does not expressly consider the human rights jurisdiction argued in article 150 (1) of the Constitution.[818] Nevertheless, the exercise of its constitutional review power can contribute to protecting the right of access to medicines in one way or another. For instance, an a priori review of constitutional provisions allows the constitutional court to declare void any bill contrary to the Constitution, preventing it, therefore, from being promulgated or applied.[819] Equally, a posteriori review of constitutional provisions permits the constitutional court to declare void or unenforceable upon individual's request any laws or regulations, which are contrary to the Constitution.[820] Finally, the general prosecutor can seize the constitutional court motu proprio for any laws or regulation, the provisions of which infringe the fundamental rights and freedoms.[821]

The above provisions mean that both natural persons and the prosecutor general can resort to this constitutional court's jurisdiction to challenge any of the above acts that violate people's right of access to medicines. However, individuals are not entitled to any form of reparation before the constitutional court.[822] It is worth recalling that, in one of its decisions dealing with the control of constitutionality of one decision taken by the Congolese Senate, the constitutional court reaffirmed its constitutional competence to ensure the guardianship of human rights and fundamental freedoms protected by the Constitution. It rightly ruled that

> the DRC Constitution edicts in its article 149 (2) that the constitutional court forms part of the judiciary, which, in terms of article 150 (1) is the guarantor of individual freedoms and fundamental rights of citizens. Among the fundamental rights recognized to citizens is the right to be elected to a political mandate. The court notes that, as guardian of the Constitution, it is called upon to ensure that public authorities and citizens respect its provisions. Therefore, it is competent to deal with any request submitted by any individual who feels aggrieved by any decision that violates his constitutionally guaranteed rights and freedoms such as the right to be elected to a political mandate.[823]

The constitutional court bases and defines its competence on a combined reading of articles 149 (2) and 150 (1) of the Constitution, even though the organic law on its working and jurisdiction fails to recognize and organize its constitutional

---

818 Organic Law on the Constitutional Court, art 42.

819 DRC Constitution, arts 123 (3), 139 and 160.

820 Ibid. art 162. See also Organic Law on the Constitutional Court, arts 48 and 50.

821 Organic Law on the Constitutional Court, art 49.

822 Ibid. art 106.

823 Cour Constitutionnelle, Affaire R. Const. 0038 RH 010/CC, 2015.

human rights jurisdiction. Moreover, this court ruling confirms and reaffirms the view that all constitutionally protected rights, including access to medicine, are judicially enforceable.

(b) Administrative courts and tribunals

Article 155 of the DRC Constitution states that an organic law sets forth the organization, competence, and working of administrative courts and tribunals. Adopted in 2016, the organic law on the administrative courts and tribunals[824] does not operationalize the exercise of their human rights jurisdiction. However, the provisions of the organic law under discussion bestows the council of state,[825] administrative courts,[826] and tribunals[827] with the power to repeal or suspend any decision taken by national, provincial, and local administrative authorities, which is contrary to the law or regulation, as the case may be. Such competence implies that administrative courts and tribunals have jurisdiction to repeal or suspend regulations and decisions that violate access to medicines as argued under other domestic laws than the DRC Constitution. Moreover, in the absence of any different competent courts, the council of state may consider claims for compensation for exceptional, material or moral damage resulting from a measure taken or ordered by the authorities of the Republic.[828] This provision does not expressly deal with human rights. Nevertheless, it can serve as an alternative to the Constitutional court's lack of competence in ordering reparation, including in case of violation of human rights such as access to medicines.

(c) Civil courts and tribunals

Article 153 of the DRC constitution calls for the adoption of an organic law on the organization, operation, and jurisdiction of civil courts and tribunals. Adopted in 2013, the organic law on civil courts and tribunals[829] does only provide for criminal, civil, commercial and social jurisdiction without reference to human rights jurisdiction.[830]Considering these legal shortcomings in the judicial enforcement

---

824 Loi Organique N° 16/027 portant organisation, compétence et fonctionnement des juridictions de l'ordre administratif, 2016 (hereinafter Organic Law on the administrative courts).

825 DRC Constitution, art 155, and Organic Law on the administrative courts, art 85.

826 Organic Law on the administrative courts, art 96.

827 Administrative tribunals are further competent if these acts violate the Constitution and ratified treaties. Ibid. art 104.

828 DRC Constitution, art 155.

829 Loi Organique N° 13/011-B portant organisation, fonctionnement et compétences des juridictions de l'ordre judiciaire, 2013, art 112 (hereinafter Organic Law on civil jurisdictions).

830 Ibid. title II.

of ESCRs as argued under the DRC Constitution, Ngoy[831] proposes two solutions. First, he suggests that the Tribunal of Grande Instance, which is competent for "all the disputes that do not fall within the jurisdiction of the Tribunal de Paix (TRIPAIX),"[832] can serve as a jurisdiction of the first instance in all human rights issues. Secondly, to avoid the adoption of a specific law on the exercise of human rights jurisdiction, the competence of the Tribunal de Grande Instance should be read in conjunction with article 1 of the 1886 Ordinance,[833]which allows Congolese tribunals to adjudicate matters that fall within their jurisdiction according to the local customs, general principles of law, and equity if a decree or ordinance does not determine the relevant procedure in that regard.

These two suggested solutions call for the following observations. First, it is plausible that the expression "all the disputes that do not fall within the jurisdiction of the TRIPAIX" is broad enough to include human rights issues. However, a close look at the law under discussion suggests that it only deals with the jurisdiction of these two tribunals in civil matters.[834] Therefore, the reference to "all the disputes'' mainly means those civil disputes that do not expressly fall within the jurisdiction of the TRIPAIX. Secondly, the 1886 Ordinance the author refers to is already repealed.[835]Thirdly, the above-suggested solution seems minimalist as it confines the judiciary's human rights jurisdiction into the Tribunal of the Grande Instance only.

(d) *Military courts and tribunals*

According to article 156 of the DRC Constitution, an organic law determines the competence, organization, and working of military courts and tribunals.[836] Adopted in 2002 and revised in 2017,[837] the Military Code does not consider the human rights jurisdiction of military courts and tribunals provided by article 150 (1) of the DRC Constitution. Instead, it entirely and exclusively deals with the criminal jurisdiction of military courts and tribunals. As a result, the existing law on the military courts and tribunals's exercise of human rights jurisdiction, including ESCRs, is incomplete in that regard.

---

831 Ngoy, "Contrôle et protection des droits,"160.

832 Organic Law on civil jurisdictions, art 112.

833 Ordonnance de l'Administrateur Général du Congo, 1886.

834 Organic Law on civil jurisdictions, arts 110-112.

835 Décret portant code de procédure civile, 1960, art 199.

836 DRC Constitution, art 156.

837 Loi N°023/2002 portant Code judiciaire militaire telle que modifiée et complétée par la Loi Organique N° 17/003 du 10 mars 2017 modifiant et complétant la Loi N° 023-2002 du 18 Novembre 2002 portant Code judiciaire militaire, 2002.

(3) *Some concluding observations to the judicial enforcement of access to medicines*

The law dealing with the organization and competence of each court and tribunal does not expressly consider their constitutional human rights jurisdiction. Regarding the right to access medicines for instance, existing laws remain silent on the competent jurisdiction to adjudicate violations of the right to health related to

> the State's failure to regulate the activities of individuals or corporations, including the manufacturers of medicines, the failure to adopt or implement a national health policy designed to ensure the right to health for everyone and the failure to take measures to reduce the inequitable distribution of health facilities and services.[838]

These laws do not expressly organize the courts and tribunals' jurisdiction regarding the adjudication of the right to health. Furthermore, unlike the African Charter and the NCHR Law, which establish the rule of procedure regarding individual complaints, existing laws on the organization and competence of courts and tribunals do not provide a similar procedure in case of the violation of access to medicines. It is worth noting that, unlike the NCHR, courts and tribunals cannot deal with the breach of the right to health motu proprio.[839] Moreover, none of the above laws explicitly recognize the courts and tribunals' competence to provide reparation for violation of access to medicines, including restitution, compensation, satisfaction, or guarantees of non-repetition.[840] These legal gaps may, to some extent, justify the lack of individual complaints on the violation of the right to health against the Congolese government. Other factors include the burdensome character of the judicial procedure, people's ignorance of their rights, lack of trust in the judiciary system, especially in cases against the government,[841] financial and geographical constraints in getting access to justice.[842] Consequently, individuals prefer the NCHR to the courts and tribunals. The NCHR received in 2018 about 4,194 human rights violation complaints, including on the right to health, as discussed earlier.[843] Three reasons can explain the examination of human rights violations by the NCHR compared to the courts. First, unlike before the courts and

838 General Comment 14, paras 50-52.

839 Mbwisi Mumbanika, "The Protection of the right to health under the Constitution of the Democratic Republic of Congo", *Verfassung und Recht Übersee 4*, (2014): 444.

840 Ibid. para 50.

841 Judicial decisions against the Congolese government are either hardly implemented or remain unimplemented at all. See Ngoy, "Contrôle et protection des droits," 306.

842 Human Rights Committee's Concluding Observations to DRC, 2017, para 37, United Nations Joint Human Rights Office in the Democratic Republic of the Congo, Progress and obstacles in the fight against impunity for sexual violence in the Democratic Republic of the Congo, 2014, paras 52-53.

843 CNDH Annual Report 2019, 35.

tribunals, the procedure to the NCHR is free of charge. Secondly, unlike the laws on different courts and tribunals, the law establishing the NCHR institutes the complaint procedure for victims of human rights violation. Finally, unlike courts and tribunals, the NCHR acts motu proprio while inquiring about human rights violations. Therefore, in handling violations of human rights cases, the NHRC can either settle them amicably or transfer them to the courts and tribunals. Unfortunately, however, the NCHR's annual report on the above cases related to the right to health does not provide detailed information in that regard.

The same observation applies to the general prosecutor who is competent to bring laws and regulations that violate the right to health to the constitutional court's scrutiny. Thus, the absence of court's decisions on access to medicines challenges the theoretical possibility of the judicial enforceability of the said right in DRC.

(4) Some suggested solutions

Courts and tribunals in the DRC have human rights jurisdiction over all rights, including access to medicines. Without undermining the identified legal gaps in that regard, courts and tribunals can still discharge their constitutional and legal role of adjudicating violations of the right to health. For example, assume that the general prosecutor,[844] or individuals[845] bring to the constitutional court laws or regulations that infringe access to medicines. In this case, the constitutional court is under the legal obligation to declare such laws or regulations void and unconstitutional.[846] Similarly, when the NCHR assists complainants and victims of the right to health violation in taking legal action[847] or sues on their behalf,[848]courts or tribunals seized in that regard should settle these complaints. The same should also apply when individuals access the courts and tribunals directly.

Pending the revision of the law regulating the organization and competence of each court and tribunal, courts and tribunals can adjudicate the violation of the right to health in drawing from the above constitutional court's decision and ratified human rights treaties, which they also apply without further formality. Furthermore, they should rely on the jurisprudence and works of human rights treaty bodies, including views, recommendations, concluding observations, general comments or judgments. Like the African Commission, courts and tribunals should seize the first opportunity to adopt the principle of progressive realization in the implementation of ESCRs, including the right to health.

844 Organic Law on the Constitutional Court, art 49.

845 Ibid. art 48.

846 DRC Constitution, art 168.

847 NHRC Law, art 6 (2).

848 Règlement Intérieur de la Commission Nationale des Droits de l'Homme, 2015 (hereinafter NHRC Rule of procedure), 153.

B. Domestic laws and their implementation on access to medicines in the URT

The present section discusses the constitutional protection of human rights, focusing on access to medicines, adopted implementation measures, and the justiciability of the right of access to medicines.

1. Protection of human rights under the URT Constitution

In addition to the vote-related rights protected under its chapter on the United Republic and people,[849] the URT Constitution protects human rights as fundamental rights and directive principles of State policy. Part III of the URT Constitution covers basic rights, including the right to equality and its variants, the right to life, freedom of movement, freedom of expression, and the right to work and property.[850] The constitutional provisions on the directive principles of State policy protect human rights both expressly and impliedly. Expressly protected rights include the rights to education, social welfare in case of old age, sickness, disability, or any other cases of incapacity,[851] and human dignity following the spirit of the UDHR.[852] The explicit and express reference to human dignity in the spirit of the UDHR indicates that constitutionally protected human rights reflect those promulgated rights in the UDHR.[853] Article 9 (f) of the URT Constitution reaffirms this assertion by expressly incorporating the UDHR.[854]Impliedly protected rights derive from article 9 (a) of the URT Constitution, which provides the obligation to respect and cherish other human rights. This constitutional provision does not enumerate other human rights it mentions. However, the expression "other human rights" is broad enough to encompass all human rights that the Constitution does not explicitly mention as basic rights or directive principles of State policy. Expressly protected rights under the human rights instruments to which the URT has subscribed at international, African and SADC levels and other domestic laws[855]can fill in the content of other human rights referred to in article 9 (a). Therefore, article 9 (a) under discussion covers all categories of human rights, whether CPRs, ESCRs, or collective rights.

However, human rights under the URT Constitution do not theoretically have the same legal status. Unlike basic rights, which are justiciable, the courts cannot

---

849 URT Constitution, art 5.

850 Basic rights are protected from articles 12 to 24 of the URT Constitution.

851 Ibid. art 11.

852 Ibid. art 9 (f).

853 High Court, Manento J.K and others vs. the Attorney General, 2006.

854 Legal and Human Rights Centre and Others vs. Attorney General (1) (Miscellaneous Civil Case No 77 of 2005).

855 Commission for Human Rights and Good Governance Act, 2001.

enforce human rights protected as directive principles of the State policy.[856] In practical terms, this constitutional provision makes these rights inaccessible to the people.[857]

a. Constitutional protection of access to medicines

The URT Constitution protects health-related rights, including access to medicines outside its Bill of Rights,[858] as directive principles of State policy from different perspectives. To begin with, article 11 (1) of the URT Constitution provides the right to social welfare at times of old age, sickness or disability and in other cases of incapacity. Although this provision does not expressly use the expression right to health or access to medicines, it constitutes the primary constitutional basis of a human right to health in URT.[859] One can argue that access to medicines forms part of the right to social welfare, which is akin to security in the event of sickness under article 25 of the UDHR. Furthermore, article 9 (f) protects everyone's human dignity following the spirit of the UDHR. Once read conjointly with article 22 of the UDHR, article 9 (f) of the URT Constitution reaffirms the view that the enjoyment of all ESCRs, including access to medicines, constitutes an integral part of human dignity. For its part, article 9 (a) protects "human dignity and other human rights." The reference to "other human rights" is broad enough to cover human rights, including access to medicines, protected under other domestic laws, the UDHR,[860] and ratified human rights treaties, such as the ICESCR and the African Charter.

Like under the DRC Constitution, the constitutional protection of the right to life in the URT Constitution[861]provides a legal avenue for protecting access to medicine.

The URT is urged to adopt or frame a new Bill of Rights that protects all categories of humans, including the right to health, as basic and justiciable rights.[862] In 2011, the URT embarked on writing a new Constitution through the Constitutional Review Act.[863] Accordingly, the established Commission drafted a Draft Constitution and submitted it to the President for publication in the Gazette and

856 URT Constitution, art 7 (2).

857 Chris Peter, Justice and dignity for All: the state of human rights in Tanzania, in *Justice and dignity for all. Current issues of human rights in Tanzania*, ed. Kennedy Gaston et al. (Dar es Salaam: Dar es Salaam University Press, 2010), 32.

858 URT's Report to the African Commission, 2006.

859 Temba, "Right to health in Tanzania," 35.

860 In the URT, the UDHR is recognized and granted due importance in the Constitution itself. Peter, "Justice and dignity," 8.

861 URT Constitution, art 14.

862 Ibid. 59-60.

863 Constitutional Review Act, 2011.

other local newspapers.[864] Upon authorization of the President in agreement with the President of Zanzibar, the Chairperson of the Commission presented the Draft Constitution to the constituent assembly, which made and passed the provisions on the proposed new Constitution.[865] The Bill of Rights in the Draft Constitution[866] make explicit provisions for access to healthcare for children, persons with disabilities, minority groups of the society, women, and the elderly.[867] To come into force, Tanzanian citizens are required to validate the proposed Constitution through a referendum.[868] However, the government has never organized the said referendum on the Draft Constitution.

b. The relationship between the treaty and constitutional health-related rights

According to article 63 (3) (e) of the URT Constitution, the National Assembly deliberates upon and ratifies all treaties and agreements to which the United Republic is party, the provisions of which require ratification. This constitutional provision makes the URT a dualist State,

> in which terms of an international treaty becomes applicable in Tanzania upon both ratifying and domesticating the treaty terms. This means that a treaty becomes incorporated into law by either amending or repealing existing legislation or enacting new legislation altogether.[869]

For its part, article 64 (5) of the URT Constitution provides that

> this Constitution shall have the force of law in the whole of the United Republic, and in the event any other law conflicts with the provisions contained in this Constitution, the Constitution shall prevail and that other law, to the extent of the inconsistency with the Constitution, shall be void.

It follows from these constitutional provisions that once domesticated through legislation, treaty rights acquire a relatively lower legal status than constitutional rights.

However, the theoretical higher legal status of constitutional rights over the domesticated treaty rights becomes meaningless for two main reasons. First, like constitutional basic rights, domesticated treaty rights become justiciable before

864 Ibid. arts 19-20.

865 Ibid. arts 20 (4), 25-26.

866 International Institute for Democracy and Electoral Assistance, The proposed Draft Constitution of Tanzania, 2014 (hereinafter Draft Constitution).

867 Ibid. arts 50 (1) (e), 52 (f), 53 (2), 54 (f) and 55 (c).

868 Constitutional Review Act, art 31.

869 URT's Report to the African Commission, 2006.

the courts. Secondly, unlike constitutional rights protected as directive principles of State policy, domesticated treaty rights that fall within the category of these constitutional rights, such as access to medicines, become as justiciable as constitutional basic rights. Suppose the treaty rights are not domesticated. In that case, they enjoy the same legal status as constitutional rights protected as directive principles of State policy, unless the Constitution simultaneously protects them as basic rights.

c. *The nature of the State's obligations in respect with access to medicines*

The State's obligations towards access to medicines comprise of specific and general duties. Accordingly, articles 9 (a) (f) and 11 (1) of the URT Constitution set forth specific duties. In contrast, article 7 (1) relates to general obligations.

aa) Specific State's obligations

According to article 9 (a) (f) of the URT Constitution, the state authority and all its agencies direct their policies and programmes towards ensuring that human dignity and other human rights are respected, cherished, preserved and upheld following the spirit of the UDHR. Under article 11 (1) of the URT Constitution, the State authority makes appropriate provisions for the realization of a person's right to social welfare at times of old age, sickness or disability and in other cases of incapacity. As discussed earlier, the right to access medicines forms part of the rights to human dignity, social welfare and other human rights. Therefore, it entails the State's obligations to respect, cherish, preserve, uphold, and make appropriate provisions for its realization.

bb) General State's obligations

Article 7 (1) of the URT Constitution states that it shall be the duty and responsibility of the government, including authorities exercising executive, legislative and judicial functions to take cognizance of, observe and apply the provisions of this part of this chapter. The phrase "the provisions of this part of this chapter" refers to the fundamental objectives and directive principles of the State policy. It covers, among others, the right to social welfare, human dignity, and other human rights. Regarding the government, it consists of the executive power vested in the President of the United Republic and the government of the United Republic,[870] the legislative power in parliament,[871] and the judicial power in, among others, the High Court of the United Republic, the Court of Appeal of the United Republic and the

---

870 URT Constitution, arts 33-34.

871 Ibid. art 64.

Special Constitutional Court of the United Republic.[872] Therefore, each branch of the government shall, within its jurisdiction, observe and apply the constitutional provisions relating to access to medicines protected as directive principles of the State policy through the adoption of various and complementary measures, including laws, regulations, court decisions, policies, budgets, and programs.

However, article 7 (2) of the URT Constitution undermines and restricts the judiciary's ability to fulfil the above constitutional obligations. Accordingly, it states that the provisions of this Part of this Chapter are not enforceable by any court. It further provides that no court shall be competent to determine the question whether or not any action or omission by any person or any court, or any law or judgment complies with the provisions of the Chapter *on* the fundamental objectives and directive principles of the State policy. This provision does not recognize the courts' jurisdiction in adjudicating questions relating to non-compliance with the State's duty to implement the right of access to medicines protected in this part of the URT Constitution. Pending the amendment of article 7 (1), the judiciary, like other State's organs, is still bound by the provisions of article 7 (1),[873]and should not serve any purpose to the contrary. As Wambali points out,[874] by ensuring that all State's organs comply with the above directive principles, courts are bound to assume a supervisory role in the defense of individual complainant's rights.

2. Existing implementation measures relevant to access to medicines

This section analyses the implementation of access to medicines through different adopted measures as required by both the Constitution and ratified human rights treaties. It focuses on adopted measures that aim to ensure the quality of medicines, their availability and accessibility, and their enforceability before both judicial and quasi-judicial bodies.

a. Quality medicines and regulation of the pharmaceutical sector

The primary laws that govern the pharmaceutical sector in the URT consist of the Pharmacy Act[875] and the Tanzanian Food, Drugs and Cosmetics Act[876]

872 Ibid. arts 108, 117, and 125.

873 Palamagamba Kabudi, "The judiciary and human rights in Tanzania: domestic application of international human rights norms," *Verfassung und Recht in Übersee / Law and Politics in Africa, Asia and Latin America 24*, no. 3, (1991): 278.

874 Michael Wambali, "The Enforcement of basic rights and freedoms and the state of judicial activism in Tanzania," *Journal of African Law 53*, no. 1, (2009): 37 and 46.

875 Pharmacy Act, 2011.

876 Tanzania Food, Drugs and Cosmetics Act, 2003.

supplemented by, among others, the Medical Practitioners Act.[877] The present subsection examines their provisions, which relate to the profession of pharmacist, the control of pharmaceutical activities, and the sanctions regime.

aa) Regulation of the profession of a pharmacist and pharmaceutical business

To qualify as a pharmacist, the applicant must hold a pharmacy degree or any other qualification recognized by the Council as being equivalent and meet other criteria set out under the Pharmacy Act.[878] Other medical personnel involved in providing medicines, including pharmaceutical technicians, pharmaceutical assistants,[879] and medical professionals,[880]must also meet education requirements.

The pharmaceutical legislation recognizes the monopoly of pharmaceutical business to the pharmacist. Following article 43 of the Pharmacy Act, a person shall not carry pharmacist's business unless that person is a pharmacist. However, this monopoly encounters some limitations in that non-pharmacists may deal with some pharmaceutical activities under some prescribed conditions. These include persons or associations that manufacture for sell, supply or dispense medicines under the supervision of a pharmacist,[881] entitled persons to deal with some pharmaceutical activities,[882] including for the public interest,[883] and medical practitioners of any health institution.[884] These exceptions are flexible and consider the country's realities. Indeed, regulating pharmaceutical activities by non-pharmacists constitutes an appropriate alternative to pharmacists' shortage in countries, such as the URT or DRC. Moreover, such exceptions deserve the merit of reducing the prevalence of pharmacy's illegal practice by non-pharmacists. It is worth recalling that the competent authority has a discretionary power to revoke, suspend or cancel the issued permit if it is satisfied that entitled entities or persons violate the terms and conditions of the permit's issuance.[885]

The law also prescribes conditions that must be complied with regarding the pharmaceutical premises and medicines' quality. Accordingly, pharmaceutical premises are subject to a previous registration.[886] The registration can only be successful if the regulatory authority is satisfied that the following conditions are

877 Medical Practitioners Act, 2007.
878 Pharmacy Act, art 16.
879 Ibid. arts 24 and 28.
880 Medical Practitioners Act, art 3.
881 Pharmacy Act, arts 43 and 44 (1).
882 Ibid. arts 36 and 37.
883 Ibid. art 40.
884 Ibid. arts 41-42.
885 Ibid. art 37 (5), 42 (3).
886 Ibid. arts 1 and 34.

met which are namely: that the premises meet the prescribed standards, equipment is available for storing the medicines, and related medical supplies with the suitability of the equipment and facilities used for distributing the medicines.[887] This provision aims to ensure that registered entities produce or keep medicines in good conditions.

Regarding the quality of medicines, the law prohibits any pharmaceutical business to deal with medicines, of which the composition has been affected by the addition thereto or subtraction therefrom of any substance and medicines that are not of nature or quality demanded by the purchaser.[888] The law further forbids medicines that are unfit for the intended purpose and counterfeit medicines.[889] In sum, the law prohibits both the manufacturing and the supply of medicines of poor quality.

bb) Control quality of medicines

The control quality of medicines in the URT falls within the Tanzania Food and Drugs Authority (TFDA) competence, which is the regulatory authority for medicines.[890] Its power consists of regulating all matters relating to the quality and safety of drugs, and taking legal measures on consumers' complaints against pharmaceutical manufacturers. To appropriately fulfil its functions, the TFDA has at its disposal the Tanzania Food and Drugs Authority Laboratory,[891] which performs all the tasks relating to the quality of medicines, namely the analysis of drugs and raw materials, packaging material, and drug delivery systems. The TFDA appoints pharmaceutical inspectors among pharmacists, medical practitioners, health officers, pharmaceutical technicians, and public officers or officers appointed under any written laws.[892]It is worth noting that quality control can occur before and after the entry of pharmaceuticals into the market.

(1) An a priori control quality

According to articles 75 and 76 of Tanzania Food, Drugs and Cosmetics Act, one cannot add any substance to a drug or subtract any substance from it with the intention of selling it in that changed state, or manufacture the counterfeit drug. Though not expressly mentioned, the reference to "add or subtract any substance" and "manufacture counterfeit drug" suggests that these provisions concern mainly the manufacture of medicine, which is also subject to inspection. They aim to

887 Ibid. art 36.

888 Tanzania Food, Drugs and Cosmetics Act, arts 75-76.

889 Ibid.

890 Ibid. arts 4 and 5.

891 Ibid. art 14.

892 Ibid. art 105.

ensure quality medicines. Moreover, the law subjects the import of drugs to a prior permit or authorization.[893] Finally, to ensure the quality of donated medicines, the applicable regulation provides that these medicines must originate from a reliable source and comply with quality standards in both the donor country and the URT, including having a remaining shelf-life of at least one year.[894] In sum, whether locally produced or imported, the law regulates the quality of medicines before they reach the patients or consumers.

(2) Postmarketing quality control

Pharmaceutical inspectors can, following article 106 of the Food, Drugs, and Cosmetics Act, enter all the pharmaceutical premises, including any premises suspected of dealing with medicines, to ensure compliance with the existing regulation. To this end, they can seize and detain any drug that appears to them to constitute or contain evidence of a contravention of any provision of the pharmaceutical legislation. Furthermore, pharmaceutical inspectors can close the premises found to have contravened the law, institute criminal proceedings, and order the return to the country of origin of any product imported without regard to the existing pharmaceutical regulation. Finally, the TFDA can order the destruction of any product found to be unfit for its intended use.[895]

To sum up, simultaneous and complementary implementation of both types of control is relevant for medicine quality. They supplement each other and aim to ensure that entitled entities produce, keep, and sell medicines of good quality in good conditions.

cc) Sanctions

Under the Pharmacy Act and Tanzania Food, Drugs and Cosmetics Act, sanctions depend on the violated provisions' nature. For instance, persons who contravene the provisions relating to the premises and issuance of the permit for pharmaceutical business are liable to a fine not exceeding ten million shillings or imprisonment for a term not exceeding two years or to both.[896] In contrast, persons carrying out the pharmaceutical business without being pharmacists or without being under the supervision of a pharmacist are liable to a fine of not less than one million shillings or imprisonment for a term not less than six months or to both.[897] Further, persons who modify the drug's composition are liable to a fine of not less than five hundred thousand shillings or to imprisonment for a term of not

893 Tanzania, Food, Drugs and Cosmetics Act, art 73.
894 Guidelines for medicines and medical supplies donations for Tanzania Mainland, 2015.
895 Tanzania, Food, Drugs and Cosmetics Act, art 6.
896 Pharmacy Act, art 34.
897 Ibid. art 43.

less than three months or to both such fine and imprisonment.[898] For their part, persons involved in counterfeit medicines are liable to a fine of not less than five million shillings or to imprisonment for a term of not less than two years or to both such fine and imprisonment.[899] Finally, in case of professional misconduct by the pharmacists, the pharmaceutical technician, and the pharmaceutical assistant, the Council may cancel, suspend, or remove their name from the register, roll, or list.[900]

These sanctions discourage illegal pharmaceutical activities to protect both people's lives and health. At the same time, fine sanctions may constitute a significant financial resource for the government. However, compared to both the threat that counterfeit or altered medicines pose to people's life and the economic benefit provided to its offenders, sanctions against these offenses seem too low and unrealistic to deter the problem of counterfeit drugs.[901] The situation becomes worse with the judge's discretionary power to prosecute the offenders of counterfeit medicines with both fine and imprisonment.

Indeed, reports reveal that the URT experienced more than twenty cases of counterfeit medicines between 2001 and 2013.[902] These documented cases of counterfeit medicines partly indicate that the postmarketing control quality in the URT works relatively well. At the same time, they also suggest that the control undertaken before marketing did not prevent these unfit medicines from entering the market. Factors that can justify the prevalence of counterfeit medicines in URT include, among others, the lack of proper and qualified laboratories, insufficient capacity of the regulatory authority to control all manufacturers and drug dealers, the limited number of drug inspectors and the high number of ports of entry.[903] They also include failure for most domestic manufacturers of medicines to comply with minimum good manufacturing practices.[904] Yet, for a least developed country such as the URT, the fight against counterfeit medicines remains a real challenge.

---

898 Tanzania Food, Drugs and Cosmetics Act, art 75.

899 Ibid. art 76.

900 Pharmacy Act, art 45.

901 Phoibe, Magili, "The efficacy of the law and regulatory mechanisms in combating counterfeit drugs in Tanzania," *Mzumbe University*, (2014): 50.

902 Hiiti Sillo, "Regulatory enforcement and the risk of counterfeit and substandard medicines in Africa: the case of Tanzania," 2013, https://medeor.de/images/themen/konferenz/HiitiSillo.pdf (accessed July 12, 2018). See also Robert Mhamba and Shukrani Mbirigenda, "The pharmaceutical industry and access to essential medicines in Tanzania," *Institute of Development Studies, University of Dar es Salaam*, (2010): 16.

903 Sillo, "Regulatory enforcement," 12, Magili, "Efficacy of the law," 56-57.

904 Tanzania Food and Drugs Authority, Ten years of regulating food, medicines, cosmetics and medical devices 2003-2013: Milestones attained, (2013) 71.

However, and regrettably, the number of the above-documented cases does not correspond to the number of prosecutions.[905] It means that the government has the discretion to prosecute or not flagrant cases of counterfeit medicines. For instance, in the case of Tanzania Pharmaceutical Industry dealing with counterfeit drugs, the accused were dismissed from their positions without being convicted to serve any punishment.[906] Failure to punish these offenders following the existing sanctions regime of fine and imprisonment violates the State's duty to protect people's health.

b. Availability and accessibility of medicines

The present subsection argues that to make medicines available and accessible, the URT government resorts to both its traditional function to protect its citizens' health and regulatory function.

aa) State's traditional function to protect people's health

The law recognizes and organizes the government's traditional function to protect people's health. To this end, the Public Health Act expressly vests the national minister responsible for health with the primary duty to promote, preserve, and maintain a comprehensive, functional, and sustainable public health system, which prevents and controls living infectious or communicable and other diseases.[907] To reach this goal, the government sets up a national health system that operates in a decentralized governance system. The national health system consists of three main stages: district, regional and national levels.[908] Dispensaries, health centres, and district hospitals deliver primary health care services, which constitute the national health system's main approach of delivering health services.[909]

Regarding the availability of medicines at public health facilities, the Medical Stores Department (MSD), an autonomous department within the ministry of health and social welfare, procures, stores, and distributes pharmaceutical products that are then sent to zonal stores, which in turn supply health facilities within the respective districts.[910]

---

905 In 2013 for instance, five prosecutions were ongoing. See Sillo, "Regulatory enforcement," 12, and Magili, "Efficacy of the law," 55.

906 Magili, "Efficacy of the law," 55.

907 Public Health Act 2009, art 4.

908 Ministry of Health and Social Welfare, Tanzania Human Resource for Health and Social Welfare Strategic Plan 2014–2019 (hereinafter Human Resource Strategic Plan), 2014.

909 Ministry of Health and Social Welfare, Primary Health Services Development Programme 2007–2017 (hereinafter Primary Health Services Programme).

910 Ministry of Health and Social Welfare, Mapping of the medicines procurement and supply management system in Tanzania, 2008 (hereinafter Mapping of the

bb) The government regulatory function and access to medicines

Through the regulatory function, the government authorizes and controls the exercise of pharmaceutical activities by non-state actors. The URT government regulates drug donations.[911] It also enables several partners to get involved in the country's medicines supply chain, namely multilateral and bilateral donors, NGOs, faith-based organizations, the private sector, and pharmaceutical industries. However, most partners have varied and diverse interests in health programs, which results in an uncoordinated multiple vertical supply chain arrangement, wastage of scarce resources, and inefficiency in supply system management.[912] Furthermore, they give little weight to the quality control of received medicines. These partners do not systematically take samples from batches procured to send for quality analysis to the in-country quality control laboratories.[913] Ignoring such procedures may constitute a threat to quality medicines.

Regarding pharmaceutical industries, studies report that domestic manufacturing output covers only 10% of the pharmaceutical market.[914] Like most sub-Saharan African countries, the URT relies and depends on imports.[915]

Despite the above government's efforts, several factors impede it from ensuring that good quality medicines are available and accessible within its jurisdiction.[916] These mainly include the existence of doubtful quality medicines, the shortage of skilled human health resources,[917] and their unequal distribution to the detriment of rural areas[918]where most Tanzanians live. Regarding the availability of medicines, the "out of stock" phenomenon of essential drugs and supplies within public facilities constitutes one of the main identified factors that render more challenging access to medicines. As a result, the population's needs and demands for medicines are higher than the available medicines,[919] the impact of which is alarming in rural areas. Indeed, people in rural areas have to travel long-distance

---

Medicines Procurement). See also Business Monitor International Ltd, Tanzania Pharmaceuticals and Healthcare Report Q3, 2016 (hereinafter BMI Report), 38.

911 Guidelines for medicines and medical supplies donations for Tanzania Mainland, 2015.

912 Mapping of the Medicines Procurement.

913 Ibid. 39.

914 BMI Report, 45.

915 Ibid.

916 Ministry of Health and Welfare, Tanzania National Health Strategy June 2013–July 2018, 2013 (hereinafter National Health Strategy). See also CESCR's concluding observations to URT, 2012.

917 Statistics show that qualified health workers in the URT health sector fill only 35% of positions. See National Health Strategy, and the Primary Health Services Programme.

918 Human Resource Strategic Plan.

919 Primary Health Services Programme.

or many hours to reach health services delivery points.[920] Their chance to get access to better health services is relatively lower than those living in urban areas.[921]

cc) Financial accessibility to medicines

Financial accessibility to medicines depends on, among others, the national health system's funding, the regulation of the price of medicines, and the management of a universal health coverage system.

(1) Funding health system

The primary sources of the national health system funding consist of the State's budget allocation to the health sector,[922] as supplemented by inter alia, development partners and non-governmental funding outside the government system.[923] The URT has subscribed to the Abuja declaration, which urges African States to allocate at least 15% of their budget to the health sector. However, the budget allocation to the health sector in URT has never reached 15%.[924] Health budget remains insufficient[925] to adequately meet people's health needs. Inherent to implementing the budget allocated to the health sector, the disproportion between the funds disbursed and the given amount makes it difficult for the government to cope with the shortage of medicines.[926]

Funds from the State's partners add substantially to the revenue available for the health sector. However, great dependence on funds from the State's partners compromises the move towards universal health coverage. Not only are donor funds sometimes unreliable due to delays in disbursement or changes in donor commitments, but also most development activities, such as the construction of

---

920 Ibid.

921 Ibid. See also Peter, "Justice and dignity," 34.

922 Mapping of the Medicines Procurement.

923 URT's Report to the CESCR, 2009, para 110.

924 For instance, the budget portion allocated to health secton in 2017 and 2018 was respectively of 6.1% and 7%. See "World Bank. Tanzania Public Expenditure Review 2020. © World Bank,"2020, Tanzania-Health-Sector-Public-Expenditure-Review-2020.pdf (accessed March 15, 2020), and Bryant Lee and Kuki Tarimo, "Analysis of the Government of Tanzania's Budget Allocation to the Health Sector for Fiscal Year 2017/18,"2018, 7183-7323_TanzaniaBudgetAllocationHealthSectorBrief.pdf (accessed January 12, 2019).

925 CRC's concluding observations to URT, 2015, para 54, and CESCR's concluding observations to URT, 2012, para 24. See also Primary Health Services Programme.

926 BMI Report, at 36-38.

health facilities, and some of the purchasing of drugs, are dependent on these external sources.[927]

(2) Price regulation for medicines

The Tanzanian government is under the obligation to prevent unreasonably high prices for needed medicines in both the public and private sectors.[928] Legislations on the price regulation in the URT are significantly underdeveloped.[929] Indeed, the prices of key medicines in the URT vary greatly between location and sector. For instance, medicines are more expensive in private health facilities than in the public sector, with many Tanzanians unable to afford medication from these private health facilities.[930] As a result, many people would rely on services provided by public health facilities,[931]despite the risk of not getting needed medicines on time due to the out-of-stock phenomenon. In contrast, patients and consumers with limited financial resources would resort to some private health facilities providing unfit medicines while using low-priced medicines to attract people.[932]

(3) Universal health care coverage

The URT is under both the constitutional and treaty's obligation to ensure access to medicines for all its inhabitants without discrimination.[933] An essential aspect of providing such access without discrimination consists of establishing a universal health care coverage system. However, like the DRC, the URT lacks universal healthcare coverage.[934] Instead, it provides limited coverage of health insurance schemes.

dd) Different ways of accessing medicines

People in the URT get access to medicines using mainly health insurance and out pocket money. Some persons, namely prisoners access medicines at public expense. Others, such as children and people affected by HIV can receive medicines

---

927 Gemini Mtei and Suzan Makawia, "Universal health coverage assessment: Tanzania," *Global Network for Health Equity*, (2014): 4.

928 African Commission Resolution 141.

929 BMI Report, 33.

930 Primary Health Services Programme. See also, BMI Report, 33.

931 Primary Health Services Programme.

932 One of the identified challenges in combating counterfeit medicines in the URT is the wide price gaps due to the lack of medicines price regulation. See Sillo, "Regulatory enforcement," 12.

933 URT Constitution, art 13, ICESCR, art 2 (2), and African Charter, art 2.

934 CESCR's concluding observations to URT, 2012, para 23.

with the government's assistance. The law also protects access to medicines for people with mental disorders and people with disabilities.

(1) Access to medicines through medical insurance

This subsection deals with access to medicines through health insurance under the National Health Insurance Fund Act,[935] the National Social Security Fund Act[936] the Worker's compensation Act,[937]and the Community Health Fund Act.[938]

(a) Access to medicines under the National Health Insurance Fund Act

The National Health Insurance Fund Act establishes a National Health Insurance Fund, which consists of the employer's and employee's contributions.[939] It applies to civil servants other than those employed in the local government, defense, police, prisons, and those covered by the National Social Security Fund.[940] Its established insurance scheme covers civil servants, their spouses, and children or dependants not exceeding four in number.[941] The limited number of children or dependents seems detrimental to civil servants with more than four children, especially when they decide about the four children to be covered. Granted health services include the inpatient hospital care fee and the outpatient care consisting of drugs and medicines in generic prescription.[942] Accredited health institutions deliver covered health services and medicines to insured persons.[943] The Fund pays the healthcare provider[944]since insured persons do not directly pay for medical treatment. However, the National Health Insurance Fund covers only about 7% of the population, and most of its beneficiaries live in urban areas.[945]

(b) Access to medicines under the National Social Security Fund Act

The National Social Security Fund Act establishes a National Social Security Fund, which consists of contributions and other amounts of money required by this Act. Insured persons include, among others, every person member of the existing Fund, every person who is self -employed, a non-pensionable employee in the

935 National Health Insurance Fund Act, 1999.
936 National Social Security Fund Act, 1997, art 3.
937 Worker's Compensation Act, 2015.
938 The Community Health Fund Act, 2001.
939 National Health Insurance Fund Act, arts 9 and 32.
940 Ibid. art 2.
941 Ibid. art 11.
942 Ibid. art 16.
943 Ibid. art 17 and 20.
944 Ibid. art 28.
945 Mtei and Makawia, "Universal health coverage," 5.

government service and parastatal organization, or every employee registered by the employer who registers under this Act.[946] According to article 41 of the Act under examination, health insurance benefits apply to the insured person, his/her spouse, and four children. Like under the National Health Insurance Fund Act, beneficiaries of this insurance scheme receive preventive and curative care, including essential drugs from doctors, nurses, and other medical providers in the accredited hospitals.[947] However, they cannot receive health care services at non-accredited health facilities, including in an emergency.

(c) Access to medicines under the Worker's compensation Act

The Worker's compensation Act applies to all employers and employees. It provides adequate and equitable compensation for employees who suffer occupational injuries or contract occupational diseases arising out of and in the course of their employment.[948] According to article 62, the Director-General shall pay the reasonable cost incurred by or on behalf of an employee in respect of medical aid necessitated by the accident or disease. The same article provides that the Director-General pays the cost incurred in respect of further medical aid that may reduce the employee's disablement. Medical aid under the Worker's Compensation Act includes medical, surgical, or hospital treatment, skilled nursing services, and any remedial treatment.[949] Moreover, the Worker's Compensation Act covers only work accidents and occupational disease. Therefore, medical aid under the Worker's compensation Act does not extend to the employee's spouse or children.

(d) Access to medicine under the Community Health Fund Act

The Community Health Fund Act allows local government authorities to establish a Community Health Fund, a voluntary community-based financing scheme, whereby households pay contributions to finance part of their basic health care services.[950] The Council determines the level of annual contributions after consultation with the community concerned.

More interestingly, the government contributes to the Fund any specified amount of money through the respective Council.[951] This pre-payment mechanism entitles every household member, including the spouse and children under the age of eighteen without number limitation, to medical services of his/her choice at a preselected health care facility within the respective district.[952] However, the

946 National Social Security Fund Act, art 6 and 11.

947 Ibid. art 42.

948 Worker's Compensation Act, arts 2 and 3.

949 Ibid. art 4.

950 The Community Health Fund Act, 2001, art 4.

951 Ibid. art 8.

952 Ibid. arts 3 and 9.

beneficiaries under the present Act cannot access health services in a health facility other than the preselected one within or outside the community. This limitation also applies to any case of emergencies, including accidents or sudden sicknesses.

It is worth stressing that the Ward Health Committee exempts some categories of persons from paying the Community Health Fund's annual contribution upon the Village Council's recommendations.[953] This provision considers the incapability of peoples who cannot pay their annual contributions. It reflects the principle of equity in the enjoyment of access to medicines. To compensate the Fund, the Ward Health Committee seeks alternative financial supports,[954]which can include the government's specified amount of money referred to earlier. However, although people themselves determine the premiums, they are still unaffordable to some people.[955] As a result, the Community Health Fund covers only about 8% of the population.[956]

(2) Access to medicines through the out-of-pocket money

Direct purchasing of health services through out-of-pocket payments does still play a significant role in the URT. The main factors that justify its practice include the limited coverage of health insurance schemes, limited tax funds to fund free health care, and the shortage of medicines within public[957]and affiliated health facilities.

The lack of universal health coverage makes non-insured people use out-of-pocket payments to access medicines provided by both government and non-government health facilities.[958] Furthermore, due to the shortage of medicines in public and affiliated health facilities, insured people have no other choice than to buy medicines at private pharmacies or non-affiliated health facilities using their out-of-pocket money.[959] Though out-of-pocket payment constitutes one of the essential financing sources of health system,[960]it limits the move towards universal coverage. Sometimes, health facilities deny access to health care services to a large population without financial risk protection.[961] Consequently, several people have died because they could not afford to contribute or even pay so-called registration

953 Ibid. art 10.

954 Ibid.

955 Stephen Winani, "Community Health Fund scheme in Tanzania: An exploration of its challenges and opportunities in contribution towards universal health coverage," *Royal Tropical Institute*, (2015): 18.

956 Mtei and Makawia, "Universal health coverage," 5.

957 Ibid. 6.

958 Ibid. 5

959 Winani, "Community Health Fund scheme," 20.

960 Primary Health Services Programme.

961 Ibid.

fees at health centres or hospitals.[962]In sum, reducing the out-of-pocket retail cost of medicines and improving affordability remains a challenge for the URT government.[963]

(3) Access to medicines with the government's assistance

This subsection discusses access to medicines for children and people with HIV.

(a) Access to medicines for children

The Law of the Child Act explicitly gives effect to international and regional conventions on the rights of the child.[964] It contains various provisions that deal with the right to health. For instance, article 9 entitles every child to the rights to life, dignity, and health from his parents. Moreover, according to article 8, parents maintain the child, including providing him with medical care. The same article 8 provides that a person shall not deprive a child access to health and medical care necessary for his development or deny a child medical care because of religious or other beliefs. These provisions make parents the sole persons who are responsible for their children's access to health care, including pharmaceuticals. It is worth recalling that under ratified international and regional conventions on the rights of the child,[965] State parties, including the URT, assist parents in implementing the child's right to a standard of living adequate for the child's physical, mental and social development, and health. The Law of the Child Act partly incorporates this treaty's obligation under article 94 (4) and (5). Accordingly, the local government authority assists the most vulnerable children in growing up with dignity and developing their potential and self-reliance. It is also the local government's duty to provide assistance and accommodation for any abandoned child or refugee child. Due to the lack of definition for "most vulnerable children" by the Child Act, one can argue that they may also include those children whose parents cannot provide medical care services. Moreover, assistance due to abandoned and refugee children is broad enough to include medicines, which is indispensable for the growing up of the children with dignity.

However, children in the URT, especially those living in poverty and remote areas, still face limited access to health care services, resulting in persistent high morbidity and infant mortality rates.[966]

---

962 Peter, "Justice and dignity," 33-34.

963 BMI Report, 33.

964 Law of the Child Act.

965 CRC, arts 27, and African Children Charter, art 20 (2)(a).

966 Committee on the Rights of the Child, concluding observations to URT, 2015 (hereinafter CRC's concluding observations URT, 2015) para 54. See also Committee on the Rights of the Child, concluding observations to URT, 2012 (hereinafter CRC's concluding observations URT, 2012), para 24.

(b) Access to medicines for people living with HIV

Several provisions of the HIV and AIDS Act[967] deal with the right to health and related rights. For instance, under article 33 (1), "any person living with HIV and AIDS shall, using available resources, have a right to the highest attainable standard of physical and mental health; and a right to treatment of opportunistic infections."[968] Moreover, depending on available resources, it is the government responsibility to ensure that persons living with HIV and AIDS, including vulnerable children and orphans, receive basic health services[969] and ARVs.[970] Like under the ICESCR, the State's obligation to implement these provisions depends on its available resources. It follows that access to medicines by people living with HIV is not free of charge. However, under article 34, local government authorities should design, formulate, establish, and coordinate mechanisms and strategic plans to grant the most vulnerable children, including orphans, access to basic health care and livelihood services. It is the health Minister's task to set out criteria for identifying the most vulnerable children.[971] Focus on the vulnerable children and orphans suggests that they could have free access to basic health care with the government's support.

Conscious of financial constraints, the HIV and AIDS Act erects into a crime the misuse of received aid and assistance by all the involved actors in the fight against HIV. In addition to criminal prosecution, the offenders are under the legal obligation to restitute the misused funds.[972] The refund of any misuse aid and assistance shall be re-allocated to meet the purpose of fighting HIV throughout the country.[973]

However, the URT remains one of the countries with the high prevalence of HIV/AIDS among women and girls, the high rate of mother-to-child transmission, and the high number of disadvantaged women facing difficulties in gaining access to health services.[974]

967 HIV and AIDS Act, 2008.
968 Ibid. art 33 (1).
969 Ibid. arts 19 and 23.
970 Ibid. art 24.
971 Ibid. art 34 (2).
972 Ibid. art 35.
973 Ibid.
974 CEDAW, Concluding Observations to the URT, 2016, paras 36 and 40, URT's 2009 Report to CESCR, para 116.

(4) *Access to medicines for people with disability and people with mental disorders*

Access to medicines for this group of people is dealt with respectively in the Persons with Disabilities Act[975] and Mental Health Act.[976] According to article 26 of the Persons with Disability Act, every person with a disability has the right to enjoy the attainable standard of health care services without discrimination. Moreover, health facilities take all reasonable and necessary measures to grant people with disability access to health services, including providing all health and rehabilitation personnel, with appropriate education and training to increase their knowledge, disability sensitive awareness and respect for the rights, dignity and needs of persons with disabilities.[977] The above right entails the State's obligation to encourage the development of sufficient numbers of health and rehabilitation professionals at all levels.[978] However, the law remains silent on financial accessibility to health care services for persons with disabilities.

Under the Mental Health Act, persons taking care of a mentally ill person ensure that the person's treatment and care received at a mental health care facility are adequate.[979] Moreover, it is the State's obligation to establish mental health care facilities of varying degrees of specialization for the care and treatment of mentally disordered offenders and persons with mental disorders.[980] This provision entails the State's duty to make available health services, including medicines for people with a mental disorder. Furthermore, the Mental Health Act establishes a Mental Health Board to supervise and monitor mental health care services and assurance of quality.[981] This provision indicates that the State ensures that people with mental disorders access good quality medicines provided by skilled medical personnel within appropriate conditions. However, like under the Persons with Disability Act, the Mental Health Act does not expressly address financial accessibility to mental health care services.

(5) *Access to medicines for prisoners at the public expense*

The Prison Act[982] requires a medical officer to be responsible for prisoners' health. The medical officer can take or cause to be taken such action, including the forcible vaccination and any other treatment of the prisoner as he may consider necessary

---

975 Persons with Disabilities Act, 2010.

976 Mental Health Act, 2008.

977 Persons with Disabilities Act, arts 3 and 26.

978 Ibid.

979 Mental Health Act, art 28.

980 Ibid. art 27.

981 Ibid. arts 16-17.

982 Prisons Act, 1967.

to safeguard or restore the health of the prisoner or to prevent the spread of disease.[983] In the event of serious illness of a prisoner confined in a prison where adequate facilities do not exist for his treatment, the medical officer should order his removal to a government hospital.[984] Finally, article 57 of the Prison Act expressly provides for treating a prisoner with an unsound mind at the government expenses. In one of its decisions, the High Court ordered the transfer of an accused charged with murder to a mental health hospital.[985] One can interpret these provisions as protecting every prisoner's access to medicines at the public expense.

However, prison conditions in the URT are harsh and life-threatening. Due to limited treatment offered by prison dispensaries, friends and family members of prisoners provide medications or the funds to purchase them.[986]

c. *Justiciability of access to medicines*

The present section discusses the possibility to enforce access to medicines protected under the domestic laws of the URT and its ratified treaties before the Commission for Human Rights and Good Governance (CHRGG) and the High Court. It considers that judicial and non-judicial remedies can promote access to medicines.[987]

aa) Enforcement of access to medicines before the CHRGG

Article 131 of the URT Constitution establishes a CHRGG. Its functions include promoting the protection and preservation of human rights under the Constitution, ratified human rights treaties, and the laws of the land, receiving allegations and complaints in the violation of human rights, and instituting proceedings in court to redress the rights so violated.[988] From this scope of jurisdiction, one can legitimately argue that the CHRGG is competent to consider a violation of access to medicines as argued in the URT Constitution, its ratified human rights treaties and domestic laws as discussed earlier.

It is worth emphasizing that the CHRGG exercises its competence over any decision, recommendation, act, or omission susceptible to a breach of any of the fundamental rights and freedoms argued under the above legal instruments.[989]

983 Ibid. art 20.

984 Ibid. arts 53 and 57.

985 Republic Prosecutor Vs. Siza Pembe Maneno, Case N°. 61, 2001.

986 United States Department of State, Country Reports on Human Rights Practices for 2017: Tanzania, 4.

987 General Comment 14, para 59, ICCPR, art 2 (3)(b).

988 Commission for Human Rights and Good Governance Act, 2001, art 6.

989 Ibid. art 28.

Reference to "omission," especially, may include the government's failure to take appropriate measures to give effect to access to medicines.

The CHRGG acts either motu proprio or upon receipt of complaints submitted by individuals or groups of persons.[990] In case of a violation of rights or freedoms, the CHRGG has two possibilities. First, it can resolve complaints through negotiation, mediation and conciliation.[991] This competence is akin to that of treaty bodies, such as the African Court, the African Commission, and the CESCR, which also settle violations of human rights through an amicable arrangement.[992] The fulfilment of these CHRGG's functions can constitute an alternative to judicial remedies. Secondly, the CHRGG can report its decision and recommendation to the appropriate authority concerned, which in turn informs it within three months of any action taken to redress the impugned fundamental rights. Though not dealing with the right to health, in the Nyamum case,[993] the CHRGG found the District Commissioner and the District Police Chief at fault and recommended payment of compensation to the villagers. However, the government refused to heed the CHRGG's decision.[994] In such circumstances, the CHRGG can bring an action before any court to enforce its recommendations.[995] The CHRGG's findings are a mere recommendation.[996]

However, the CHRGG has never received cases on the violation of access to medicines.

bb) Enforcement of access to medicines before the High Court

Article 30 (3) of the URT Constitution provides that a citizen has a right to seek a judicial remedy for violation of one's rights. It reads as follows,

> Any person alleging that any provision in this Part of this Chapter or any law concerning his right or duty owed to him has been, is being or is likely to be violated by any person anywhere in the United Republic, may institute proceedings for redress in the High Court.

---

990 Ibid. arts 15 and 22.

991 Ibid. art 28 (4).

992 Optional Protocol to ICESCR, art 7, and African Court Protocol, art 9.

993 In Nyamuma, the whole village was uprooted from its land, homesteads burnt, and lives lost to execute state policies that did not recognize the human rights of Nyamuma villagers. See Edmund Mvungi, Sixty years of the Universal Declaration of Human Rights and twenty years of the Bill of Rights in Tanzania, in *Justice and dignity for all. Current issues of human rights in Tanzania*, eds. Kennedy Gaston et al. (Dar es Salaam: Dar es Salaam University Press, 2010), 70.

994 Ibid. See also Peter, "Justice and dignity," 58.

995 Commission for Human Rights and Good Governance Act, art 28 (3).

996 Ibid. art 17 (1).

The words "any provision in this part of this chapter" refers to part III of the URT Constitution, which deals with basic rights and duties. Strictly read, it deals exclusively with basic constitutional rights. In contrast, the phrase "any provision in any law concerning his right or duty" should mean to include all human rights, whether basic rights or not, protected in other laws than the URT Constitution. The Constitution itself does not use the word "basic rights" protected in any law.

Article 30 (3) under discussion vests the High Court with a full[997] exclusive human rights jurisdiction over all constitutional basic rights, and all rights protected under any law. However, the implementation law on the exercise of the High Court's human rights jurisdiction organizes only its competence over constitutional basic rights, including the rights to work and property.[998] It leaves aside the exercise of the High Court's jurisdiction over human rights protected in other laws.

In case of any law or government's action that abridges one of the basic rights, the High Court has two options. The first consists of declaring such law or government's action void, invalid, or unconstitutional.[999] The second option is to allow the authority concerned to correct any effect in the impugned law or action within a specified period.[1000] However, the second option gives rise to the following issues. The offending law or act remains in force pending the corrective action of the concerned authority.[1001] It continues to cause damage to people involved in the litigation. Moreover, it is not clear whether the High Court still provides a remedy for the victims in such cases. Finally, by ordering other institutions to correct the impugned law or action within a specific period instead of declaring it merely unconstitutional and void, the Court interferes with the principle of separation of powers.[1002]

More specifically, the High Court makes all necessary and appropriate orders to secure the applicant the enjoyment of his/her basic rights.[1003] These orders may include different forms of human rights reparation, such as restitution, compensation, satisfaction or guarantees of non-repetition.[1004]

Further legal avenues for judicial enforcement of access to medicines under the domestic laws of the URT include, among others, implemented human rights

997 Wambali, "Enforcement of basic rights," 37.

998 Basic Rights and Duties Enforcement Act, art 3.

999 Ibid. art 13 (2), and URT Constitution, 30 (5).

1000 Ibid.

1001 Chris Maina Peter, *Human rights in Tanzania: selected cases and materials* (Köln: Rüdiger Köppe Verlag, 1997), 765.

1002 The principle does not envisage one power ordering the other. Ibid.

1003 Basic Rights and Duties Enforcement Act, art 13 (1).

1004 African Commission General Comment N° 4, para 35.

treaties legislation and the indirect protection of access to medicines through the rights to dignity and life.

(1) Enforcement of access to medicines through implemented human rights treaties legislation

As mentioned above, ratified treaties by the URT become incorporated into law by either amending or repealing existing legislation or enacting new legislation altogether.[1005] Only after their domestication, the courts can enforce human rights herein protected. However, the URT government seems to have free hands and discretion concerning its ratified treaties' domestication. For instance, the URT does not provide accurate information about the domestication of the SADC Treaty, its protocols, and the ICESCR. Instead, it claims to have incorporated and domesticated some African Charter principles in some selected legislations.[1006] This selective and partial way of incorporating the provisions of the African Charter reinforces the government's discretion in that regard. Express recommendations made to the government of URT to domesticate both the African Charter[1007] and the ICESCR[1008] prove sufficiently that it has not yet domesticated these treaty provisions, including those relating to the right to health. As a dualist State, signing and ratifying human rights treaties without domesticating them is not sufficient.[1009]

The absence of domestication of ratified treaties prevents individuals from seeking redress before the courts. However, it does not allow the URT to clean itself of its treaty´s obligations. Indeed, on acceding and ratifying human rights treaties, the URT took a solemn declaration to respect and ensure that all individuals within its jurisdiction enjoy human rights herein protected.[1010] As an illustration, the URT's reports to the African Commission and the CESCR inform about the measures the country has taken to implement the right to health, including access to medicines.[1011] Moreover, although they do not deal with access to medicines, several cases submitted against the URT to the African Court relate to the violation of human rights protected in ratified human rights treaties.[1012]

1005 URT's 2006 Report to the African Commission.

1006 These include Penal Code CAP. 16 R.E. 2002, Criminal Procedure Act CAP. 20 of R.E. 2002, Evidence Act CAP. of 6 R.E. 2002, and the Sexual Offences (Special Provisions) Act 2002. Ibid.

1007 African Commission, concluding observation to URT, 2006, para 32.

1008 CESCR's concluding observations to URT, 2012.

1009 Peter, "Justice and dignity," 12.

1010 URT's Report to the African Commission, 2006.

1011 URT's 2009 Report to the CESCR, 2009, para 112. See also URT's Report to the African Commission, 2006.

1012 African Court's Activity Report 2018, 6-7.

(2) Enforcement of access to medicines through the right to human dignity

The URT Constitution recognizes human dignity as the cornerstone of all human rights. Accordingly, article 9 of the URT Constitution emphasizes twice human dignity that the State shall respect, cherish, preserve, and uphold following the spirit of the UDHR. Furthermore, the URT Constitution protects human dignity as a basic right. According to article 12 (2) of the URT Constitution, every person has the right to recognition and respect for his dignity. However, these constitutional provisions do not define human dignity, nor do they determine its content. Once read in conjunction with the UDHR, the Constitution refers to, human dignity constitutes the foundation of freedom, justice, and peace globally,[1013] including in the URT. Besides, the right to dignity is inherent to all human beings upon birth, the full enjoyment of which includes realizing the right to social security and all ESCRs, including the right to health.[1014]

In sum, as part of the basic right to human dignity, which is justiciable, the High Court can enforce access to medicines.

(3) Enforcement of access to medicines through the right to life

It is worth emphasizing that the right to life and right to access medicines are two distinct and autonomous human rights. However, some health-related rights form part of other fundamental rights such as the right to life.[1015]

Article 14 of the URT Constitution protects every person's right to live and to the protection of his life as a basic right. One way to give effect to this right is to increase life expectancy through efforts that aim to reduce infant and maternal mortality and eliminate epidemics by establishing functioning health systems.[1016] The URT government itself subscribes to this approach. In its efforts to protect people's life under article 6 of the ICCPR, the URT has taken various actions to reduce child and maternal mortality and fight HIV/AIDS, malaria, pneumonia, and acute diarrhoea.[1017] Access to medicines is one of the State's main used means to combat these diseases and reduce child and maternal mortality. Moreover, these State's actions underline the close relationship between the right to health and the

1013 Preamble to the UDHR.

1014 Ibid. arts 1 and 22.

1015 Collen Flood and Aeyal Gross, "Introduction: marrying human rights and health care systems: contexts for a power to improve access and equity," in *The right to health at the public/private divide. A global comparative study*, eds. Collen M. Flood and Aeyal Gross (Cambridge: Cambridge University Presse, 2014), 9.

1016 African Commission General Comment 3, paras 6 and 42. See also Human Rights Committee, General Comment N°6: article 6 (right to life), 1982, para 5.

1017 United Republic of Tanzania, fourth periodic report to the Human Rights Committee, 2007, paras 53-54.

right to life.[1018] As Baumstark points out,[1019] the right to life can only comprise a basic and immediate life-saving content of a right to health without covering more elaborate of such a right like establishing a health care system.

In one of its decisions on environmental rights,[1020] the High Court ruled that

> it is not given to any Court to grant a prayer seeking for permission to pollute the environment and endanger people's lives regardless of their number and that, it is therefore a contradiction in terms and a denial of this basic right to life deliberately to expose anybody's life to danger or, what is eminently monstrous, to enlist the assistance of the Court in this infringement.[1021]

Due to the absence of a specific provision on environmental rights under the URT Constitution, the Court's interpretation of the right to life to include the right to a safe and clean environment is a manifestation of judicial activism.[1022] Indeed, a liberal interpretation of the basic right to life can also enforce the right to health before the High Court in URT.[1023]

However, on the ground, cases seeking redress for violation of access to medicines before the High Court through the right to life or human dignity are lacking. Factors that justify this lack of complaints include, among others, the challenge for people to access the formal justice system owing to the attendant expenses,[1024] lack of complaints from the CHRGG, NGOs, or other entitled entities.

(4) Some remarks on the partial organization of the human rights jurisdiction of the High Court

Article 30 (3) of the URT Constitution recognizes the High Court's exclusive competence for a redress of violation of basic rights provided by the Constitution, and other rights argued in any law. There is the requirement for enactment of

---

1018 Peter, "Justice and dignity," 33.

1019 Baumstark, *Human right to health*, 24.

1020 The request was submitted by the city council of Dar-es-Salaam, which sought the court´s permission to dump collected garbage in a small city located on the outskirts of Dar-es-Salaam. In support of its request, the Council argued that, it was a lesser evil to pollute and endanger the lives of people in a specific area of the City of Dar-es-Salaam than to do so in the whole City. Festo Balegele and 784 Others vs. Dar es Salaam City Council (Civil Case No. 299 of 1988).

1021 Ibid.

1022 Hamudi Majamba, "Environmental rights jurisprudence in Tanzania: Review of judicial precedents," *Lesotho Law Journal*, (2005): 16.

1023 Wambali, "Enforcement of basic rights," 45-46, Temba, "Right to health in Tanzania," 36.

1024 URT's fourth periodic report to the Human Rights Committee, para 28.

legislation to ensure the effective exercise of the High Court's powers regarding the enforcement of rights.[1025] In compliance with this constitutional requirement, Tanzanian parliament adopted the Basic Rights and Duties Enforcement Act. However, the Basic Rights and Duties Enforcement Act does not consider the High Court's jurisdiction over protected rights in other laws. From the title to its substantive provisions, the Basic Rights and Duties Enforcement Act only applies to basic rights and duties set out in part III of chapter one of the URT Constitution, which covers articles 12 to 29.[1026] Unless protected rights in any law the Constitution refers to are simultaneously constitutional basic rights, the High Court cannot enforce them following the procedure and relevant provisions of the Basic Rights and Duties Enforcement Act.

C. Partial conclusion

The present chapter has discussed the domestic protection and implementation of access to modern medicines focusing on its constitutional protection, the relationship between constitutional and treaty right to health, and its statutory application. Regarding the constitutional protection of access to medicines, the Constitution in the DRC and URT deals with it as a derivative right. Accordingly, the right to access medicines forms part of the right to health in the DRC Constitution, whereas the URT Constitution protects it through social welfare and other human rights. Furthermore, unlike under the DRC Constitution, where access to medicine is theoretically enforceable before the courts and tribunals, under the URT Constitution, it is not.

Regarding the relationship between constitutional and treaty rights to health, the DRC and URT Constitutions consecrate the formal superiority of the Constitution over other sources of law, including ratified treaties. Consequently, the constitutional health-related rights enjoy a higher legal status than the treaty's right to health. However, the State's obligations towards access to medicines under the Constitution and ratified human rights treaties, especially the ICESCR, conflict with each other. While DRC and URT have the constitutional obligation to immediately implement access to medicines within their national resources, the ICESCR subjects them to the principle of progressive realization, including available resources from international cooperation and assistance.

To give effect to access to medicines argued under the Constitution and ratified treaties, the DRC and URT resort to their regulatory and provider functions. As part of the regulatory role, both DRC and URT regulate pharmacists and other medical professionals, quality control of medicine, and sanctions in non-compliance with the relevant laws. They also control the provision of drugs by non-state actors.

1025 URT Constitution, art 30 (4).

1026 Basic Rights and Duties Enforcement Act, arts 1 (2), 3, 9 (1), 13 (2)(3).

The fulfilment of the regulatory power is consistent with the State's obligation to protect the right to health. However, the political will seems to differentiate the country's commitment. For example, unlike the URT, pharmaceutical legislation in the DRC contains some conflicting, outdated, and repealed provisions.

Both the DRC and URT have national health systems headed by the national ministry in charge of health matters regarding their provider function. In addition to funding the national health system, they provide health care services, including access to medicines within public health facilities. However, it is worth recalling that none of these two countries has compulsory universal health system coverage, but instead, they provide some alternative systems. For instance, except under the Social Security Law, the DRC government covers access to medicines for a significant part of the population through social benefits. Through an insurance scheme, the URT deals with access to medicines for some people and their dependents. Furthermore, the country studies make provisions for the protection of some vulnerable groups of the society. For instance, prisoners have access to medicines at public expense in the DRC and URT. Moreover, unlike in the DRC, where all people affected by HIV enjoy free access to medicines, only the most vulnerable children affected by HIV, including orphans, can access basic health care free of charge in the URT. Besides, some categories of children in the DRC and URT can access medicines with the government's support. Finally, unlike in the URT, mothers can access free health care in the DRC during or after deliveries.

Regarding the enforceability of access to medicines, the DRC and URT empower their national human rights commissions to deal with human rights violations for all categories of rights, including ESCRs, as argued in human rights treaties and domestic laws. However, unlike the NCHR, which dealt with some violations of the right to health, the CHRGG did not. It is worth recalling that, unlike the URT Constitution, which does not make the constitutional right to health enforceable, in the DRC, courts and tribunals have jurisdiction over violations of the right to health. However, there are no courts's decisions dealing with the violation of access to medicines on the ground.

IV. Access to traditional medicine (TM)

The present chapter examines TM protection, which is quite different from conventional/modern medicine in many cases.[1027] It discusses and examines the protection of TM under the international human rights law and its implementation at the domestic laws of the DRC and URT.

A. TM under the international human rights law

The present section deals with the protection of TM within the rights to health, natural resources, and cultural life at the global, African, and SADC levels.

1. TM at the global level

The subsection provides a brief development towards recognizing TM as part of the right to health at the global level, defines the concept of TM, and underlines the link between TM and the rights to natural resources and cultural life. Then it will discuss in detail the protection of TM under the ICESCR.

a. *Brief development towards the recognition of TM at the global level*

TM is nothing new since it is present in all human cultures.[1028] The use of TM is anterior to the codifying the right to health at the international, regional, and domestic levels. It is worth recalling that, like conventional medicines, recognizing TM as a human right at the global level is inherent to that of the right to health.

The WHO Constitution's preamble remains the first international instrument to recognize the fundamental right of all people to enjoy the highest attainable standard of health without distinction. It does not expressly mention TM. However, subsequent adopted works and instruments within the WHO's framework are the first to recognize the relevance of TM in the enjoyment of the right to health, as argued in the WHO Constitution. For instance, already in 1977, the WHO recommended the application of TM to primary health care.[1029] Applying this WHO's recommendation, the Alma-Ata Declaration expressly recognizes that primary health

---

1027 WHO General Guidelines for Methodologies on Research and Evaluation of Traditional Medicine, 2000 (henceforth WHO Guidelines 2000).

1028 World Health Organization, The Promotion and Development of Traditional Medicine. Technical Report Series 622, 1978 (henceforth WHO Report on Traditional Medicine), 9.

1029 Ibid. 38.

care relies on health workers, including traditional practitioners.[1030] The WHO adopted subsequent declarations, urging governments to protect people's health through appropriate, safe, and effective TM.[1031] Further declarations reaffirm the governments' commitment to the Alma- Ata Declaration's values and principles, including applying traditional knowledge to strengthen primary health care.[1032] It is worth observing that although the WHO acknowledges that all medicine is modern,[1033] but regrettably[1034] treats traditional practitioners involved in the provision of mental health services as informal health caregivers.[1035]

As the first human rights treaty, the ICERD protects the right to public health and medical care[1036] without explicit reference to TM. Interestingly, the Committee on ICERD has interpreted the right to medical care herein protected to cover TM.[1037] For its part, article 12 of the ICESCR protects everyone's right to enjoy the highest attainable standard of physical and mental health, including medical service and attention. Like its predecessors, the ICESCR does not mention TM. Interestingly, in interpreting the right to health under article 12 at hand, the CESCR refers to the Alma-Ata Declaration, in addition to expressly recognizing TM as an essential component of the right to health.[1038] Similarly, women's right to health care services under article 12 of the CEDAW[1039] and children's right to enjoy the highest

1030 Alma-Ata Declaration, para VII (7).

1031 Beijing Declaration adopted by the WHO Congress on Traditional Medicine, Beijing, China, 2008, para II.

1032 World Health Organization. Declaration of Astana: Global Conference on Primary Health Care, Astana, Kazakhstan, 2018.

1033 All medicine is modern in so far as it is satisfactorily directed towards the common goal of providing health care. WHO Report on Traditional Medicine, 9.

1034 Despite the vast anthropological literature supporting the importance of traditional health systems for the well-being of local communities, the recognition of traditional medicines and healers is highly marginalized within the GMH agenda. Bouso and Sánchez-avilés, "Traditional Healing Practices," 1465.

1035 Greater collaboration with "informal" mental health care providers, including traditional healers, is also needed. See World Health Organization, Mental health action plan 2013–2020 (2013), para 51.

1036 ICERD, art 5 (e) (iv).

1037 Evidence that TM falls within the ambit of the ICERD is the 2005 Conclusions and Recommendations of the CERD to Venezuela, where the Committee expressly acknowledged the right of indigenous persons to TM in the Venezuelan Constitution. See Doolan and Carne, "Evolution and Complementarity? Traditional and complementary medicine," 78. See also Conclusions and Recommendations of the Committee on the Elimination of Racial Discrimination: Venezuela, 67th sess, UN Doc CERD/C/VEN/CO/18, 2005.

1038 General Comment 14, paras 34 and 43.

1039 CEDAW, art 12.

attainable standard of health,[1040] do not explicitly cover TM. However, Burkina Faso, for instance, explicitly uses TM to implement women's right to health under the CEDAW.[1041] For its part, like the Alma-Ata Declaration, Zimbabwe acknowledges the role of traditional birth attendants in the deliveries of mothers, including reducing perinatal mortality and morbidity and preventing infections during antenatal care.[1042] These illustrations provide evidence that nothing prevents one from reading the rights to medical care and health services under the UDHR,[1043] the International Convention on the Protection of the Rights of all Migrant Workers and Members of their Families[1044] and the Convention on the Rights of Persons with disabilities[1045] to include TM. Like other human rights treaties, these human rights instruments do not expressly prescribe nor prohibit TM.

It is essential to mention further global non-binding instruments, which expressly call for the proper use of TM and its integration into healthcare systems,[1046] and recognize indigenous peoples' right to TM, including the conservation of their vital medicinal plants, animals and minerals.[1047] These instruments supplement each other in that they relate either to traditional practitioners and traditional practices or traditional medicinal products.

b. The concept of TM

Human rights treaties protecting the right to health, such as the ICESC and the African Charter, do not define TM. Similarly, although they expressly use the word TM, the CESCR and the African Commission do not define it.[1048] The same legal gap is patent in the Congolese laws, which expressly provide for TM, such

1040 CRC, art 24.

1041 Committee on the Elimination of Discrimination against Women, Consideration of reports submitted by States parties under article 18 of the Convention on the Elimination of All Forms of Discrimination against Women: Sixth periodic report of States parties, Burkina Faso, CEDAW/C/BFA/6, 2009, para 127.

1042 Committee on the Rights of the Child, Consideration of reports submitted by States parties under article 44 of the Convention: initial reports of States parties due in 1992: Zimbabwe, 1995, para 122 (d).

1043 UDHR, art 25.

1044 International Convention on the Protection of the Rights of all Migrant Workers and Members of their Families, art 28.

1045 Convention on the Rights of Persons with disabilities, art 25.

1046 Report of the Special Rapporteur on the right of everyone to the enjoyment of the highest attainable standard of physical and mental health, 2006, para 50.

1047 United Nations Declaration on the Rights of Indigenous Peoples, GA Res 61/295, UN Doc A/RES/61/295 (2 October 2007, adopted 13 September 2007), art 24 (1).

1048 General Comment 14, and African Commission's Resolution 141.

as the Public Health Law.[1049] For its part, the Traditional Medicine Act in the URT describes TM as

> a total combination of knowledge and practice, whether applicable or not, used in diagnosing, preventing or eliminating a physical, mental or social disease and which may rely exclusively on past experience and observation handled down from one generation to another orally or in writing.[1050]

This definition reflects the WHO's definition of TM as

> the sum total of the knowledge, skills, and practices based on theories, beliefs and experiences indigenous to different cultures, whether explicable or not, which has been used for centuries to maintain health, prevent, diagnose, improve or treat physical and mental illnesses.[1051]

The definition under discussion sees TM as an independent health system, which is different from modern medical science. Furthermore, the definition makes it explicit that TM is used to maintain health, prevent, diagnose, improve and treat illness and diseases. It is essential to notice that the Traditional Medicine Act considers the social dimension of disease, unlike the WHO's definition. However, the description of TM under discussion remains too general[1052] and abstract. For instance, it does not determine the possessors of the knowledge, skills, and practices it refers to, nor does it enumerate their content. To fill in this gap, the WHO's Traditional Medicine Strategy 2014-2023 provides that the concept of TM involves expanding access to TM products, practices, and practitioners.[1053] As regards TM products, existing instruments refer to them simultaneously as TM, traditional preventive care, vital medicinal plants, animals, and minerals.[1054] They mainly consist of traditional medication therapies that involve herbal medicines, animal parts, and minerals[1055] for medicinal purposes.[1056] Regarding traditional

1049 Public Health Law, arts 59-60.
1050 Traditional Medicine Act, art 3.
1051 WHO Guidelines 2000.
1052 Sisai Wang, *Market access of traditional Chinese medicinal product in the EU under WTO legal framework*, (Cham: Springer International Publishing 2020):65.
1053 WHO traditional medicine strategy: 2014-2023 (2013) (henceforth WHO Strategy 2014-2023), p. 25.
1054 General Comment 14, para 27, and Resolution 141.
1055 WHO traditional medicine strategy 2022-2005 (2002) (henceforth WHO Strategy 2002-2005).
1056 Raw traditional medicinal products are used in natural states or after undergoing simple processing, such as cutting, drying or crushing. See Tanzania Food and Drugs Authority, Guidelines for application for registration of traditional medicinal products, 2014 (hereinafter Guidelines for application for registration of traditional medicinal products).

practices, diversity is the rule. They include traditional healing practices[1057] and non-medication TM therapies, such as manual and spiritual therapies.[1058] Other approaches include religious and spiritual methods, prayers, dance formulas, and other ritual acts.[1059]

Although it does not define them, the International Conference on Primary Health Care[1060] expressly recognizes the role of THPs in the delivery of primary health care. The SADC Health Protocol[1061] ratified by the DRC and URT describes THPs as peoples who use the total combination of knowledge and practices, whether explicable or not, to diagnose, prevent, or eliminate physical, mental, or social diseases. It goes further by prescribing that, in their mission, THPs rely exclusively on experience and observation handed down from generation to generation while bearing in mind the original concept of nature, which included the material world, the sociological environment, whether living or dead and the metaphysical forces of the universe.[1062] THPs act as spiritualists, exorcists, herbalists, traditional circumcisers, or midwives, depending on treated diseases and used methods.[1063] Thus, unless otherwise specified, TM in this study shall encompass TM products, practices, and THPs, as the case maybe.

c. The connection between natural resources and TM

Since prehistoric times, peoples have used natural products, such as plants, animals, micro-organisms, and marine organisms, in medicines to alleviate and treat diseases.[1064] The medicaments used in TM mostly derive from these natural resources.[1065] Located within the tropical and subtropical climate, Africa is full of fauna and flora that constitute an inexhaustible source of therapies for various ailments.[1066] It contains about 45,000 species of plants with a potential for development and out of which 5,000 species serve medicinal purposes.[1067] In the URT, people resort to about 1,000 plant species as sources of TM for human ailments.[1068]

1057 General Comment 14, paras 27 and 34. See also Resolution 141.

1058 WHO Strategy 2002-2005.

1059 Traditional Medicine Decree, art 2.

1060 Alma-Ata Declaration, para VII.

1061 SADC Health Protocol, art 1.

1062 Ibid.

1063 Traditional Medicine Decree, art 2.

1064 Haidan Yuan et ali., "The traditional medicine and modern medicine from natural products," *Molecules*, (2016): 1.

1065 Ibid.

1066 Mahomoodally, "Traditional medicine in Africa," 2.

1067 Ibid. 9.

1068 Georges Shemdoe and Loy Mhando, "National policies and legal frameworks governing traditional knowledge and effective intellectual property systems in

For its part, the DRC is one of the hotspots of plant biodiversity globally, with the potential role in developing new medicines, including anticancer agents from its flora.[1069] Medicinal plants in treating people's diseases are borrowed from substances that these plants produce to protect themselves from insect pests and pathogens.[1070] Unlike modern medicines, TM products are collected in the wild,[1071] mostly without State investment.[1072] Moreover, unlike modern medicines, one can use TM products in their natural state without any significant transformation.[1073] For this reason, TM is relatively available, accessible, and affordable compared to conventional medicines.

d. The connection between the right to cultural life and TM

The use of TM in African countries, including DRC and URT, has a very long history. It expresses people's various perceptions of illness and its etiology, including physical, supernatural, psychological, and sociological factors or causes.[1074] TM considers human beings as a somatic and spiritual entity using a holistic nature and culture-based approach.[1075] It uses various treatment methods for any illness,[1076] based on social, cultural and religious background, and the knowledge, attitudes, and beliefs prevalent in the community regarding physical, mental and social well-being and the cause of disease and disability.[1077]

It is significant that TMPs are members of patients'communities and have intimate knowledge of their lives and cultural milieu.[1078] Finally, TM deals with

---

Southern and Eastern Africa: The case of traditional healers in Tanzania," *African Technology Policy Studies Network*, (2012): 15.

1069 Koto-te-Nyiwa Ngbolua et ali., "Medicinal plants from Democratic Republic of the Congo as sources of anticancer drugs," *Journal of Advanced Botany and Zoology*, (2018):1.

1070 Scheinman, "Traditional medicine in Tanga," 1.

1071 Andrew Kaniki and Kutu Mphahlele, "Indigenous knowledge for the benefit of all: can knowledge management principles be used effectively?" *South African Journal of Library & Information Science* 68, *Issue 1*, (2002): 4.

1072 Kabengele et al., "Traditional/alternative medicines," 50. See also WHO Traditional Medicine Strategy 2014-2023.

1073 WHO Traditional Medicine Strategy 2014-2023.

1074 Harald Heggenhougen, "Health services: official and unofficial," in *Tanzania – crisis and struggle for survival*, eds. Jannik Boesen et al. (Sweden: Scandinavian Institute of African Studies, 1986), 312, Antwi-Baffour et al., "Place of traditional medicine," 51.

1075 Antwi-Baffour et al., "Place of traditional medicine," 51.

1076 Heggenhougen, "Health services," 312.

1077 Tanzanian Traditional Medicine Act.

1078 Heggenhougen, "Health services," 312.

some specific diseases present only in the African environment. Illustrations include TM's effectiveness in treating tropical and neglected diseases in which most modern medical personnel do not have expertise.[1079] Since immemorial time, the cultural aspect of TM justifies its use by African people, including Tanzanians and Congolese.

e. Protection of TM under the ICESCR

This section discusses the protection of traditional medicines through the rights to health, natural resources and cultural life under the ICESCR.

aa) TM and the right to health under article 12 of the ICESCR

Article 12 of the ICESCR provides for everyone's right to health but does not explicitly mention TM or conventional medicine.[1080] Instead, it prescribes steps to take for the full realization of the right to health. These include the provision for the reduction of the stillbirth-rate and of infant mortality, prevention, treatment, and control of diseases, and the creation of conditions that assure all medical service and medical attention in the event of sickness. It is worth stressing that article 12 at hand does not enumerate the nature of "steps" that State parties should take to achieve the right to health. The structure and formulation of article 12 in a general, abstract, and flexible way positively impact the protection of TM. It is argued that

> In analysing art 12, and whether its scope arguably includes T&CM, four important points can be made. First, none of the terms contained within art 12 are defined by the instrument. This includes the terms 'medical service and medical attention' only referred to in art 12(2)(d). Without a clear indication as to what medical service and medical attention means, an interpretation inclusive of T&CM service and attention is arguably possible... Third, art 12 neither explicitly mentions nor proscribes T&CM. Fourth, art 12(2)(c) refers to prevention and treatment but does not specify how this is to be achieved. This potentially enables an interpretation inclusive of T&CM prevention and treatment"[1081]

This quote suggests that article 12 under discussion does not prescribe or impose any medicines or establish any hierarchy between existing types of therapies. It leaves open room for State parties to decide on the kind of medicines to use in implementing the right to health. Consequently, one can legitimately argue that all types of existing treatments, including traditional and modern medicines, fall

1079 Chirwa, "Access to medicines," 28.

1080 Kabengele et al., "Traditional/alternative medicines," 49.

1081 Doolan and Carne, "Evolution and Complementarity? Traditional and complementary medicine,"69.

within the ambit of article 12 and enjoy the same legal and theoretical status. One should also acknowledge the impact of the use of TM by all human cultures since immemorial times on the elaboration and structure of article 12 of the ICESCR. The drafters of the Covenant were aware of various health systems worldwide, including TM. Therefore, they could not have included all existing medicines into a Covenant that different States with multiple health systems had to ratify at the international level.

The flexibility of the Covenant is also reflected in article 2 (1), which urges State parties to use all appropriate means and available resources within their jurisdictions to implement the right to health.[1082] In taking a broad and flexible approach that enables each State party's particularities and relevant considerations,[1083] the Covenant provision at hand does not exclude the use of TM as available resources. The practice of State parties and the CESCR to article 12 reinforces this assertion.

(1) State's reports and the protection of TM

The State parties to the ICESCR are under the treaty obligation to submit reports on the measures taken and progress made in achieving the observance of the right to health.[1084] Like conventional medicine, the implementation of TM is subject to the progressive realization clause within the country's available resources, including international assistance and cooperation.[1085] A close look at some State reports on article 12 of the ICESCR reveals that they contain information about various aspects of TM. For instance, unlike the DRC and the URT, which do not mention any elements of TM at all,[1086] China's report refers to the State Administration of Traditional Chinese Medicine as one of the entitled departments, the opinions of which are relevant in the establishment of a national basic medicines system.[1087] Furthermore, while India's report refers to the 2002 National Health Policy, which aims to mainstream the Indian systems of medicine and homeopathy to extend the public health services as a complementary system to modern medicine,[1088] Uganda recognizes traditional healers as one of the health personals categories.[1089] For their part, while the Republic of South Africa mentions the Traditional Medicine

1082 ICESCR, art 2 (1).

1083 CESCR General Comment No. 9: The domestic application of the Covenant, 1998 (henceforth General Comment 9), paras 1-2.

1084 ICESCR, art 16 (1).

1085 Ibid. art 2 (1).

1086 URT's Report to the CESCR, 2009, and DRC's Report to the CESCR, 2007.

1087 People's Republic of China, Second periodic report to the CESCR, 2010, point 10.

1088 India, Combined second to fifth periodic reports to the CESCR, 2006, para 484.

1089 The Republic of Uganda, Initial reports submitted by State parties under articles 16 and 17 of the Covenant, 2012, para 141.

Act as one of the central policies and legislations on health care,[1090] Zambia and Namibia report on TM's relevance concerning birth attendants[1091] and mental health.[1092]

The most relatively revolutionary information in this issue is that of the Republic of Zimbabwe submitted in 1995,[1093] of which more than two paragraphs refer to TM. Accordingly, TM remains acceptable to a large section of the population, and the government recognizes TM through the establishment of the Zimbabwe National Traditional Healers Association. The training of midwives (both traditional and conventional) and the upgrading of all traditional midwives with provision for the child's healthy development constitutes some of the government's adopted measures to reduce the stillbirth rate and infant mortality.[1094] More specifically, while the government upgraded traditional midwives' skills with emphasis on hygiene and referral of women at risk to clinics and hospitals, it taught traditional healers about the dangers of spreading diseases like AIDS through the use of unsterilized razor blades.[1095]

All in all, these reports on the implementation of article 12 of the ICESCR constitute evidence on TM as an essential component of the human right to health. They cover various aspects of TM and reflect its place and role within their national health systems. These include, among others, the establishment of traditional national bodies and the relevance of their views in implementing the national health policy, the contribution of TMPs, the collaboration between modern health professionals and THPs, adoption of laws on TM, and training of THPs.

(2) The CESCR's practices and the protection of TM

The CESCR can deal with article 12 of the ICESCR in various ways, including through concluding observations, views and recommendations from communication procedure, and general comments. However, unlike some State's reports on various aspects of TM, the corresponding CESCR's concluding observations do not expressly address TM's question. Furthermore, the CESCR has never issued views or recommendations that deal with TM. Interestingly, the CESCR has partly filled in this gap in the General Comment 14.[1096] In interpreting the abstract right

1090 The Republic of South Africa, Initial reports submitted by State parties under articles 16 and 17 of the Covenant, 2017, para 116.

1091 The Republic of Zambia, Initial reports submitted by State parties under articles 16 and 17 of the Covenant, 2003, para 214.

1092 Namibia, Initial reports submitted by State parties under articles 16 and 17 of the Covenant, 2012, para 337.

1093 The Republic of Zimbabwe, Initial reports submitted by State parties under articles 16 and 17 of the Covenant, 1995.

1094 Republic of Zimbabwe's Report, 1995, para 180.

1095 Ibid. paras 147-148.

1096 General Comment 14, para 27.

to health under article 12 of the ICESCR, General Comment 14 gives it concrete content. Considering the Covenant's flexibility on the formulation of the right to health, General Comment 14 broadly interprets its content and the nature of the State's obligations to encompass TM. To begin with, the CESCR states that all health goods and services must be respectful of the culture of individuals, minorities, peoples, and communities.[1097] One of the striking features of TM is its cultural acceptability.[1098] Besides, General Comment 14 identifies indigenous peoples' right to traditional preventive care, healing practices, and medicines as part of article 12 of the Covenant.[1099] It therefore, calls for the protection of vital medicinal plants, animals, and minerals necessary to the full enjoyment of the said right.[1100] However, the CESCR's interpretation regarding TM gives rise to two main criticisms. The first criticism is that in only referring to indigenous people, the CESCR takes a reductionist view, which does not consider TM's use by everybody.[1101] The counter-argument is that the CESCR has dealt with indigenous people as one of the special topics of broad application.[1102] Furthermore, CESCR has interpreted the State's obligation to respect the right to health to include refraining from prohibiting or impeding traditional preventive care, healing practices, and medicines.[1103] This obligation is of general application. The Special Rapporteur on the right of everyone to the enjoyment of the highest attainable standard of physical and mental health also confirms the assertion that national measures should support the proper use of TM for all.[1104]

The second criticism is that the CESCR's recognition of TM can be in tension with paragraph 51 of General Comment 14, which erects the State's failure to discourage the continued observance of harmful traditional medical or cultural practices into the violation of the obligation to protect the right to health.[1105] Against this criticism, one can argue that paragraph 51 only prohibits "harmful traditional medical practices" that hinder the efficacy and safety of TM, such as practices that interfere with access to pre-and post-natal care and family planning.[1106] Within this context,

---

1097 Ibid. para 12 (c).

1098 WHO Regional Committee for Africa, Promoting the role of traditional medicine in health systems: a strategy for the African Region, 2000, (henceforth African WHO Strategy), para 9.

1099 General Comment 14, para 27.

1100 Ibid.

1101 *Kabengele* et ali., note 20, p. 49.

1102 General Comment 14, paras 24-27.

1103 Ibid. para 34.

1104 Report of the Special Rapporteur on the right of everyone to the enjoyment of the highest attainable standard of physical and mental health, 2006, para 50.

1105 Maria Stuttaford et al., "The right to traditional, complementary, and alternative health care," *Glob Health Action*, (2014): 3.

1106 General Comment 14, paras 22 and 35.

the CEDAW Committee calls for respect of women's, including rural and indigenous women's access to high-quality sexual and reproductive health services, covering family planning, the prevention of early pregnancies.[1107] It is therefore, the State's obligation to promote good and positive TM practices through the abolishment of harmful practices and the dissemination of appropriate information in that regard.[1108] Thus, compliance with positive or good traditional medical practices cannot violate the right to health.

Overall, General Comment 14 has a positive impact on the protection and recognition of TM as part of the right to health. Like in article 12 of the ICESCR, the use of TM within and by State parties has significantly influenced the CESCR's interpretation of the right to health. However, General Comment failed short in not recognizing explicitly other types of medicines, such as complementary medicine or alternative medicine. The WHO describes "complementary medicine" or "alternative medicine" as a broad set of health care practices that are not part of that country's tradition or conventional medicine and are not fully integrated into the dominant healthcare system.[1109] As mentioned above, the content of the right to health protected in various human rights treaties, especially under article 12 of the ICESCR, is broad enough to include these types of medicines. From these, one can infer that the scope of the right to health necessarily consists of a right to traditional and complementary medicines.[1110]

bb) TM and the right to natural resources

According to article 1 (2) of the ICESCR, all peoples have the right to dispose of their natural wealth and resources freely. It further prescribes that one cannot deprive peoples of their means of subsistence. Without explaining further, the treaty provision under discussion identifies natural wealth and resources as people's means of subsistence. One can legitimately argue that medicinal plants, animals, and minerals that serve as TM constitute an essential part of natural wealth and resources. Therefore, their use for medical purposes meets the criteria of people's means of subsistence.

In its report on the implementation of article 1 (2) under examination, the DRC mentions, among others, the constitutional protection of the right to enjoy national resources and adopted measures, such as the law governing general property, land ownership, and real estate, the Mining Code, the Forestry Code, and

---

1107 CEDAW Committee, Concluding observations on the eighth periodic report of the Democratic Republic of the Congo, 2019, para 37 (e).

1108 Ibid. paras 22 and 37.

1109 WHO Strategy 2014-2023, p. 15.

1110 Angela Doolan and Greg Carne, "Evolution and complementarity? Traditional and complementary medicine as part of the international Human Rights Law Right to Health", *Bond Law Review, 32,* no. 1, (2020): 82.

other regulations.[1111] The report does not explicitly refer to TM. However, some provisions of these laws, as will be seen later, entitle people to use natural resources for medicinal purposes. For its part, the URT's report states that, in the pursuit of economic rights, the government grants Tanzanian people ownership of land, which is the essential means of subsistence under the Land Act.[1112] Land use as a necessary means of subsistence can include its utility in the gathering of TM products.

Regarding the CESCR, it emphasizes the link between natural resources and TM through its General Comment 14 and concluding observations. According to General Comment 14, the protection of vital medicinal plants, animals, and minerals is necessary to indigenous peoples' health.[1113] Therefore, the forced displacement of indigenous peoples from their traditional territories has negative impacts on their health.[1114] Moreover, in its concluding observations to the DRC, the CESCR observed that abusive exploitation of the country's forests undermines indigenous peoples rights to manage their forests according to their traditional practice and amounts to the violation of article 1 (2) of the ICESCR.[1115] Although the CESCR talks only about indigenous populations, article 1 (2) protects everyone's right to natural resources. Therefore, one can argue that the protection of medicinal plants, animals and minerals is necessary for everyone's right to health.

cc) The right to cultural life and TM

TM forms part of the cultural component of the right to health.[1116] The ICESCR recognizes and protects the right to cultural life. According to article 15 (1) (a) of the ICESCR, everyone has the right to take part in cultural life. The treaty provision under discussion does not expressly mention TM. However, the word "cultural life" can cover TM's practice by individuals and communities. The CESCR also broadly interprets the right to cultural life to involve TM. Its General Comments and concluding observations address the relationship between the right to cultural life and TM. According to General Comment 21, the right to cultural life is an explicit reference to culture, which encompasses the total way of life of a particular group, including customs and traditions through which individuals and communities produce items for survival.[1117] The General Comment 21 does not explicitly use the

1111 DRC's Report to the CESCR, 2007, paras 40-42.
1112 URT's Report to the CESCR, 2009, para 28.
1113 General Comment 14, para 27.
1114 Ibid.
1115 CESCR's concluding observation to RDC, 2009, para 13-14.
1116 General Comment 14, para 12 (c).
1117 Committee on Economic, Social and Cultural Rights, General Comment N°21: Right of everyone to take part in cultural life (art 15 (1) of the ICESCR, 2009 (hereinafter General Comment 21), para 13. See also Okiegs case, para 179.

word TM. Nevertheless, it refers to "total way of life" and "customs and traditions through which individuals produce items for survival," which can include the production of TM necessary for their lives and survival. It is the CESCR's view that forced eviction of pygmies, pastoralists, and hunter-gatherer communities from their traditional lands[1118] constitutes a significant obstacle to the enjoyment of their right to the manifestations of their cultures, including genetic resources, medicines, and knowledge of the properties of fauna and flora.[1119] Altogether, the cultural acceptability of medicine constitutes its principal determinants. TM meets this criterium, given that people perceive it as part of their daily life or cultural life.

2. TM under the African human rights law

The present section begins with a brief history of TM in Africa, which underwent a negative colonial impact. It will then focus on protecting TM under the African Charter.

a. A Brief history of the use of TM in Africa

This subsection comprises three points relating to TM in pre-colonial, colonial, and post-colonial Africa.

aa) TM in pre-colonial African societies

African people's attempts to protect themselves against disease and illness through TM are as old as humankind. Indeed, all the people in the world have used TM to various degrees.[1120] In African societies, TM remains the oldest of all therapeutic systems.[1121] Before missionaries' arrival, TM was the only available health system.[1122] During this period of self-reliance in health matters, African TMPs controlled, prevented, alleviated, or cured diseases and pandemics using African

1118 CESCR's concluding observations, DRC, 2009, paras 6, 14 and 36, and CESCR's concluding observations to URT, 2012, para 29.

1119 General Comment 21, para 37.

1120 Kamgoui Kuitche, *Médecine traditionnelle et droit de la santé pour une intégration du droit dans le système traditionnel* (Paris: L'Harmattan, 2017), 24.

1121 Fawzi Mahomoodally, "Traditional medicines in Africa: An appraisal of ten potent African medicinal plants," *Evidence-Based Complementary and Alternative Medicine* (2013): 2.

1122 Sekaya Yahaya, Warren Aryeija, and Unice Bitwari, "Traditional medicine in Uganda: historical perspective, challenges, and advances," *IK Notes*, no. 67, (2004): 2, Ali Abdullahi, "Trends and challenges of traditional medicine in Africa," *African Journal of Traditional, Complementary, and Alternative Medicines 8*(S), (2011): 120.

means and healing methods, including medicinal plants, animals, and minerals.[1123] African TMPs, including herbalists, diviners, mediums, surgeons, midwives, or psychiatrists, have a varied knowledge of diseases, their cause, treatment, and prevention. They acquire medical knowledge through others' teaching, which passes orally from father to son through generations.[1124] TMPs also use methods that have been tried and tested over many generations, making it possible to discard ineffective methods and maintain and preserve those that proved effective for current and future generations.[1125] Thus, one cannot perform as TMP without education or training. TMPs simultaneously appear as botanists, pharmacists, doctors, psychologists, or sociologists when approaching medicines and diseases.[1126] In sum, during this period, African peoples did not undergo any restriction in TM.

bb) TM in colonial Africa

Two main events marked this period regarding TM. The first event was the encounter between traditional and modern medicines introduced by Christian missionaries[1127] and colonists[1128] to survive in tropical Africa.[1129] The second event dealt with some express limitations that colonists imposed on TM because Africans' conception of disease and illness supposed to be embedded in witchcraft, was contrary to colonial religion and Western medicine ideals.[1130] Consequently, TM acquired an inferior legal status compared to imported conventional medicine. In the DRC, for instance, the 1952 Decree, taken during the colonial period but still in force, does not allow the practice of TM in urban areas. During the same period in the URT, the conventional health care system took dominance over

---

1123 David Scheinman, "Traditional medicine in Tanga today: The ancient and modern worlds meet," *Indigenous Knowledge Notes*, no. 51, (2002): 1-2.

1124 Samuel Antwi-Baffour et al., "The place of traditional medicine in the African society: The science, acceptance, and support," *American Journal of Health Research 2*, no. 2, (2014): 49.

1125 Chirwa, "Access to medicines," 25.

1126 Rashim Ahluwalia et Bernard Méchin, *La médecine traditionnelle au Zaïre: fonctionnement et contribution potentielle aux services de santé* (Ottawa: CRDI, 1979), 18.

1127 Chirwa, "access to medicines,"26.

1128 Bruce Fetter, "Health care in twentieth century Africa: Statistics, theories, and policies," *Africa Today 40*, no. 3, (1993):12.

1129 Conventional medicines were administered unevenly, with Europeans receiving favored access and rural Africans the least. See the Republic of South Africa, combined second periodic report under the African Charter on Human and Peoples' Rights, 2015, para 275.

1130 Abdullahi, "Trends and challenges," 116, and Yahaya, Aryeija and Bitwari, "Traditional medicine in Uganda," 2.

TM.[1131] Thus TM acquired an inferior status as compared to conventional therapy. As Chirwa[1132] rightly points out, in superimposing their home laws on African customary statutes and marginalizing African medicine, colonial governments intended to suppress African beliefs, promote a Western way of life, and introduce African dependence on the West for health care. Though intensely fought, TM was still practiced less explicitly in colonial times[1133]and continues to satisfy people's health needs even in the post-colonial period.

cc) TM in post-colonial Africa

The main characteristic of this period is the relative mismatch between the joint determination of African States to promote TM at the regional level and the weak mobilization of individual States to concretize this regional commitment at the national level. Regarding regional determination, for instance, African governments are committed to promoting TM within the framework of the WHO Regional Office for Africa, the African Union, and the African human rights system.

In 1976, African countries members of the WHO provided the first definition of TM and traditional health healers during their meeting in Brazzaville.[1134] Furthermore, within the framework of the African Union, African governments adopted resolutions, strategies, and declarations dealing with various aspects of TM. For instance, adopted in 1981, the Resolution on traditional medicine and African medicinal plants,[1135] recognizes the availability of potential medicinal plants with tested therapeutic value within African countries. The Resolution also calls for regulations on forest protection and their application to medicinal plants, which excessively benefit foreign pharmaceutical firms or their local agencies to the detriment of African peoples.[1136] In its declaration on the Decade of African Traditional Medicine,[1137] the AU Summit acknowledges that about 85% of the African population satisfies their health delivery services through TM. The Summit, therefore, urges member States and their governments to use TM in achieving the goal

---

1131 ZH., Mbwambo, R. Mahunnah, and Edmund Kayombo, "Traditional health practitioner and the scientist: bridging the gap in contemporary health research in Tanzania," *Tanzania Health Research Bulletin* 9, no. 2, (2007): 115.

1132 Chirwa, "Access to medicines," 27, 28, and 43.

1133 Yahaya, Aryeija and Bitwari, "Traditional medicine in Uganda," 2.

1134 WHO Report on Traditional Medicine, 8-9.

1135 OAU Council of Ministers, Resolution on traditional medicine and African medicinal plants– joint project, 1981.

1136 Ibid.

1137 OAU Assembly of Heads of State and Government, Decision on the declaration of the period 2001-2010 as the OAU decade for African traditional medicine, Zambia, 2001 (henceforth OAU Declaration on TM), para 2.

of health for all.[1138] Furthermore, based on the OAU Declaration on TM, the African Health Strategy 2007-2015[1139] urged African governments to integrate African TM into their health systems.[1140]

It is also important to note that African human rights treaties protecting the right to health, similar to global human rights instruments, are framed to allow a broad interpretation to include TM. According to article 16 of the African Charter, every individual has the right to enjoy the best attainable state of physical and mental health, including medical attention. Like the ICESCR, this Charter's provision does not explicitly mention TM. However, in its interpretation of the right to health, the African Commission explicitly considers TM an integral part of article 16 of the African Charter.[1141] Like the African Charter, subsequent African human rights instruments dealing with the right to health for various persons do not expressly mention TM. Illustrations include children's and youth's right to enjoy the best attainable state of physical, mental, and spiritual health,[1142] women's right to health, including reproductive rights,[1143] and displaced persons' right to medical care and health services.[1144] The structure and formulation of these treaty provisions are broad enough to cover TM. For example, in reporting on children's right to health, the government of Uganda expressly recognizes the critical role of a significant number of traditional birth attendants in assisting births in this country.[1145] It is important to note that TM as part of the right to health under article 16 of the African Charter applies to everybody, including children, youth, women, and displaced persons.

However, individual governments seem slow in implementing their regional commitment to TM into appropriate laws and regulations at the domestic level. As a result, like in the colonial period, TM still enjoys an inferior status compared with conventional medicines. The case studies of DRC and URT in this thesis will show that the governments in these two countries do not make TM accessible and available within public health hospitals. Furthermore, existing laws dealing with health insurance in these two countries do not expressly cover TM.

1138 Ibid. para 3.

1139 African Union Conference of Ministers of health, Africa Health Strategy: 2007-2015, 2007 (hereinafter African Health Strategy), paras 72-73.

1140 Ibid. para 72-73.

1141 African Commission's Resolution 141.

1142 Children Charter, art 14, and African Youth Charter, art 16.

1143 African Women Protocol, art 14.

1144 Convention for the Protection and Assistance of Internally Displaced Persons in Africa, art 9.

1145 Republic of Uganda, Periodic report to the African Committee of Experts on the Rights and Welfare of the Child on the implementation of the African Charter on the Rights and Welfare of the Child, 2020, 28.

b. TM and the right to health under article 16 of the African Charter

Article 16 of the African Charter protects everyone's right to enjoy the best attainable state of physical and mental health. It further obligates State parties to take all necessary measures to protect the health of citizens and ensure that they receive medical attention when they are sick. However, like the ICESCR, the Charter's right to health does not expressly mention TM. Moreover, like the ICESCR's drafters, the founders of the African Charter do not explicitly mention any medicines. The implication of such formulation of the right to health is that it leaves State parties with a margin of discretion in filling in its content, which can cover TM. Similarly, African peoples'use of TM before the codification of the right to health in Africa had influenced the Charter's protection of the right to health. Without undermining the implicit protection of TM under article 16 at hand, it is legitimate to express concerns about the absence of an explicit reference to TM in the African context for two main reasons. First, the preamble to the African Charter expressly claims to eradicate all forms of colonialism from Africa. As discussed earlier, colonialism has negatively affected the perception of TM's use in Africa. One way of doing this would be explicitly recognizing TM under article 16 of the African Charter. Secondly, the African Charter's preamble expressly considers the virtues of African States' historical tradition and African civilization's values, which would inspire and characterize their reflection on the concept of human and peoples' rights. Applied to the human right to health, this would imply that the Charter, unlike the ICESCR, expressly mentions TM as a fundamental part of African people's culture, which has been an integral part of the African health care system since time immemorial.[1146] Nonetheless, as already mentioned, the necessary measures that State parties take to implement the right to health in article 16 under discussion are broad enough to include the protection of TM. Moreover, considering the role of TM in millions of Africans,[1147] State parties to the African Charter report on various aspects of TM as part of the right to health.

aa) State's reports and TM under article 16 of the African Charter

State parties to the African Charter report on the legislative and other measures taken to give effect to the right to health, including TM.[1148] The obligation to implement TM is immediate and does not expressly consider the country's available resources.[1149] Like under the ICESCR, State's practices on TM under article 16 of the African Charter are not uniform. The DRC, for instance, does not mention any single word on TM in its periodic reports.[1150] Interestingly, unlike the DRC, and

---

1146 Mahomoodally, "Traditional medicine in Africa," 9.

1147 Antwi-Baffour et al., "Place of traditional medicine," 50.

1148 African Charter, art 62.

1149 Ibid. art 1.

1150 DRC's 11th to 13rd Reports to the African Commission, 2015.

contrary to its report under the ICESCR, the URT's report to the African Commission[1151] expressly reports on the role of TM and alternative healing systems by the national health policy. More importantly, it mentions the Traditional Medicine Act, which governs the practices and issues of research regarding TM and alternative healing systems. As an Act of parliament, people's representatives publicly examined, discussed, and adopted the relevant provisions of the Traditional Medicine Act.

Along with the URT, the Republic of South Africa[1152] and the Republic of Zimbabwe[1153] also mention adopted legislations on TM among implementation measures to enjoy the right to health. Further information from Zimbabwe includes the establishment of the Zimbabwe National Traditional Healers Association,[1154] the upgrading skill of more than 30 000 traditional midwives,[1155] and interdiction for TMPs to sell their medicines from unhygienic premises.[1156] Another relevant report is from Burkina Faso,[1157] which provides information relating to the recognition, development, efficiency, modernization, and integration of TM into its public healthcare system. Besides 30,000 stakeholders who carry out TM's practice as self-employed persons, the government adopted national policy and texts regulating the profession's practice, and established a framework for collaboration, supervision of THPs, and traditional drug marketing approvals.[1158] Following the OAU Decade on TM, Burkina Faso incorporated TM in the 2001-2010 and 2011-2020 National Health Development Plans.[1159]

1151 URT's Report to the African Commission, 2006, 26.

1152 Other important developments in health care policy and legislation include the Traditional Health Practitioners Act, 2004. Republic of South Africa, combined second periodic report under the African Charter on Human and Peoples' Rights and initial report under the Protocol to the African Charter on the Rights of Women in Africa, 2015, para 286

1153 The Act permits TMPs to practice TM without interference. The Republic of Zimbabwe, 7th, 8th, 9th and 10th combined Report submitted to the African Commission on Human and Peoples' Rights, 2006.

1154 Republic of Zimbabwe, second and third reports in terms of article 62 of the African Charter on Human and Peoples' Rights, 1997, 23.

1155 Ibid.

1156 The Republic of Zimbabwe, 7th to 10th combined Report submitted to the African Commission on Human and Peoples' Rights, 2006.

1157 Periodic Report of Burkina Faso within the framework of the implementation of article 62 of the African Charter on Human and Peoples' Rights, 2015, paras 185-186.

1158 Ibid. para 185.

1159 Ibid. para 186.

In sum, these State reports indicate that TM forms an integral part of the right to health under article 16 of the African Charter. They also reveal that each State party can deal with TM according to its population's health needs. Therefore, State parties can, among others, adopt legislations, policies, or plans on TM, provide training for TMPs, establish national associations for TMPs, and issue permits allowing TMPs to practice. It is worth recalling that the African Commission has endorsed the principle of progressive realization of all the Charter's ESCRs within the country's available resources, and international aid.[1160]

bb) The practice of the African Court and the African Commission towards TM under article 16 of the African Charter

The African Court can deal with article 16 of the African Charter using its contentious or advisory jurisdiction.[1161] However, it never issued any judgment or advisory opinion dealing with TM as part of article 16 of the African Charter. Unlike the African Court, the African Commission has already dealt with article 16 of the African Charter regarding communications,[1162] concluding observations, and resolutions.[1163] However, the African Commission's views and concluding observations do not adress TM.

Interestingly, like General Comment 14, Resolution 141 interprets the right to health under article 16 of the African Charter to include TM. Unlike the founders of the African Charter, African Commission's members expressly mention TM as a component of the right to health. Accordingly, the African Commission reads the obligation to promote access to medicines to include the State's duty not to prohibit or refrain from using TM and healing practices that are scientifically sound and medically appropriate.[1164] Unlike General Comment 14, Resolution 141 expressly states that TM and healing practices should be science-based and medically appropriate. In doing so, Resolution 141 enhances and stresses the quality aspects of TM. However, as mentioned earlier, some practices combined with TM cannot be science-based. Finally, unlike the General Comment 14, which addressed some questions of TM for indigenous people, Resolution 141 does not.

It is worth observing that Resolution 141 seems not to seriously consider the place of TM compared to General Comment 14. It does not reflect the African States' commitment to TM's protection as expressed in existing instruments

---

1160 African Commission's Guidelines on ESCRs.

1161 African Court Protocol, arts 4 (1) and 5.

1162 See for instance, the Zaïre Case, Ogoni case, the Saro Case, the Gambia Case, and Mauritania Case.

1163 African Commission Resolution 141. See also African Commission, Resolution on State's obligation to regulate private actors involved in the provision of health and education services-ACHPR/Res.420 (LXIV), 2019.

1164 African Commission Resolution 141.

adopted within the OAU framework, namely the OAU Declaration on TM and the 2007 Africa Health Strategy 2007-2015 (African Health Strategy).[1165]

The OAU Declaration on TM considers the vital role TM plays in African societies,[1166] where about 85% of the African population satisfy their health delivery services through TM.[1167] It, therefore, urges Member States and their governments to acknowledge and build upon this traditional knowledge resource-base to make the goal of health for all easier to achieve through effective mobilization and use of TM.[1168] To give effect to the provisions of the Declaration under discussion, the OAU General Assembly requires the General Secretariat in collaboration with WHO to assist Member States to prepare a Plan of Action for implementation and regularly report to it on progress.[1169] It is worth mentioning that Member States adopted the recommended Plan of Action in 2003.[1170] Progress made so far by some African countries during the period from 2001 to 2010 includes, among others, the facilitation of the collaboration between TMPs and conventional health practitioners, conduction of research on TM for malaria, HIV/AIDS, diabetes, and hypertension, and the inclusion of TM in their national essential medicines lists.[1171] It is worth acknowledging that African countries do still face permanent challenges in implementing the Plan of Action. These include limited financial and human resources, weak regulatory capacity, and unfavourable policy, economic, and regulatory environments for local production of TM.[1172] The AU conference of African ministers of health renewed the decade period from 2011 to 2020. For its part, based on the OAU Declaration on TM, the African Health Strategy pursues the vision for an integrated and prosperous Africa free of its heavy burden of disease, disability, and premature death.[1173] It focuses on strengthening the best practices of TM following the OAU Declaration on TM.[1174] Therefore, it urges the AU member States to implement the Plan of Action on TM, promote, and fund

1165 African Union Conference of Ministers of health, Africa Health Strategy: 2007-2015, (2007).

1166 Some African countries make local production of various plant-based preparations for cough, diabetes, malaria, mental health, and HIV/AIDS. See African WHO Strategy, paras 6-9.

1167 OAU Declaration on TM, para 2.

1168 Ibid. para 3.

1169 Ibid. paras 9-10.

1170 WHO Regional Office for Africa, Progress Report on decade of traditional medicine in the African region, 2011, para 3.

1171 Ibid. paras 7-14.

1172 Ibid. para 15.

1173 African Health Strategy, paras 23 and 25.

1174 Ibid. para 71.

research in TM to identify safe traditional medicines, and integrate African TM into their health systems.[1175]

To sum up, the OAU Declaration on TM has positively impacted on the recognition and protection of TM. Therefore, the African Commission ought to have learned from the above AU's declarations and strategies to formulate and lay down principles and rules on TM, upon which African governments would base their legislations to solve health problems.[1176]

c. *TM and the right to natural resources*

Article 21 of the African Charter on the protection of natural resources provides, among others, that

> all peoples shall freely dispose of their wealth and natural resources and that States parties shall undertake to eliminate all forms of foreign economic exploitation to enable their peoples to benefit from the advantages derived from their national resources fully.

This Charter's provision does not explicitly say that natural resources shall serve as TM. However, the expression "fully benefit from the advantages derived from national resources," is broad enough to include various types of advantages, including peoples' well-being[1177] and TM. The Charter's provision under discussion has a historical foundation. It aims to heal the wounds of colonial time, where outside powers have exploited African material resources to the detriment of African peoples, depriving them of their birthright and alienating them from the land.[1178]

In the Ogieks Case, the applicant contended that the Kenyan authorities had violated the rights of the Ogieks to freely dispose of their wealth and natural resources by evicting them from the Mau Forest and denying them access to the vital resources therein.[1179] In its judgment, the African Court ruled that the respondent's violation of the rights of Ogieks people to use and enjoy the produce of the land through forced eviction also entails that of the rights of the same people to enjoy and freely dispose of the abundance of food produced by their ancestral lands,[1180] including their means of survival such as animals, honey, and TM[1181] as argued under article 21 of the African Charter. In sum, the use of TM constitutes one of

1175 Ibid. para 72-73.
1176 African Charter, art 45 (1)(b).
1177 Ogoni case, para 58.
1178 Ibid. para 56.
1179 Ogieks Case, para 191.
1180 Ibid. para 201.
1181 Ibid. paras 179-183.

the advantages that may derive from the enjoyment of national resources, of which natural resources are an essential element.

d. TM and the right to cultural life

Article 17 (2) and (3) of the African Charter entitles everyone to the right to take part in his community's cultural life. At the same time, it enjoins State parties to protect and promote both morals and traditional values recognized by the community. The Charter provision under discussion does not expressly mention TM. However, the word "traditional values recognized by the community" is broad enough to cover the practice of TM by both individuals and communities. The African Court broadly interpreted the right to cultural life to include TM in the Ogieks case against the government of Kenya, which restricted Ogieks people's access to their cultural sites through forced eviction.[1182] Accordingly, the African Court ruled that the restrictions and forced displacement interfered with the enjoyment of cultural rights of Ogieks people, including their ways of practising TM and other traditional values.[1183] Therefore, it recalled the State's obligations to respect and protect indigenous peoples' cultural productions, including their natural medicines.[1184] The above development reveals that the use of medicinal plants, animals, and minerals by people is part of their cultural life. Therefore, health laws in the DRC and the URT should consider arguments based on African culture, virtues, and values, recognized by African countries to incorporate and treat TM as a genuine aspect of the African health system.[1185]

3. TM under the SADC human rights law

Like the previous development, the present section examines the protection of TM through the rights to health, natural resources and cultural life under the SADC Treaty, the SADC Health Protocol and SADC Gender Protocol.

a. Protection of TM as part of the right to health under the SADC Treaty and its Protocols

Article 4 (c) of the SADC Treaty obligates the Member States to act following the principle of human rights, democracy, and the rule of law. As discussed earlier, this SADC Treaty provision covers access to medicines protected in both SADC and other human rights instruments. SADC human rights instruments, namely the SADC Gender Protocol and the SADC Health Protocol safeguard access to health

1182 Ogieks Case, para 170.
1183 Ibid. paras 182-83.
1184 Ibid. para 50.
1185 Stuttaford et al., "The right to traditional health care," 6.

care, universal HIV and AIDS treatment,[1186] and health services,[1187] without explicitly distinguishing between conventional and traditional medicines. However, like articles 12 of the ICESCR and 16 of the African Charter, these provisions are broad enough to cover TM. The SADC Treaty urges Member States to follow the principle of human rights in implementing the Community's objectives to combat HIV/AIDS and other diseases.[1188] In achieving these SADC' objectives, Member States can use a human rights approach to access to medicine, including adopting measures promoting and regulating TM. More especially, under article 20 of the SADC Health Protocol, State parties develop mechanisms to regulate the practice of traditional healing and cooperate with THPs. At the same time, the SADC Health Protocol obligates State parties to cooperate and assist one another in the research, documentation, and utilization of TM.[1189] These provisions suggest that State parties can use TM to control, prevent and treat human diseases. Moreover, the regulation of traditional healing practices is consistent with the State's obligation to protect people's health from possible violation by third parties. Indeed, the State's failure to appropriately address TM can pose a challenge to health-related rights.[1190] Besides, cooperation between the State parties and THPs considers the latter's contribution as an essential component of the health workers, capable of responding to the expressed health needs of the community.[1191] For instance, in mental health, recent studies[1192] reveal that traditional healers are more numerous than mental health workers in the Global South countries. They constitute the primary health resource that local populations believe in and use.[1193] Finally, international cooperation between the Member States in the documentation and utilization of TM aims at setting up a sub-regional databank of identified medicinal plants, animals, and minerals and the ailments they treat, heal, or prevent. It further enables other Member States to learn from a given State's experience about the specific use of some TM.

Regarding human rights instruments outside the SADC framework, like in the Campbell case, article 4 (c) of the SADC Treaty covers access to medicines protected in, among others, the African Charter and the ICESCR, ratified by DRC and URT. Therefore, SADC Member States are under the treaty obligations to protect TM, which forms an essential component of the right to health under articles 16 of the African Charter and 12 of the ICESCR as developed in the previous sections.

1186 SADC Gender Protocol, arts 11 and 27 (c) (b).

1187 SADC Health Protocol, arts 2 (d), 3 (h).

1188 SADC Treaty, arts 4-5.

1189 SADC Health Protocol, article 29 (e).

1190 Bouso and Sánchez-avilés, "Traditional Healing Practices," 146.

1191 Alma-Ata Declaration, para VII (7).

1192 Bouso and Sánchez-avilés, "Traditional Healing Practices," 1465.

1193 Ibid.

It is important to recall that like under the ICESCR, the implementation of TM under the SADC human rights regime is subject to the principle of international cooperation. However, unlike the ICESCR, SADC human rights instruments do not expressly provide for the progressive realization of the right to access TM.

b. *Protection of TM through the right to natural resources under the SADC Treaty and its Protocols*

Unlike the ICESCR and the African Charter, the SADC Treaty does not expressly provide for a human right to enjoy natural resources. Instead, it erects into one of its objectives the achievement of sustainable utilization of natural resources,[1194] which shall be implemented in accordance with the principle of human rights. Like the ICESCR and the African Charter, it does not expressly connect the utilization of natural resources to the enjoyment of TM. However, once read in the light of the Treaty's principle of human rights and objectives of combating HIV/AIDS and other diseases,[1195] one can submit that the sustainable utilization of natural resources the Treaty refers to shall be achieved in conformity with the human right to natural resources. Moreover, in implementing the Treaty's objectives to combat HIV/AIDS and other diseases, the sustainable utilization of natural resources can extend to their medicinal utilization. This interpretation is reinforced by the provision of article 29 of the SADC Health Protocol, which urges State parties to cooperate and assist one another in the research and documentation on TM. The same provision emphasizes the establishment of a databank for medicinal plants. It derives from this article that research and documentation of TM would not be successful if they do not consider medicinal plants, animals, and minerals, which form part of the natural resources. Moreover, the goal of research and documentation on medicinal plants is to enable SADC people to enjoy access to TM. One of the advantages of documentation of TM consists of recording the treatment successes and failures of traditional health remedies, which in turn can contribute to the evaluation of TM.[1196]

c. *TM and the right to cultural life*

According to article 4 (c) of the SADC Treaty, SADC Member States shall act by the principle of human rights, democracy, and the rule of law. As discussed earlier, the SADC Tribunal interpreted this provision to entail the State's obligations to respect, protect and fulfil human rights. In explaining the rights protected under the SADC Treaty, the SADC Tribunal relied on human rights instruments adopted outside the SADC framework, such as the UDHR and the African Charter. Therefore,

---

1194 SADC Treaty, article 5 (g).
1195 Ibid, art 5 (a) (i).
1196 Habtom, "Perceptions and attitudes," 18.

one can argue that human rights under article 4 (c) of the SADC Treaty include the right to cultural life protected in the ICESCR and the African Charter as discussed in the previous section. Like these two legal instruments, the right to cultural life protected in article 4 (c) of the SADC Treaty covers TM. Moreover, the right to cultural life is implicitly protected in the SADC Gender Protocol, which obligates State parties to comply with their obligations under the human rights instruments they subscribed to at international and regional levels. Therefore, SADC Member States are under the treaty obligations to protect TM as part of the right to cultural life protected under the African Charter and the ICESCR.

B. Protection of TM under the domestic law of the DRC and URT

The present section discusses the protection of TM through the constitutional provisions on the right to health in the DRC and URT. More specifically, it focuses on adopted regulations and legislation on the practice and quality of TM. Finally, it examines the extent to which existing laws in these two countries make accessible natural resources for medicinal purposes.

1. Relevance of TM in the enjoyment of access to medicines in DRC and URT

Various arguments justify the relevance of TM in the enjoyment of access to medicine in the DRC and URT. To begin with, both treaty and constitutional provisions on the right to health, as discussed earlier, implicitly recognize traditional medicine. Thus, implementing access to TM is consistent with the State's obligations regarding the right to health. Furthermore, TM shares the common goal of providing health care[1197] with other treatment systems, including conventional medicine. Therefore, it prevents and treats the main human pathologies, such as tuberculosis,[1198]malaria,[1199]and HIV-related

1197 WHO Report on Traditional medicine, 9.

1198 Philipp Anochie et al., "African medicinal plants that can control or cure tuberculosis," *International Journal of Pharmaceutical Sciences and Developmental Research 4*, no. 1, (2018): 2, Sebua Semenya and Alfred Maroyi, "Medicinal plants used for the treatment of tuberculosis by Bapedi traditional healers in three districts of the limpopo province, South Africa," *African Journal of Traditional, Complementary and Alternative Medicines 10,* no. (2013): 318-19.

1199 TM has been used to treat malaria for thousands of years and is the source of the two main groups (artemisinin and quinine derivatives) of modern antimalarial drugs. Merlin Willcox and Gerard Bodeker, "Traditional herbal medicines for malaria," *BMJ*, (2004): 1156.

infections.[1200] Moreover, the culture-based approach to traditional healthcare[1201]practiced in DRC and URT has been part of their people's cultural lives since immemorial time. These historical and cultural reasons still maintain TM's popularity[1202] despite the colonial impact on its practice and its current lower legal status compared to modern medicine. Thus, as an essential aspect of the acceptability of the right to health, TM respects the culture of individuals, minorities, peoples, and communities.[1203] It is important to note that people obtain TM products from natural resources, namely medicinal plants, animals, and minerals. The DRC and URT have various natural resources to meet their people's health needs. To this end, the Public Health Law in DRC[1204] and the Traditional Medicine Act in URT[1205] make explicit provisions to protect medicinal plants, animals, and minerals. Finally, as two African countries facing challenges in providing equitable access to conventional medicines for all, both DRC and URT should use all medical resources at their disposal, especially TM[1206] and TMPs.[1207] Therefore, the country studies should consider the positive aspects of TM,[1208] promote the collaboration between THPs and MHPs,[1209] and ensure the complementarity between modern and traditional health systems.[1210]

1200 Dale Babb et al., "Use of traditional medicine by HIV-infected individuals in South Africa in the era of antiretroviral therapy," *Psychology, Health & Medicine*, (2007): 315.

1201 Antwi-Baffour et al., "Place of traditional medicine," 53.

1202 African WHO Strategy, paras 6-9.

1203 General Comment 14, para 12 (c).

1204 Public Health Law, art 58.

1205 Traditional Medicine Act, art 6 (1).

1206 Kamgoui, *Médecine traditionnelle*, 19.

1207 TMPs are one of the key actors in delivering primary health care, which includes essential medicine. See Alma-Ata Declaration, para VII (3) and (7).

1208 Robert Smith, *Medicinal chemistry-fusion of traditional and Western medicine*, (Sharjah: Bentham Science Publishers, 2013), 4. See also Kamgoui, *Médecine traditionnelle*, 15 and 18.

1209 Integration of TM in health systems increases coverage and access to health care. See African WHO Strategy, para 32.

1210 Gebremichael Habtom, "Perceptions and attitudes of modern and traditional medical practitioners about traditional medical practice in Eritrea," *International Journal of Alternative and Complementary Medicine 11*, no. 1, (2018): 18.

2. Significance of TM regulation in the enjoyment of the right to health

Appropriate regulation of TM is a prerequisite for its total contribution to the enjoyment of the right to health. Regulation mainly tackles some concerns associated with TM, such as issues relating to the quality of TM products and THPs, and the integration of traditional medicine into the country's national health system. Concerning TM products' quality, expressed concerns mainly include the lack of therapeutic effectiveness, poor-quality products, and unacceptable hygiene conditions.[1211] These concerns undermine the quality of TM, which is a crucial component of the right to health. It is the State's responsibility to address all these issues. For instance, the State can create conditions that allow conventional investigation methods to study and analyse physical ingredients used in TM scientifically.[1212] These methods can apply to medication therapies involving herbal medicines, animal parts, and minerals.[1213] Scientific research has revealed that medicinal herbs contain active ingredients,[1214] and that modern drugs can derive from natural products.[1215] However, the application of conventional scientific methods to TM can encounter some limitations. As an illustration, unlike in biomedical systems where clinical trials can demonstrate the safety and efficacy of medicines, the long history of use of TM products determines their safety and effectiveness.[1216] Moreover, the spiritual realm of TM makes it difficult for modern scientists to fully determine the efficacy and effectiveness of all TM's aspects.[1217] One cannot tell whether modern scientists are well equipped to test TM non-medication

1211 Emmanuel Kabengele Mpinga et al., "Traditional/alternative medicines and the right to health: key elements for a convention on global health," *Health and Human Rights 15,* no. 1, (2013): 50. See also WHO Traditional Medicine Strategy 2014-2023, (2010).

1212 Kabengele et al., "Traditional/alternative medicines,"119.

1213 WHO Strategy 2002-2005.

1214 Zargaran A, Karimi M, Rezaeizadeh H., "COVID-19: Natural Products and Traditional Medicines; Opportunity or Threat?" *Traditional Persian Medicine, 6,* no. 1, (2021):1.

1215 Yuan et ali., "The traditional medicine and modern medicine from natural products,"11.

1216 The conceptions of safety and efficacy in conventional and traditional medicines may not be equivalent. See Carlos Bouso, and Constanza Sánchez-avilés, "Traditional Healing Practices Involving Psychoactive Plants and the Global Mental Health Agenda," *Health and Human Rights 22,* no. 1, (2020):146-47.

1217 Kabengele et al., "Traditional/alternative medicines,"119.

therapies, such as spiritual therapies[1218] provided following religious and spiritual methods.[1219] Appropriate regulation can also tackle the issue of unhygienic conditions.

Like concerns about TM products of lousy quality, worries about TMPs include charlatanism and lack of qualification,[1220] which constitute a severe threat to TM services' quality. Moreover, these concerns affect the appropriate integration of TM into the national health system giving rise to mutual mistrust between modern and traditional health practitioners[1221] and hampering the collaboration between them. Furthermore, to qualify as THP, one needs to meet some requirements, including education and training. Therefore, appropriate regulation on the practice of THPs can adequately tackle issues of lack of qualifications, including charlatanism.[1222] Finally, the government's responsibility is to create necessary conditions for collaboration between TMPs and clinicians through law or policy that recognizes and makes such cooperation compulsory as part of TM's integration into the national health system.[1223]

3. Protection of TM at the domestic law of the DRC

Article 47 of the DRC Constitution protects the right to health without express mention to modern or TM. Since TM contributes to the enjoyment of the right to health, one may assume that it forms part of the constitutional right to health. Adopted to implement article 47 of the DRC Constitution, article 59 of the Public Health Law unequivocally recognizes TM in DRC. Along with the Public Health Law, various official documents deal with different aspects of TM. These include, among others, the National Pharmaceutical Policy,[1224] laws,[1225] and ministerial

1218 TM non-medication therapies are carried out primarily without medication, as in the case of acupuncture, manual, and spiritual therapies. See WHO Strategy 2002-2005.

1219 TM Decree, art 2 (3).

1220 WHO Traditional Medicine Strategy 2014-2023. See also Kabengele et al., Traditional/alternative medicines, 50.

1221 Angela Akol et al., ""We are like co-wives": Traditional healers' views on collaborating with the formal Child and Adolescent Mental Health System in Uganda," *BMC Health Services Research*, (2018): 6, Markus Müller et Innocent Balagizi, "La médecine moderne ou traditionnelle: le besoin de coopération," *Tearfund*, no. 48, (2001): 3.

1222 Appropriate legal frameworks to checkmate the quacks and charlatans in the practice of TM constitute an urgent need. Abdullahi, "Trends and challenges," 120.

1223 Akol et al., "We are like co-wives," 6.

1224 Politique Pharmaceutique Nationale, 2008.

1225 Public Health Law.

decrees.[1226] A number of reasons have been given to justify the use of TM. They include the lack of formal health services in some areas,[1227] financial constraints to get modern medicine, the efficacy of TM in dealing with some peculiar pathologies to Congolese,[1228] negative cultural perception of modern medicine,[1229]and the government's intent to improve health care coverage through the development of TM and the harmonization of partnerships between modern conventional and TM systems. Other justifications include integrating medical plants into the national pharmaceutical arsenal and the government commitment to promote and organize TM.[1230] Though no reliable statistics that provide the number of people who use TM. About 70% of patients in the DRC do not have access to modern health services.[1231]One can assume that an essential fraction of these patients relies on TM in one way or another.

a. *Regulation of TM as part of the right to health*

Article 59 of the Public Health Law explicitly recognizes TM in the DRC.[1232] It further places TM under the tutelage of the national health minister,[1233] who is responsible for the organization, regulation and promotion of TM, including traditional pharmacopeia and medicinal plants.[1234] The Public Health Law also vests the national health ministry with the power to set out the conditions for the practice of TM, including the rights and obligations of TMPs.[1235]

Pending the adoption of this provision's implementation measures, a panoply of uncoordinated legal texts addresses various aspects of TM. These include, among

1226 Arrêté Ministériel N° 1250/ CAB/MIN/S/CJ/KIZ/32/2002 portant organisation de l'exercice de la profession de praticien de la médecine traditionnelle, 2002 (hereinafter Traditional Medicine Decree).

1227 Pygmy communities suffer various issues of discrimination in areas of modern health care. See CESCR, concluding observations to DRC, 2009, paras 14 and 17. See also Human Rights Committee, Concluding observations to DRC, 2017, paras 40-50.

1228 PNDS 2016-2020.

1229 About 33% of married women do not have access to modern health care because of their husbands' lack of consent. Ibid.

1230 Arrêté Ministériel N° 1250/ CAB/MIN/S/AJ/DJK/12/2002 portant création et organisation d'un programme national de promotion de la médecine traditionnelle et des plantes médicinales, 2002 (hereinafter Decree on the National Program of Traditional Medicine).

1231 PNDS 2011-2015.

1232 Public Health Law, art 59.

1233 Ibid. art 60.

1234 Ordonnance N° 20/017 fixant les attributions des ministères, 2020, art 24.

1235 Ibid.

others, the Children Act,[1236] the Criminal Code,[1237] the 1952 Decree, the Traditional Medicine Decree, and the Decree on the National Program of Traditional Medicine. The Children Act and Criminal Code confine themselves in only mentioning traditional healers among the category of health personals without further details. Therefore, the present subsection focuses on other decrees, which have in common the fact of being anterior to both the DRC Constitution and the Public Health Law. Regarding the 1952 Decree, it regulates TM since colonial time and will be dealt with separately.

aa) Regulation of TM under the 1952 Decree

The 1952 Decree is about 69 old years and is still in force in the DRC. Accordingly, article 15 reads as follows,

> the provisions of the present decree do not apply to the natives of the Belgian Congo or those of the bordering African territories who provide care or administer remedies in the customary areas according to the habits and customs without disturbing the public order.

This provision does not explicitly use the word TM. Instead, it refers to TM as "care or remedies administered according to the habits and customs." Moreover, the word "natives of the Belgian Congo" may be understood to refer to Congolese THPs. However, the provision under discussion does not set out the conditions for qualifying as a THP, except providing remedies in customary regions according to the habits and customs. The fact that the 1952 Decree relegates the practice of TM to customary areas is not random. Instead, it reflects the discriminatory character of colonial health legislation in most African countries, which did not allow conventional medicines and TM coexistence, especially in urban areas.

In sum, the 1952 Decree does not ban the practice of TM. Instead, it demotes its exercise to rural areas, excludes it from any regulation through its provisions, and subjects its practice to "public order," a concept which it does not define. Sanctions for violation of the 1952 Decree do not apply to peoples that exercise TM without regard to public order. Thus, its provisions do not cover control quality of both THPs and TM products.

bb) Regulation of TM under the Traditional Medicine Decree

The Traditional Medicine Decree regulates the profession of TMPs. Its main and explicit intended objectives are the government's commitment to improving health care coverage through the development of TM and the harmonization of partnerships between modern conventional and TM systems.

1236 Children Law, art 170 (4).

1237 Criminal Code, art 171 bis.

The Traditional Medicine Decree describes a TMP as any individual who usually advises on methods to preserve or improve health and treats human, physical and mental diseases through the virtue of faith and spiritual guidance or by means traditionally used in the community and which can heal by helping or stimulating nature.[1238] TMPs can perform as naturalists, spiritualists, exorcists, ritualists, herbalists, or traditional birth attendants.[1239] One can use various means and methods to practice TM. Like under the 1952 Decree, the Traditional Medicine Decree reiterates that TMPs mainly exercise TM in rural areas.[1240] However, it also recognizes its exercise in urban areas under some prescribed conditions.[1241] Such provision conflicts with the Public Health Law, which does not provide for the divide of rural-urban areas. In that case, it does not seem helpful for an independent government that intends to integrate TM into its health system.

Regarding the collaboration between conventional and traditional health professionals, any THP who wants to provide his services in a modern health facility has the burden to apply in that regard and sign a partnership agreement with the concerned medical institutions.[1242] It would be recommendable that the government itself decides without ambiguity on the integration of TM into the national health system.

cc) *Regulation of TM under the Decree on the National Program of Traditional Medicine*

The Decree on the National Program of Traditional Medicine intends to integrate medicinal plants into the national pharmaceutical arsenal, integrate TM into the national health system, promote and organize TM. It establishes a National Program for the Promotion of Traditional Medicine and Medicinal Plants (National Program for TM) to develop and promote TM and integrate it into the national health system.[1243] The National Program for TM further shall contribute to medicinal plants' availability by organizing and coordinating research on medicinal plants, promoting the cultivation of medicinal plants, and carrying out the inventory of all the Congolese medicinal plants. It is responsible for protecting herbal and animal-based medicines and promoting local production of improved TMs.[1244] Reference to local production of improved TMs implies that one can also use TM in dosage forms, such as tablets, syrups, capsules, creams, lotion, or solutions.[1245]

1238 Traditional Medicine Decree, art 1.

1239 Ibid. art 2.

1240 Ibid. art 9.

1241 Ibid.

1242 Ibid. art 7.

1243 Decree on the National Program of Traditional Medicine, art 2.

1244 Ibid, arts 2–3.

1245 Guidelines for Application for registration of traditional medicinal products, 5. See also Decree on the registration of pharmaceutical products, arts 1 (20) and 2.

dd) Quality of TM and their facilities

The Traditional Medicine Decree makes provisions, which aim to ensure the quality of TM. For instance, it subjects THPs to some conditions. Accordingly, THPs in rural areas exercise their profession in conformity with public order and after registration. Whereas those performing in urban areas need a license for the art of traditional healing, an authorization to open a traditional medical care centre, or a collaboration agreement with modern hospitals.[1246] Furthermore, all TMPs are subject to the duty of integrity and honesty, and shall respect human life, physical and moral integrity of their patients. Moreover, they shall keep their TM care centres clean and respectful of hygiene rules.[1247] All these provisions aim to ensure that qualified persons administer TM in good conditions. However, the Traditional Medicine Decree falls short in two aspects. First, it does not expressly provide a regulatory authority responsible for TM products' control quality, health facilities, and THPs. Secondly, it does not offer an appropriate sanction regime in case of non-compliance with its relevant provisions. Regarding quality control of TM products, the Decree on the registration of pharmaceutical products partially fills in this gap. To this end, it subjects improved traditional medicines (improved TMs)[1248] to the same procedure of registration as modern medicines. The goal of this obligation is to guarantee quality control of this category of TM products.

ee) Inadequate sanction regime

The Decree on the registration of pharmaceutical products refers to the sanction regime provided by article 64 of the 1933 Ordinance. Its intended goal consists of discouraging lousy practices associated with improved TMs. It partly fills in the gap regarding lack of sanctions in both the 1952 Decree and the Traditional Medicine Decree. However, the sanction regime it refers to, lacks vigor. Consequently, non-compliance with the Traditional Medicine Decree and the Decree on the registration of pharmaceutical products relating to improved TMs remains unpunished. The absence of an appropriate sanction regime amounts to the State's failure to protect people's health from third parties, namely TMPs, who can provide their services without qualification[1249] or good manufacturing practices and distribution.[1250]

1246 Traditional Medicine Decree, arts 10-11.

1247 Ibid. art 20.

1248 Decree on the registration of pharmaceutical products, arts 1 (20) and 2.

1249 PNDS 2016-2020.

1250 Bofoe, *La criminalité pharmaceutique*, 30.

b. Natural resources and TM

Article 58 of the DRC Constitution expressly provides that all Congolese have the right to enjoy the national resources and that the State has to redistribute them equitably. As part of national resources, natural resources include any product provided by nature that can serve as a means of livelihood for a population, including land resources, water resources, forest resources, air, and wildlife species.[1251] One can argue that medicinal plants, animals, and minerals which are essential components of natural resources, constitute livelihood for the Congolese people.

Several legal texts explicitly deal with the protection of some medicinal natural resources. The Public Health Law defines a medicinal plant as any terrestrial or aquatic plant owning at its natural state active ingredients with healing or preventive properties for human or animal diseases.[1252] It further creates a national service for medicinal plants within the national health ministry, the organization and operation of which shall be set out by a decree of the Prime Minister.[1253] The provision under discussion does not determine the attributions of the national service for medicinal plants. However, its establishment can lead to conflict of interest with the National Program for TM. As discussed earlier, the National Program for TM is responsible for protecting herbal and animal-based medicines, promoting the cultivation of medicinal plants, and carrying out an inventory of the Congolese medicinal plants.[1254]

For its part, the Forest Code expressly[1255] entitles people living in or near the forest estate to the forest use rights, including the harvest of forest resources to satisfy their domestic needs by gathering fruits, food, or medicinal plants. It also stresses that the exercise of these rights for domestic purposes is free of charge and does not give rise to the payment of any tax or forest fee.[1256]

Finally, the Mining code[1257] obligates the mining operators to compensate the rights holders of the land for any occupation of land depriving them of the enjoyment of the soil or any modification rendering the land unfit for cultivation. Furthermore, in the displacement of the population, the mining operators must first make the reimbursement, compensation, and resettlement of the populations concerned. These provisions highlight the relevance of various advantages that people can take from their land, including TM. Moreover, the condition of compensation

1251 Loi N° 14/003 relative à la conservation de la nature, 2014 (hereinafter the Conservation of Nature Law), art 1 (42)

1252 Public Health Law, art 58.

1253 Ibid. art 57.

1254 Decree on the National Program of Traditional Medicine, arts 2 and 3.

1255 Loi N°11/2002 portant Code Forestier, 2002, arts 36 and 39.

1256 Ibid. art 43.

1257 Loi N°18/001 modifiant et complétant la Loi N° 007/2002 du 11 Juillet 2002 portant Code Minier, 2018, art 281.

in that regard is crucial, as it allows the affected occupants to find other ways of dealing with, among others, their health-related needs. However, it is deplorable that the Mining Code does not consider the consent of the rights-holders of the soil.

4. Protection of TM under the domestic law of URT

The URT Constitution does not directly and expressly provide for the right to health. Instead, it contains some provisions that address various aspects of health. These include, among others, the government's obligation to use national resources towards eradicating disease and making appropriate provisions for the realization of the right to social welfare at times of sickness, including adopting public health law.[1258] All these constitutional provisions do not expressly mention TM. However, the expression "use of national resources towards eradicating disease" is sufficient enough to include use of TM. Furthermore, the URT government can use TM to realize the social welfare during sickness or solve any public health issue.

Interestingly, TM constitutes one of the components of healthcare in URT, aiming to promote the integration between traditional and biomedical health systems. About 60% of Tanzania's population access healthcare through TMPs.[1259] Reasons that justify reliance on TM are manifold. They mainly include cultural belief models, limited access to modern medicine, safety concerns of conventional medicine, and TM's effectiveness, especially in mental health management.[1260] To appropriately benefit from TM, the URT adopted a law, which exclusively deals with TM's regulation.

a. Regulation of TM under the Traditional Medicine Act

Adopted in 2002, the Traditional Medicine Act is the main legislation on TM in URT.[1261] Its heading reads as follows, "An Act to make provisions for promotion, control, and regulation of traditional and alternative medicines practice, to establish the Traditional and Alternative Health Practice Council and to provide for related matters." As its title suggests, the Traditional Medicine Act aims to, among others, promote, control, and regulate TM in the URT. The adoption of the Traditional Medicine Act in the form of an Act of parliament is a manifestation of the government's political commitment to promoting and recognizing TM.[1262] The present subsection examines the regulation of the profession of TMPs, TM quality, and its integration into the national health system.

1258 URT Constitution, arts 7 (1), 9 and 30 (2).

1259 Ministry of Health, Community development, Gender, Elderly and Children, The National Health Policy, 2017 (henceforth National Health Policy 2017).

1260 Ibid.

1261 Traditional Medicine Act.

1262 Mbwambo, Mahunnah, and Kayombo, "Traditional health practitioner," 117.

aa) Legally qualified as TMPs

Article 3 of the Traditional Medicine Act refers to a TMP as a person who is recognized by the community in which he lives as competent to provide health care by using plants, animal, mineral substances and other methods based on social, cultural and religious background as well as on the knowledge, attitudes and beliefs that are prevalent in the community regarding physical, mental, and social well-being and the cause of disease. This definition implies that a THP must be a community member competent to provide health care. Moreover, provided health care should not include modern medicines. Instead, they shall consist of medicinal plants, animal, and mineral substances. Furthermore, THPs administer health care following the community's culture, beliefs, and attitude.

The Traditional Medicine Act also urges TMPs to present any relevant identification documents to the Registrar, including a written statement from the local government authority within which they perform.[1263] This requirement helps to identify all THPs and ensures that the local government authority recognizes them.

bb) Regulation of TM quality

Tanzanian health authorities consider that, like modern medicine, TM has side effects and some ethical issues.[1264] To tackle these concerns, several provisions of the Traditional Medicine Act ensure TM's quality. These include the obligation to treat patients with clear knowledge, skills, and light attitude, the observance of cleanness of traditional healers, their used appliances, and premises.[1265] Further provisions include the proscription of any practice which is or likely to be dangerous to people's health and life,[1266] and the obligation for THPs to only collect medicinal herbs from areas that are free from environmental contaminants, such as industrial pollution, mining areas and pesticides.[1267]

The Traditional and Alternative Health Practice Council carries out control quality of TM services by supervising and controlling the practice of THPs and protecting the society from their abuse.[1268] In carrying out its functions, the Council inspects and scrutinizes practitioners' practicing premises, terminates or suspends operation, permits, or professional certificates to practice as an aid or THP, and revokes permits to perform illegal practices.[1269]

1263 Traditional Medicine Act, art 14(1).

1264 National Health Policy 2017.

1265 Traditional Medicine Act, arts 31-35.

1266 Ibid. art 30.

1267 Guidelines for application for registration of traditional medicinal products.

1268 Traditional Medicine Act, arts 4 and 6.

1269 Ibid. art 7.

cc) *Sanctions regime*

Non-compliance with the provisions of the Traditional Medicine Act gives rise to sanctions. For instance, any person who practices as THP without being registered commits an offence and is liable on conviction to a fine not exceeding two hundred thousand shillings or to imprisonment for a term not exceeding two years or to both.[1270] Moreover, the court can order forfeiture or destruction of any TM remedies or diagnostic instruments or appliances used by, or belonging to, or found in possession of a person convicted.[1271] These sanctions intend to discourage anyone exercising the practice of TM without quality or qualification. They also put out of reach of the population any material, instrument, or product used by the offender. In sum, they aim to ensure that qualified TMPs provide TM within good conditions.

dd) *Collaboration between THPs and MHPs*

TMPs in the URT do not perform their activities in isolation from modern medicine. Instead, they are under a legal obligation to cooperate, not only with other THPs but also with MHPs. To this end, TMPs can make transfers to hospitals below the district level where circumstances demand, including the transfer of complex cases.[1272] Furthermore, the Health Minister prescribes the mechanisms for transferring patients from one traditional medical facility to another.[1273]These transfers underline the idea of complementarity between modern medicine and TM, which contribute to the enjoyment of the right to health. However, the Traditional Medicine Act remains silent on the transferring cases from modern hospitals to TMPs.

b. *Natural resources and TM*

Article 9 (c) and (i) of the URT Constitution urges the State authority and all its agencies to direct their policies and programs towards ensuring that the use of national resources eradicates poverty and disease. The word "national resources" includes natural resources, consisting of all materials or substances occurring in nature such as soil, subsoil, water resources, flora, fauna, genetic resources, aquatic resources, and micro-organisms.[1274] As part of both national and natural resources, medicinal plants, animals, and minerals can eradicate poverty and disease. The Traditional Medicine Act explicitly emphasizes the use of natural resources for medicinal purposes. Accordingly, it empowers the Council to provide for the protection of Tanzanian medicinal plants and other natural resources of therapeutic

1270 Ibid, art 45 (1), (2).
1271 Ibid, art 45 (3).
1272 Ibid. arts 34 (1) and 35 (2) (e).
1273 Ibid. art 34 (2).
1274 Natural Wealth and Resources (Permanent Sovereignty) Act, 2017, art 3.

value, such as animals, minerals, aquatic, and marine products and their parts thereof.[1275] Focus on TM-based product protection highlights the utility and relevance of TM for people's health in the URT.

Interestingly, the 1979 National Institute for Medical Research Act establishing the National Institute for Medical Research vests the latter with the functions to carry out and promote the carrying out of research into various aspects of local traditional medical practices to facilitate the development and application of herbal medicine. The National Institute for Medical Research benefits from funds and resources provided by Parliament, donations, grants bequests, and loans in order to adequately carry out its work.[1276] In sum, such research aims to make available and accessible herbal medicine and other aspects of TM.

5. Some concluding remarks: governments' double attitude towards TM

Despite the DRC and URT's commitment to make TM part of their national health system, TM enjoys a relatively lower status than modern medicine. Human right demands that States make TM available and accessible. However, the government in these two countries does not use its provider function to make TM available and accessible within public hospitals and facilities. Instead, the country studies regard TM as an exclusive private business for traditional healers. In doing so, the Congolese and Tanzanian governments fail to comply with their treaty obligations to create conditions that ensure all medical services and medical attention in the event of sickness.

Furthermore, existing laws on health insurance in these two countries do not expressly cover TM. As an illustration, in the DRC, the 2012 Circular and article 31 of the Public Physicians Decree reimburse only medical care costs and pharmaceuticals in official hospitals. Similarly, in the URT, both the National Health Insurance Fund Act[1277] and the National Social Security Fund Act[1278] do not cover health care services and drugs not prescribed in accredited hospitals. These provisions do not consider TM products or services provided by THPs argued under the existing legislation on TM discussed in this section. As a result, they reduce access to TM without explicit and justified grounds and infringe insured people's freedom to choose modern medicine or TM. Denouncing the lack of automatic reimbursement for many traditional therapies in countries with insurance systems, some commentators report that, in many cases, such reimbursement depends on the evidence of TM therapeutic effectiveness.[1279] This justification cannot stand in

1275 Traditional Medicine Act, art 6 (1).

1276 National Institute for Medical Research Act, 1979, art 20.

1277 National Health Insurance Fund Act, art 17.

1278 National Social Security Fund Act, art 42.

1279 Kabengele et al, "Traditional/alternative medicines," 51.

the case of DRC and URT because it would conflict with the legal recognition and protection of TM. Once again, these legal texts violate the obligation to fulfil access to TM through public health insurance systems.

It is important to note that two provisions under the Congolese law exceptionally cover TM. First, article 31 of the Public Physicians Decree allows the physician, in case of absolute necessity, to use other medical means upon prior authorization from the competent authority or information of the latter within the short period. Other medical means refer to health care services other than those provided in accredited State's hospitals. Therefore, they extend to health care delivered by non-state actors, including TMPs. Secondly, under the Social Security Law, the public institution in charge of the social security system accepts financial responsibility for health services provided by a non-selected medical facility in force majeure or an emergency justified by the state of health of the insured person.[1280] One can argue that "services provided by a non-selected medical facility" are broad enough to include health care provided by TM facilities. In these two cases of exception, the beneficiary of received health services has the burden to justify the emergency and the impossibility of resorting to State's hospitals or selected medical facilities. These exceptions emphasize the relevance of ensuring an appropriate collaboration of modern and traditional health systems to provide patients with a wide choice of healthcare providers.[1281] Good cooperation between these two health systems requires a full recognition and integration of TM into all areas of healthcare delivery, including national medicines policy, registration of TM products, regulation of TM practice, the establishment of TM hospitals, inclusion of TM in national insurance schemes as reimbursable items, the establishment of relevant research institutions on TM, and training of TMPs at all levels of education, including universities.[1282]

C. Chapter summary

TM forms part of the rights to health, natural resources, and cultural life under the international and domestic human rights laws. Regarding the protection of TM through the right to health, like modern medicine, treaty provisions on the right to health in the ICESCR, the African Charter, the SADC Treaty, and its two protocols do not expressly mention TM. However, their scope of the right to health is sufficient enough to include TM. For instance, State's reports under the ICESCR and the African Charter explicitly mention various aspects of TM as an essential component of the right to health. Although the corresponding concluding observations

1280 Social Security Law, art 69.
1281 Habtom, "Perceptions and attitudes," 17.
1282 Ibid, 18.

issued by the African Commission and the CESCR do not address TM, these treaty bodies acknowledge TM as an essential aspect of the right to health. Accordingly, the CESCR's General Comment 14 and the African Commission Resolution 141 identify TM as a crucial component of the right to health. Interestingly, the SADC Health Protocol that supplements the SADC Treaty expressly calls for regulating traditional healing practices and cooperating with TMPs. In providing for cooperation with TMPs, the SADC Health Protocol considers the currently suggested fusion approach between traditional and Western medicine[1283]for the reasonable enjoyment of the right to health.

Concerning indirect protection of TM, the chapter showed that appropriate implementation of the rights to enjoy natural resources and cultural life implies TM's protection from two perspectives. First, people obtain TM remedies from medicinal plants, animals, and minerals, which form natural resources. Secondly, people's use of natural resources for medicinal purposes has a longer tradition than the advent of chemistry, pharmacology, or even modern science. Therefore, it forms part of the right to cultural life. Finally, it is worth recalling that the CESCR and the African Court have established the relationship between TM and natural resources and cultural life rights.

At the domestic level, like human rights treaties, constitutional provisions on the right to health and health-related rights in the DRC and URT do not mention TM. However, like the treaty provisions, these constitutional provisions are broad enough to include TM. Parliaments and governments have adopted legislation and regulation on TM within the country studies. The Traditional Medicine Act regulates and recognizes TM in the URT and provides a control quality mechanism and appropriate sanction regime. In contrast, in the DRC, a panoply of laws and regulations govern various aspects of TM. Unlike in the URT, the protection of TM is relatively weak because of some conflicting provisions and the absence of appropriate sanctions. Regulating TM is part of the State's obligation to protect people's health.

Regarding indirect protection of TM through the right to natural resources, both countries have explicit provisions allowing the use of some natural resources for medicinal purposes. Illustrations in the DRC include the Public Health Law and the Forestry Code, which protect natural resources for people's health needs. In the URT, the Traditional Medicine Act makes provisions for protecting Tanzanian medicinal plants, animals, and minerals. Besides, the Land Act considers the use or ownership of land as a significant means of subsistence. However, once assessed in the light of their treaty obligations, the country studies fall short in making TM of good quality available and accessible. For instance, public health institutions do

1283 Smith, *Medicinal chemistry-fusion*, 4.

not deliver TM services, nor do health insurance legislations explicitly cover TM services.

V. General conclusion

The present study dealt with the State's obligations vis-à-vis the human right to access medicines within the framework of the right to health under the applicable law to DRC and URT, consisting of ratified human rights instruments and domestic laws. It considered the scope of the right to health to include conventional and traditional medicines.

A. Access to modern medicines under the international human rights law

Both DRC and URT are parties to various human rights treaties protecting the right to health, at the global, the African continental and sub-regional levels. At the global instance for example, the ICESCR protects everyone's right to the enjoyment of the highest attainable standard of physical and mental health, without expressly guaranteeing access to modern medicine as a specific, independent, and autonomous right. However, the full enjoyment of this treaty right requires access to medicines. To this end, State's reports on the implementation of the right to health mention various adopted measures that facilitate access to medicines, such as legislative, budgetary and social measures. Likely, in fulfilling its treaty supervisory tasks, the CESCR recognizes access to medicines as an essential component of the right to health through the General Comment 14 and concluding observations.

Almost similar to the ICESCR, article 16 of the African Charter guarantees the right to enjoy the best attainable state of physical and mental health without explicit reference to medicines. Nevertheless, the right to health herein protected is broad enough to encompass medicines. In its views, concluding observations, and Resolution 141, the African Commission interprets article 16 under discussion to include medicines. Furthermore, State' reports inform about adopted implementation measures on access to medicines as part of their commitment in implementing the right to health under the African Charter.

Under the SADC human rights law, the SADC Treaty urges the SADC and Member States to act following human rights principles. However, it does not explicitly list these human rights. While interpreting compliance with SADC Treaty's principle of human rights, the SADC Tribunal in the Campbell Case ruled that the provision gives rise to the State's obligations to respect, protect and fulfil human rights. Moreover, SADC Tribunal used human rights instruments to which Member States have subscribed, such as the UDHR, the African Charter, and the ICCPR, to explain the scope of human rights in the SADC Treaty. Therefore, the right to health argued in the African Charter and the ICESCR ratified by the DRC and URT falls within the ambit of the SADC Treaty. It is worth recalling that the SADC Health Protocol and SADC Gender Protocol help fill in this Treaty's gap regarding the right to health. For instance, in addition to protecting access to health services for all following the SADC Treaty's human rights principle, the SADC Health Protocol makes explicit provisions for distributing affordable essential drugs and pharmaceuticals. The SADC Gender Protocol protects the boy and girl child's equal access to health care and guarantees universal access to HIV and AIDS treatment for infected people. Thus, access to health services in the SADC Health Protocol, and children's access to health care and universal treatment for HIV and AIDs in the SADC Gender Protocol, is broad enough to comprise access to medicines. Overall, despite some language differences in the formulation of the right to health, all these legal instruments have in common the fact that they allow a broad interpretation to cover access to medicines.

The above treaty provisions on access to medicines call for implementation measures, including legislation. However, they subject these implementation measures to different approaches. For instance, unlike the ICESCR, which consecrates the clause of available resources and progressive realization,[1284] the African Charter,[1285] the SADC Treaty, and its two Protocols[1286] do not. Regarding the African Charter, especially, its founders did not expressly refer to the principle of the progressive realization of ESCRs, including the right to health. Consequently, State parties are under the obligation to immediately and individually implement access to medicines in all its aspects, including the provision of judicial remedy, irrespective of the country's available resources. For the same right, State parties, such as the DRC and URT, are bound to different and conflicting types of obligations. To bring the State's duties into harmony, the African Commission admits the principle of progressive realization within the State's available resources, including regional and international aid, in implementing the Charter's ESCRs, such as the right to health.[1287] The African Commission's interpretation considers the country's developmental level regarding the implementation of access to medicines. However, the lack of or limited resources cannot explain the State's failure to meet its minimum core obligations regarding the provision of essential medicines under the ICESCR and the African Charter.[1288] Both the African Commission and the ICESCR overlooked the fact that even the provision of essential drugs as part of minimum core obligation depends on the State party's availability of resources.[1289]

Moreover, unlike the African Charter, both the ICESCR and SADC Protocols consider the relevance of international assistance and cooperation in implementing

---

1284 ICESCR, art 2 (2).

1285 African Charter, art 1.

1286 SADC Treaty, arts 4, 5 and 6.

1287 African Commission's Guidelines on ESCRs, paras 13-15.

1288 Ibid. para 17. See also General Comment 14, para 47.

1289 Sellin, *Access to medicines*, 92.

access to medicines. Accordingly, article 2 (2) of the ICESCR provides appropriate means through international assistance and cooperation. For its part, article 14 (3) of the Optional Protocol to ICESCR establishes a Trust Fund to assist State parties concerned for the enhanced implementation of the Covenant's rights. Though these provisions apply to all State parties, they should benefit indigent State parties, such as the DRC and URT. Under the SADC human rights law, article 25 (4) of the SADC Treaty makes available SADC's resources to the Member States to pursue the Treaty's objectives, including the fight against HIV/AIDS and other diseases. Furthermore, State parties to the SADC Health Protocol and SADC Gender Protocol cooperate and assist one another in the pharmaceuticals to address health problems within the region.[1290] Again, it is the DRC's and URT's right to request the SADC resources or assistance to enhance the implementation of the right of access to medicines within their jurisdictions. It is worth recalling that, in its Guidelines on ESCRs, the African Commission also acknowledges the relevance of regional and international aids in the implementation of the Charter's ESCRs, including access to medicines.

Each treaty provides enforcement mechanisms to ensure compliance with its provisions. Under the ICESCR, the only enforcement mechanism for the DRC and URT remains the state reporting procedure. Accordingly, both DRC and URT submit some reports on the implementation measures for the right to health, including access to medicine. However, in addition to the delay in sending the State reports, the content of these reports is often incomplete regarding specific measures that make medicines of good quality available and accessible. For instance, submitted reports do not provide information about the State's minimum core obligations regarding essential medicines. For its part, the CESCR has also issued some concluding observations to some of these reports, in which it recommended improving the right to health. However, the CESCR made no recommendations on the State's minimum obligations, nor did it deal systematically with the elements of quality, availability, and accessibility of medicines. Finally, the CESCR has no power to compel State parties concerned to comply with its recommendations or sanction them in case of delay in submitting their reports.

At the African regional level, enforcement mechanisms consist of non-judicial and judicial mechanisms. Non-judicial mechanisms include the state reporting procedure, inter-state and individual communications before the African Commission. With respect to the state reporting procedure, the DRC and URT report to the African Commission by providing information on implementing the right to health, including some aspects of access to medicine. However, there are challenges regarding state report procedures. Similar to the reporting procedures under the ICESCR, State parties submit their reports with a considerable delay, while the reports lack detailed and specific information regarding the quality,

1290 SADC Health Protocol, arts 3 and 29, and SADC Gender Protocol, art 2 (1)(c).

availability, and accessibility of medicines. Additionally, these reports remain silent on implementing essential medicines that form part of the State's minimum obligations developed by the African Commission. It is worth noting that, like the CESCR, the African Commission did not consistently issue concluding observations for every received State report, nor did it examine access to medicines following its established elements of availability, accessibility, and quality.

Concerning individual and inter-state communications, they allow individuals and States to complain about the violation of any Charter's right, including access to medicines, by a State party to the African Charter. However, none of the State parties has submitted to the African Commission an inter-state communication on the violation of access to medicines by the DRC or URT. Moreover, the only individual communication on the violation of access to medicines by the DRC (Zaïre) goes back to 1996. The African Commission ruled that the shortage of medicines within the respondent's public hospitals was a violation of article 16 of the African Charter. However, the African Commission's views in this communication did not contain any recommendation or remedy.

Regarding judicial mechanisms, they involve individual and inter-state complaints before the African Court. However, entities with the locus standi to seize the African Court have never lodged any application on the violation of access to medicines by DRC or URT. Regarding individual complaints, unlike the DRC, which never recognizes the African Court's competence to receive complaints from natural persons, the URT has withdrawn its declaration allowing the African Court's competence in that regard. Therefore, individuals within the country studies cannot claim violation of access to medicines before the African Court.

It is worth noting that, unlike the CESCR's decisions, the AU General Assembly can enforce through sanctions the African Commission's views and concluding observations and the African Court's judgments.[1291] However, the AU General Assembly has never adopted sanctions against State parties to the African Charter that fail to comply with their state reporting obligations, including failure to implement the African Commission´s concluding observations.

Like under the African Charter, the SADC human rights law provides both judicial and non-judicial enforcement mechanisms. These include individual and inter-state communications before the SADC Tribunal, the procedure before the SADC Summit, and the state reporting procedure. However, unlike under the ICESCR and the African Charter, the SADC Gender Protocol does not determine the implementation modalities for the state reporting procedure it establishes. Moreover, none of the SADC enforcement mechanisms have engaged the DRC or URT regarding the violation of access to medicines.

Factors that can justify the lack of complaints on the violation of access to medicines against DRC and URT before these treaty bodies are not clear-cut. One

1291 AU Act, art 23(2).

may presume that they include, among others, the absence of acts and omissions that amount to the violation of access to medicines, the lack of power of the supervisory bodies to enforce their decisions, or the absence of domestic implementation framework for the treaty bodies' decisions.

Having ratified the above human rights treaties, the DRC and URT are under the treaty obligation to implement access to medicine herein guaranteed within their jurisdictions.

B. Implementation of access to modern medicines under the domestic law of DRC and URT law

The study examined the domestic implementation of the right to access modern medicines in DRC and URT by looking at the constitutional protection of access to medicines, the relationship between treaty and constitutional rights to health, the State's obligations, and the enforcement mechanism. It further examined adopted measures to implement both the treaty and constitutional right to access medicines.

Regarding the constitutional protection of access to medicines, like ratified treaties, the DRC and URT Constitutions do not explicitly provide an independent and specific human right of access to medicines. Instead, the Constitution in these countries protects access to medicine as a derivative right. Accordingly, unlike the DRC Constitution, which protects access to medicines through the right to health, the URT Constitution guarantees access to medicines as part of the right to social welfare and other human rights. Furthermore, unlike under the DRC Constitution, where access to medicines enjoys the same legal status as all constitutional rights, including CPRs, the URT Constitution regards access to medicine as directive principle of State policy. Therefore, if access to medicines under the DRC Constitution is theoretically enforceable before the courts of law, under the URT Constitution, it is not. The State's traditional role in protecting people's health, and adherence to the UDHR and ratified human rights treaties can justify the constitutional protection of health-related rights in the DRC and URT, albeit in different ways. The constitutional history of each country can partly justify the difference in the constitutional protection of access to medicines by the DRC and URT.[1292] Indeed, adopted in 2006 and revised in 2011, the DRC Constitution explicitly proclaims the country's adherence to human rights protected under the UDHR, the African Charter, and other international human rights instruments, making provisions for the right to health. Whereas the 1977 URT Constitution came into force 29 years before the DRC Constitution. Its Bill of Rights goes back to 1984, a period when the

---

1292 More recent constitutional texts seem to include stronger commitments, possibly reflecting the positive influence of the global development of the right to health in the past 50 years. See Perehudoff, Laing, and Hogerzeil, "Access to medicines in national constitutions,"800.

right to health was not enforceable under the ICESCR or under the Constitution in force in the DRC.[1293]

Concerning the relationship between the treaty and the constitutional right to access medicines, articles 215 of the DRC Constitution and 64 (5) of the URT Constitution consecrate the supremacy of the Constitution over treaty provisions. Therefore, the treaty right of access to medicines enjoys an inferior legal status than constitutional health-related rights. However, the protection of access to medicines as directive principles of State policy under the URT Constitution does not have any practical relevance for two reasons. Firstly, once domesticated, the treaty right of access to medicines becomes as justiciable as basic constitutional rights before the High Court. Secondly, unlike the constitutional right to health, domesticated treaty rights of access to medicines make it judicially enforceable. However, the URT still has to domesticate treaty provisions on access to medicines. It is worth noting that, unlike in the DRC, courts in the URT can only apply ratified human rights treaties after being domesticated.

Regarding the enforcement mechanisms, both the DRC and URT Constitutions provide for non-judicial and judicial mechanisms. In respect of non-judicial mechanism, the DRC' NCHR Law and the URT Commission for Human Rights and Good Governance Act empower the NCHR and CHRGG to receive complaints on the violation of access to medicine, assist complainants and victims in bringing to justice all proven cases of violation, and settle some complaints through conciliation. Moreover, unlike the NCHR Law, the Commission for Human Rights and Good Governance Act entitles the CHRGG to settle claims of human rights breaches through negotiation and mediation, and make its recommendations enforceable before the courts.

In practice, unlike the CHRGG in the URT, which has never dealt with cases of violation of access to medicine, the Congolese NCHR has received more than two complaints on the violation of various aspects of access to medicines. These violations related to the illegal running of pharmacies, shortage of medicines within public hospitals, bad quality medicines and prisoners' lack of medical care. However, information is lacking on whether the NCHR settled these cases through a conciliation procedure or it assisted the complainants in seizing the courts and tribunals.

Concerning the judicial mechanism, articles 150 (1) of the DRC Constitution and 6 (2) of the NCHR Law bestow the human rights jurisdiction upon all courts and tribunals. Unlike in the DRC, article 30 (3) of the URT Constitution vests human rights jurisdiction exclusively with the High Court. Further, while the judiciary's human rights jurisdiction in DRC relates to all the categories of rights, under the

1293 The Constitution that was in force in the DRC from 1977 to 1984 did not protect the right to health. See, la Constitution de la République Démocratique du Congo du 24 Juin 1967.

URT Constitution, the High Court can only address the violation of the constitutional basic rights and rights protected in any law. However, unlike in the DRC, where the law does not provide for the administration of the exercise of the court's human rights jurisdiction, the Basic Rights and Duties Act in URT manages only the High Court's jurisdiction over basic rights. It remains incomplete about the High Court's jurisdiction over rights protected in other laws. However, none of the courts or tribunals in these two countries had already enforced the treaty or constitutional right to access medicines. Therefore, any distinction between a monist and dualist State or between a country with an explicit constitutional right to health and a government that protects it as a non-enforceable right becomes worthless and meaningless.

Overall, one can assume that the similarity in providing both non-judicial and judicial enforcement mechanisms is partly due to the influence of international human rights instruments to which DRC and URT subscribed. Examples include articles 8 of the UDHR and 2 (3) of the ICCPR, which entitle everyone to an effective remedy for acts violating the rights granted him by the Constitution or law. Moreover, the non-binding nature of their decisions can explain the broader jurisdiction of the national human rights commissions over all ESCRs compared to courts in these two countries.

Regarding the State's obligations, the DRC Constitution subjects access to medicines to the State's duties to guarantee and respect. In contrast, the URT highlights the government and all its agencies' responsibilities to take cognizance of, observe and apply constitutional provisions on the right of access to medicines. All these constitutional provisions imply that each government branch shall take appropriate measures within its competence to implement access to medicines. However, unlike the ICESCR, and similar to the African Charter, the constitutional provisions on the State's duties in DRC and URT do not explicitly subject the implementation of health-related rights to the clause of progressive realization or available resources. These constitutional obligations do not consider the country's developmental level. It is the State's competent organs to bring constitutional obligations in conformity with the principle of progressive realization of all ESCRs, including access to medicines, as argued in the ICESCR and reiterated by the African Commission.

To give effect to access to medicines, the DRC and URT resort to the government regulatory and provider functions. As part of the regulatory function, both DRC and URT have adopted legislations that regulate the exercise of the profession of pharmacists and other medical professions, pharmaceutical business, including by non-state actors, and quality control. Regulating the pharmaceutical sector forms part of the State's obligation to protect people's health.

In DRC, a panoply of laws and regulations governs the pharmaceutical sector. However, some provisions are uncoordinated and conflict with each other. For instance, some legislations in force still refer to the abrogated provisions of the 1933 Ordinance and the 1952 Decree relating to pharmaceutical activities. Unlike in DRC, the laws that regulate the pharmaceutical sector consist mainly of the

Pharmacy Act and the Tanzania Food, Drugs and Cosmetics Act. Furthermore, unlike in DRC, where pharmacy inspectors work with inadequate equipment and without public laboratories to ensure control quality for medicines, the Tanzania Food, Drugs and Cosmetics Act puts a public laboratory at the disposal of TFDA for appropriate control quality.

Regarding sanction regime, except the Public Health Law, which provides fine in the legal currency in use in DRC for any activity on pharmaceuticals of bad quality, the 1972 ordinance-law, the 1991 Ordinance- Law, and the Decree on the trade of pharmaceuticals refer to a currency which is no longer in use in DRC. Moreover, the 1991 Ordinance- Law and the Decree on the trade of pharmaceuticals refer to the abrogated sanctions regime of the 1933 Ordinance and 1952 Decree. In contrast, the Pharmacy Act and the Tanzania Food, Drugs, and Cosmetics Act offer an appropriate sanctions regime, including prescribing fine in the currency in use in the country. While both countries aim to protect their people's health, political will and commitment can partly explain these identified differences in the regulation of the pharmaceutical sector within their jurisdictions.

The State's provider function enables the government to deliver medicines and to facilitate financial accessibility to medicines, including through health insurance and special protection to employees and the vulnerable groups of the society. Accordingly, both the Public Health Law in DRC and the Public Health Act in URT establish a national health system headed by the national minister with health matters in his/her remit. The government mainly funds the national health system through the budget allocation to the health sector. However, the budget allocated to the national health system in these two countries has never reached 15% of the general budget. Moreover, competent authorities do not fully implement the amount allocated to the health sector. Unlike the Public Health Act, the Public Health Law in DRC establishes a Health Promotion Fund to support the national health system, even though its implementation decree has never been adopted. Given that the local production of medicines in DRC and URT contributes only to 10% of the national needs, the government in these two countries relies mainly on the imports of medicines. For medicines to reach people, the government resorts to public health institutions, including dispensaries, health centres, and district hospitals, and general hospitals.

Concerning people's access to medicines through health insurance, the Public Health Law in the DRC establishes a universal health coverage system based on equity principles, including the Health Solidarity Fund. However, the absence of the implementation decree for both the universal health coverage system and the Health Solidarity Fund makes the DRC similar to the URT, which does not have universal compulsory health coverage. In practice, both DRC and URT have adopted some alternative measures.

For instance, unlike in the URT, the Congolese law covers access to medicines of a significant fraction of the population, including the members of the national government, public servants, and members of higher education institutions, as part of social benefits at public expense or that of the higher education institutions as the case may be.

Moreover, both the DRC and URT have a law on social security. Under the Social Security Law in DRC, the public institution in charge of the social security reimburses medical costs for secured members for medical services provided by preselected medical institutions or abroad, including non-selected medical facilities in case of an emergency. In contrast, the National Social Security Fund Act in the URT covers health care of insured members provided by accredited health facilities only. However, unlike under the Social Security Law, which extends to the pregnant woman as the sole dependent of an insured member, under the National Social Security Fund dependents of secured persons extend to their spouses and four children irrespective of their age. Furthermore, unlike the Social Security Law, the National Social Security Fund Act does not explicitly cover health services received from non-accredited health institutions in case of emergency. The difference between the two legislations lies in the nature of covered health-related matters. Unlike the Social Security Law, which only deals with occupational diseases and accidents and maternity benefits, the National Social Security Fund Act covers all health issues without limitation.

Contrary to the DRC, the URT government provides further health insurance schemes through the National Health Insurance Fund Act and the Community Health Fund Act, covering insured members, spouses, and children or dependents. However, unlike under the National Health Insurance Fund Act, where the number of children or dependents cannot exceed four irrespective of their age, the Community Health Fund Act covers only children under the age of eighteen without number limitation. Like the National Social Security Fund Act, the National Health Insurance Fund Act, and the Community Health Fund Act do not contain a clause that allows their beneficiaries to receive medical care in non-accredited health facilities in the event of an emergency.

Regarding access to medicines for employees, the Labour Law in the DRC obliges every employer to cover the costs of medical services administered to his workers and all his family members when they get sick. In contrast, the Worker's Compensation Act in the URT covers only the employee's occupational injuries and diseases and does not extend to his family members. Two reasons can justify the differences in these two laws. Firstly, unlike the Labour Law, which covers all health-related problems, the Worker's Compensation Act deals with occupational diseases and injuries. Secondly, unlike the Worker's Compensation Act, the Labour Law considers the International Labour Organisation's (ILO) conventions and recommendations. For instance, since April 1987, the DRC has been a party to the 1952 ILO Social Security (Minimum Standards) Convention n° 102, which guarantees medical care to employees, their wives, and children.

Special protection for some vulnerable groups of the society covers people with HIV, prisoners, children, and women. Concerning people with HIV, the HIV Law in the DRC grants free access to preventive and curative care for people with HIV. Unlike in DRC, the provision of medicines for people affected by HIV under the

HIV and AIDS Act in URT is not free of charge and depends on the State's available resources. The legal status of people with HIV can justify the difference between these two provisions. According to article 123 (16) of the DRC Constitution, which serves as the legal basis to the HIV Law, vulnerable groups, including all people with HIV irrespective of their social status, enjoy special protection. In this context, free access to health care constitutes one of the special protection measures. Whereas under the HIV and AIDS Act, only the most vulnerable children, including orphans, have a right to special protection, namely the means to access basic health care and livelihood services from the local government authorities.

Concerning prisoners, like the Public Health Law and the Prison Ordinance in DRC, the Prisons Act in the URT protects prisoners' access to medicines at the State's expense. All these provisions consider that prisons in the country studies are the exclusive preserve of the State. Therefore, physical integrity and welfare of prisoners are the responsibility of the competent public authorities.

As far as children's access to medicine is concerned, the Children Law in DRC and the Children Act in URT do not make it free of charge. Instead, they make provisions for special protection for some categories of children. The beneficiaries of special protection under the Children Law who enjoy health services and food from the State are children with one or both parents imprisoned, children whose parents cannot ensure survival, and children with physical or mental disability. Under the Children Act in the URT, local government authorities provide assistance and accommodation to the most vulnerable children, namely lost, abandoned, and refugee children in order to grow up with dignity and develop their potential and self-reliance. The similarity in the special protection for these categories of children is as a result of the DRC and URT's compliance with ratified treaties on children rights. Like the Children Law in DRC, the Children Act in URT implements children's rights protected in regional and international human rights laws. More specifically, articles 27 (3) of the CRC and 20 (2) (a) of the African Children Charter urge State parties to assist parents in case of need about their children's health.

Finally, unlike under the discussed laws in URT, the Women Law in DRC entitles women to health care services at a reduced cost, or where appropriate, free of charge during pregnancy, childbirth, and after birth. Two factors can justify the special protection of women under the Women Law in DRC. First, unlike the URT Constitution, article 14 of the DRC Constitution explicitly urges the State to protect and promote women's rights, including eliminating all forms of discrimination against them. Secondly, the Women Law expressly implements the constitutional and treaty provisions on women's rights, including the CEDAW, the SADC Gender Protocol, the African Women Protocol, and the UN Resolution 1325.[1294]

1294 See the explanatory note to the Women Law.

C. Access to traditional medicine

The present study interprets the scope of the right to health as provided for under ratified treaties and domestic laws of the DRC and URT to include TM. It further uses an interdependence approach by recognizing the indirect protection of TM through the rights to natural resources and cultural life.

1. Access to traditional medicine under the international human rights law

The chapter discussed TM's direct protection as part of the right to health and its indirect protection through the protection of natural resources and cultural life, focusing on the ICESCR, the African Charter, SADC Treaty, and its two protocols.

Regarding the direct protection of TM as part of the right to health, relevant treaty provisions under the ICESCR, the African Charter, and the SADC Treaty do not expressly mention TM. However, their scope is broad enough to include TM. For instance, Article 12 of the ICESCR deals with the right to the enjoyment of the highest attainable standard of physical and mental health. It does not expressly mention TM nor does it prescribe any kind of medicines. Therefore, the structure of article 12 coupled with its abstract nature, permits a broad interpretation to cover all types of medicines, including traditional medicine. The drafters of article 12 of the ICESCR considered the existence of various health systems worldwide, including traditional medicine. Hence, they used a language formulation that would recognize State parties' realities regarding the implementation of the right to health. In its efforts to give a concrete content to the abstract character of article 12, General Comment 14 expressly identifies TM as an essential component of the right to health. Like the drafters of article 12 of the ICESCR, the CESCR's members took into account the use of traditional medicine within and by State parties in their elaboration of General Comment 14. However, General Comment failed short in not recognizing explicitly other types of medicines, such as complementary medicine or alternative medicine. In implementing the Covenant right to health, State's reports explicitly mention various adopted measures, including legislation, policies, and programs dealing with the multiple aspects of TM. The corresponding CESCR's concluding observations, however, do not adress TM.

Like the ICESCR, article 16 of the African Charter protects the right to enjoy the best attainable state of physical and mental health without explicit reference to TM. By not mentioning any kind of medicines, the founders of the African Charter recognize the State parties' latitude to determine the type of health systems that would meet their people's health needs, including TM. Without ignoring the impact of article 16 at hand on TM, the absence of an explicit reference to TM is questionable for two reasons. First, the preamble to the African Charter expressly claims to eradicate all forms of colonialism from Africa. Explicit mention of TM would have been an appropriate way of eradicating the negative impact that colonization had had on the African TM. Secondly, the African Charter's preamble expressly considers the virtues of African States' historical tradition and African civilization's values, which inspire and characterize their reflection on the concept of human and peoples' rights. This would imply that the African Charter, unlike the ICESCR, expressly mentions traditional medicine as a fundamental part of African people's culture, which has been an integral part of the African health care system since time immemorial. Unlike the African Charter's drafters, the African Commission's members that have adopted Resolution 141 explicitly recognize the use of TM and healing practices that are scientifically sound and medically appropriate as part of the Charter's right to health. Unlike General Comment 14, Resolution 141 stresses that traditional medicines and healing practices should be science-based and medically appropriate. However, Resolution 141 overlooks the fact that some practices combined with traditional medicines cannot be science-based. Illustrations include spiritual therapies provided using religious and spiritual approaches. It is worth recalling that, unlike the General Comment 14, which addressed some questions of traditional medicine for indigenous people, Resolution 141 does not. Like under the ICESCR, State parties to the African Charter, including the URT, report on implementation measures dealing with various aspects of TM in their efforts to give effect to the Charter's right to health. However, like the CESCR, the African Commission's concluding observations are silent regarding TM.

Under the SADC human rights law, article 4 (c) of the SADC Treaty obligates the Member States to act following the principle of human rights, democracy, and the rule of law. Applied to the human right to health, the SADC Treaty provision at hand covers access to medicines protected in both SADC and other human rights instruments. Therefore, access to health care, health services and universal HIV and AIDs treatment in the SADC Gender Protocol and the SADC Health Protocol is broad enough to cover TM. Furthermore, the SADC Health Protocol addresses TM issues in three explicit ways. First, it expressly emphasizes the regulation of traditional healing. Regulating health services provided by non-state actors is part of the State's obligation to protect the right to health. Secondly, it focuses on the internal cooperation between State parties and THPs. The underlying idea about such collaboration is the complementarity between conventional and traditional medicines, which should result in the integration of TM into the national health system. Thirdly, the SADC Health Protocol urges State parties to assist one another in the use of TM. Regarding human rights treaties adopted outside the SADC framework, the content of article 4 (c) of the SADC Treaty consists of TM protected in articles 12 of the ICESCR and 16 of the African Charter, ratified by the DRC and URT.

The above development of treaty provisions on the right to health suggests that, like modern medicines, TM contributes to the enjoyment of the right to health. However, in their discretion regarding the content of State reports, most State parties do not give information relating to TM. For instance, despite existing legislation and regulation on TM since colonial time, the DRC's reports on the domestic implementation of the right to health under the ICESCR and the African Charter are silent in that regard. The same observation applies partly to the URT whose reports to the CESCR do not mention the 2001 Traditional Medicine Act. The study commends and welcomes the broad interpretation of the right to health by the CESCR and the African Commission to cover TM. At the same time, it urges them to also address the issues of TM adequately on a case-by-case basis in their concluding observations to the corresponding State reports.

Regarding the protection of TM through the human right to natural resources, the ICESCR, the African Charter, and the SADC Treaty do not expressly provide for the medical use of natural resources. Instead, like with the right to health, these provisions are broadly framed. They recognize peoples' right to benefit from their national resources' advantages, including their use as means of subsistence.[1295] More importantly, under the SADC Health Protocol, State parties cooperate and assist one another in establishing a regional databank of TM and medicinal plants.[1296] A combined reading of these provisions reveals that they are sufficient to include natural resources' therapeutic utility, such as medicinal plants, animals, and minerals. In General Comment 14, the CESCR explicitly calls for protecting vital medicinal plants, animals, and minerals necessary to the full enjoyment of the right to health.[1297] Equally, in the Ogiek case, the African Court emphasized the importance of using traditional lands in getting means of survival, including practicing TM.[1298]

Finally, in addition to being respectful of the culture of individuals,[1299] TM is an essential component of people's cultural life. The legal basis for the human right to cultural life consists of articles 15 (1) (a) of the ICESCR, 17 (2) and (3) of the African Charter, and 4 (c) of the SADC Treaty. It is worth recalling that these treaty provisions make no explicit reference to TM. However, both the CESCR and the African Court interpret the right to cultural life as encompassing traditional healing practices. Through its concluding observations and general comments, the CESCR states that people's rights to manifest their cultures, including medicines and knowledge of fauna and flora properties, form part of the right to cultural life.[1300] At the same time, the African Court ruled that the right to cultural life includes, among others, distinct ways of practicing TM.[1301]

1295 ICESCR, art 1 (2), African Charter, art 21, SADC Treaty art 5 (g), and SADC Health Treaty.

1296 SADC Health Protocol, art 29.

1297 General Comment 14, para 27.

1298 Ogiek case, paras 179-183.

1299 General Comment 14, para 12 (c).

1300 CESCR, concluding observations to DRC, 2009, paras 14 and 36, CESCR's concluding observations to URT, 2012, para 29, and General Comment 21, para 37.

1301 Ogieks Case, paras 179-183.

In sum, appropriate protection of TM contributes simultaneously to the enjoyment of the human rights to health, natural resources, and cultural life. For having ratified the above human rights treaties, the DRC and the URT are bound to protect TM within their jurisdictions.

2. Implementation of TM under the domestic law of DRC and URT

At the national level, the study dealt with the protection of TM through the rights to health and natural resources. Regarding the guarantee of TM as a component of the right to health, the DRC and URT Constitutions do not expressly mention TM. Nevertheless, constitutional provisions on health-related rights are sufficient enough to include TM. To this end, both the DRC and URT have adopted laws and regulations dealing with TM. In the DRC, the Public Health Law recognizes TM in the country. It subjects its organization to a ministerial decree of the national minister with health in his/her remit. The implementation decree, however, does not exist. Instead, the 1952 Decree, the Traditional Medicine Decree, the Decree on the National Program of Traditional Medicine, and the Decree on the marketing of medicine provide the mandate for administration of TM's various aspects. However, some provisions of these legal texts seem uncoordinated to some extent. For instance, the 1952 Decree which was adopted in the colonial period does not recognize TM's practice in urban areas, nor does it address questions relating to TMPs and TM products' control quality. The 1952 Decree further lacks an appropriate sanction regime in case of non-compliance with its provisions. For its part, the Decree on Traditional Medicine falls short by not providing the competent authority to ensure quality control of TM products and TMPs. Like the 1952 Decree, it does not offer an appropriate and explicit sanction regime. The absence of appropriate sanctions under the laws and regulations on TM violates the State's obligation to protect individuals against unregular and potentially harmful practices and products. It is worth recalling that the law on traditional medicine in DRC does not make compulsory the collaboration between TMPs and MMPs.

Like the DRC, the URT recognizes TM. However, unlike in DRC, the Traditional Medicine Act remains the primary legal text that regulates TM's exercise throughout the country without restriction. Furthermore, unlike in the DRC, the Traditional Medicine Act empowers the Traditional and Alternative Health Practice Council to ensure control quality of healthcare provided by TMPs, including through the termination or suspension of operation, permit, or professional certificate to practice as TMP. Contrary to the DRC law, the Traditional Medicine Act makes explicit provisions for transfers from TM facilities to hospitals and between traditional medical facilities. Finally, unlike in DRC, the Traditional Medicine Act provides an appropriate sanction regime, consisting of fines, imprisonment, and the destruction and confiscation of any TM remedies or diagnostic instruments or appliances used by the convicted person.[1302] Therefore, the URT, unlike the DRC, adequately complies with the State's obligation to protect people's health from potential violation by THPs.

Regarding natural resources protection for medicinal purposes, both the DRC and URT Constitutions do not expressly provide for the specific right to natural resources. Instead, like article 58 of the DRC Constitution that guarantees the right to enjoy national resources, article 9 (c) of the URT Constitution urges the State to direct its policies and programs towards ensuring that national resources eradicate poverty and disease. In implementing these constitutional provisions, the legislator in the DRC and URT defines national resources to include products provided by nature that serve as a means of livelihood, such as land resources, forest resources, air, and wildlife species,[1303] of which medicinal plants, animals, and minerals are an essential component.

In the DRC, for instance, the Public Health Law protects medicinal plants and creates a national service for medicinal plants. Furthermore, the Decree on the National Program for TM empowers the National Program for TM to promote and organize medicinal plants' research. More specifically, the Forest Code entitles people living in or near the forest estate to harvest forest resources to satisfy their domestic needs by gathering medicinal plants. The same Code provides that the exercise of these rights for domestic purposes is free of charge.

For its part, the Traditional Medicine Act in the URT urges the Traditional Medicine and Alternative Council to protect Tanzanian medicinal plants and other natural resources of medicinal value, including animals, minerals, aquatic and marine products, and their parts thereof. Like the Decree on the National Program for TM, the National Institute for Medical Research Act establishes and empowers the National Institute for Medical Research to promote research into various aspects of local TM practices to facilitate the development and application of herbal medicine.

The similarity in the recognition and protection of TM through the rights to health and natural resources within the country studies results from internal and external factors. Internal factors include the use of traditional health systems by Congolese and Tanzanians since immemorial and the availability, accessibility, and use of medicinal plants, animals, and minerals. External factors comprise the influence and impact of treaty human rights provisions on the right to health, General Comment 14, and the OAU decade of African traditional medicine 2001-2010. As an illustration, the adoption in 2002 of the Traditional Medicine Decree, the Decree on the National Program of Traditional Medicine, and the Traditional Medicine Act took place after the issue of General Comment 14 in 2000 and the adoption of the OAU decade of African traditional medicine 2001-2010.

1302 Traditional Medicine Act, art 45.

1303 The Conservation of Nature Law, art 1 (42), and Natural Wealth and Resources, art 3.

The country studies also have some differences regarding the implementation of traditional medicines. The two factors explaining these differences are mainly political commitment and the impact of colonial legislation. Regarding political commitment, it seems relatively mixed in the DRC than in the URT in many regards. For instance, unlike under the Traditional Medicine Act in the URT, the DRC maintains the above-identified conflicting legal provisions relating to some aspects of traditional medicines. Moreover, unlike the Tanzanian government, the DRC seems lax in protecting people's health through an appropriate sanction regime under the laws and regulations on traditional medicine. Finally, unlike the Tanzanian government, the DRC seems reluctant to expressly promote transfers of patients between TM facilities and from the later to modern hospitals.

It is worth recalling that in some essential aspects of traditional medicine, the political commitment of the two countries is limited. Moreover, their domestic laws are inadequate when assessed based on international standards. For instance, public health facilities and hospitals in the DRC and URT do not provide TM services. This violates the State's obligation to make traditional medicines available and accessible. Furthermore, in not explicitly reimbursing medical costs for traditional medicine treatments, existing legislation on medical insurance or social benefits within the country studies is inconsistent with the State's obligation to fulfil access to traditional medicines through a public health insurance system. Finally, the absence of direct transfer of patients from modern hospitals to traditional medicine facilities hinders people from accessing traditional medicine, impeding appropriate collaboration between health workers.

The influence of colonial legislation is present and manifests itself in the DRC in three ways.

First, unlike in the URT, regulations in the DRC reiterate the colonial view that traditional medicine is mainly practiced in rural areas. However, the Public Health Law recognizes the general use of TM throughout the country. Secondly, like the 1952 Decree adopted during colonization, subsequent laws and regulations on traditional medicine in the DRC do not include appropriate sanctions. Thirdly, and similar to the URT, traditional medicine, like in the colonial period, continues to have an inferior legal status compared to modern medicine.

D. Concluding observations

Both the DRC and URT have taken various measures to access medicines within their respective jurisdictions. However, the study has identified common and specific factors that impede the full and appropriate implementation of the right of access to medicines by the country studies.

Identified common concerns to the country studies relate to the following:

- Relative weak implementation of the treaty provisions on the right to health, including access to medicines. Illustrations include the absence of an appropriate domestic remedy procedure regarding judicial enforcement of access to

medicines, and lack of a national enforcement mechanism for the implementation of the treaty bodies' decisions, views, recommendations, or judgments. Other factors include irregular submission of State reports to the competent treaty bodies, and the incompleteness of submitted reports regarding some specific aspects of medicines, such as compliance with the minimum core obligations towards essential medicines, relevant information on traditional medicine, or explicit request for international assistance from the CESCR.
- Lower budget allocation to the health sector: the portion of the national budget allocated to the health sector has never reached 15%, as argued in the Abuja Declaration.
- Weak commitment in the local production of medicine: the national production of medicines satisfies only 10% of the people's needs.
- Partial integration of TM into the national health system: illustrations include public hospitals' failure to deliver TM services, the ignorance by existing health insurance laws of services provided by TMPs, and the absence of transfer mechanisms from modern health facilities to TM ones.

Identified specific factors to each country study result from the comparative analysis on the one hand. They also correspond to inherent shortfalls in the country's domestic laws, on the other hand.

For the DRC, identified challenges include the following:

- The absence of a specific legislation on the exercise of the courts' human rights jurisdiction to access medicines, as argued under the DRC Constitution, ratified human rights treaties, and other domestic laws.
- Mismanagement of received international assistance.
- Limited power of the NHRC: unlike the Tanzanian CHRGG, the NHRC cannot address the violation of access to medicines through negotiation and mediation, nor can it enforce its recommendations before the courts for appropriate remedy.
- The presence of conflicting and outdated provisions regulating the pharmaceutical sector: Illustrations include reference by laws and regulations in force to sanctions regime under abrogated laws, such as the 1933 Ordinance and 1952 Decree, fixing the fines in a currency that is no longer in use, and contradictory qualification requirements for pharmacists under the 1972 Ordinance law and the 1991 Ordinance law.
- Lack of public control laboratories for medicines quality: unlike in the URT, the government in the DRC does not have State's laboratory.
- The non-inclusion in the Social Security Law of the insured family members other than the pregnant spouse.
- Weak regulation of TM: Unlike in the URT, existing laws and regulations do not offer an appropriate sanction regime, nor do they make provisions for transferring patients from TM facilities to modern health facilities or between TM facilities. Furthermore, they fail to provide a competent authority in charge of quality control compared to the URT legislation.

- Absence of implementation measures on universal health coverage: the competent authority for the universal health coverage system, the Health Promotion Fund, and Health Solidarity Fund established under the Public Health Law have not yet been implemented.
- Absence of implementation measures for the special protection of children and women regarding access to health care services provided in the Children Law and Women Law.

Identified specific challenges for the URT include:

- The lower legal status of the constitutional right of access to medicines: unlike under the DRC Constitution, the URT Constitution protects access to medicines as directive principles of State policy.
- Failure to protect access to medicine or the right to health as a fundamental right: unlike the DRC Constitution, which theoretically makes access to medicines judicially enforceable, the URT Constitution does not.
- The government's failure to domesticate ratified human rights treaties providing for access to medicines.
- The lack of provision for reimbursement of medical costs for the health care provided by non-selected health facilities: unlike under the DRC legislation, the Community Health Fund Act, the National Health Insurance Fund Act, and the National Social Security Fund Act do not allow their beneficiaries to resort to health services of non-affiliated health institutions in case of emergency.
- The incompleteness of the Basic Rights and Duties Act regarding the High Court's competence: the Act's provisions fail to expressly recognize the High Court's jurisdiction to address the violation of human rights protected in other laws than the URT Constitution.
- Absence of special protection for women regarding healthcare: unlike the DRC Constitution and the Women Law, the URT Constitution does not guarantee special protection for women.

E. Recommendations

These suggested recommendations correspond to the above-identified obstacles that impede an appropriate implementation of access to medicines by DRC and URT. They comprise common recommendations to both countries and specific recommendations for each country study. If the DRC and URT governments adopt them, these recommendations can contribute to improving the implementation of access to medicines within their jurisdictions.

Suggested recommendations to both countries include the following:

- Organization of an appropriate judicial domestic remedy mechanism for the violation of access to medicines. This recommendation is also consistent with the exhaustion of domestic remedies principle argued under the African Charter, the SADC Tribunal Protocol, and the Optional Protocol to ICESCR.
- Explicit request for international assistance within their reports to the CESCR.

- Adoption of an appropriate national implementation mechanism for treaty bodies'decisions, views, recommendations, concluding observations, or judgments as the case may be.
- Adequate integration of TM into the national health system: three things can be done in order to implement this recommendation. Firstly, the government should exercise the provider function of delivering TM services through its public health institutions. Secondly, existing laws should contain explicit provisions for transferring patients from modern health institutions to TM facilities. Thirdly, health insurance laws and regulations should explicitly cover traditional therapies.
- Adequate budget allocation to the health sector: both DRC and URT should make efforts to allocate at least 15% of their general budget to the health sector following the Abuja Declaration and ensure its complete execution.
- Increasing local production of medicines: due to the lack of public pharmaceutical industries, the DRC and URT governments can invest in developing improved TMs that private laboratories can locally produce.[1304]

Concerning the DRC, suggested recommendations are as follows:

- Extension of the power of the NHRC: Like in the URT, the parliament should amend the NHRC Law to empower the NHRC to address the violation of access to medicines through negotiation and mediation and enforce its recommendations before the courts.
- Establishment of the legal procedure for judicial enforcement of access to medicines: the parliament should amend existing laws regulating each court and tribunal in oder to include their human rights jurisdiction on ESCRs, the rule of procedure, and an appropriate reparation regime.
- Harmonization of pharmaceutical legislation: this includes the harmonization of qualification requirements for a pharmacist, abrogation of provisions that refer to the 1933 Ordinance and 1952 Decree, and the provision of an adequate sanction regime, and establishing a unique competent authority for pharmaceutical regulation.
- Extension of health coverage for family members under the Social Security Law: like in the URT, the amendment of the Social Security Law is necessary to cover family members other than a pregnant wife of an insured person.
- Reinforcement of control quality for medicines: like in the URT, the government should equip pharmacy inspectors with appropriate working materials, including a public laboratory.
- Implementation of universal health coverage: the government should implement the Public Health Law's provisions on the universal health coverage system and Health Solidarity Fund.
- Appropriate use of received international aid.

1304 See, for instance, Decree on the Program of Traditional Medicine, art 3.

- Adoption of measures for the special protection of children and women: the government should adopt implementation measures for children and women special protection regarding their health services under the Children Law and Women Law.
- Appropriate regulation of TM: Like in the URT, the Congolese parliament should adopt a law to regulate TM and related-issues practice. Adopting such a law shall put an end to the diversity of existing uncoordinated legislation and regulations on TM, including repealing article 15 of the 1952 Decree. It shall further tackle control quality of TMPs and TM products, competent regulatory authority, appropriate sanctions regime, and transfers from TM facilities to hospitals and between traditional medical facilities.
- Unifying the competent authority's functions on medicinal plants: the government should merge the national service attributions for medicinal plants under the Public Health Law into the existing National Program for TM established under the Decree on the Program of Traditional Medicine.

The following are specific recommendations for the URT:

- Protecting the right to health as a fundamental right: like under the DRC Constitution, the URT Constitution should protect access to medicines as a fundamental right that is judicially enforceable. The implementation of this recommendation can serve as an alternative to the country's lack of commitment to the domestication of ratified treaties on the right to health.
- Domestication of ratified human rights treaties: for Tanzanian people to fully enjoy access to medicines, the URT should domesticate its treaty provisions on the right to health, including the African Charter, the ICESCR, SADC Health Protocol, and Gender Protocol.
- Complete enforcement of the High Court's human rights jurisdiction: the parliament should amend the Basic Rights and Duties Act to include the High Court's jurisdiction over human rights protected in other laws than the Constitution following article 30 (3) of the URT Constitution.
- Implementation of universal health coverage: the URT government should make compulsory the membership to the Community Health Fund Act and provide necessary alternative means for compensating the Fund in case of exemptions for contribution.
- Special protection for children: like the Children Law, the Law of the Children Act should make explicit provisions for special protection of children with disabilities regarding their access to medicine.
- Special protection for women: like the Women Law in the DRC, the URT should adopt a law that provides health care services for women at reduced costs or free of charge, especially during pregnancy, childbirth, and after birth.
- Consideration of cases of emergency by existing health insurance laws: like in the DRC, the parliament should revise the National Health Insurance Fund Act, the National Social Security Fund Act, and the Community Health Fund Act to insert provisions allowing their beneficiaries to resort to health care services

provided by non-preselected health facilities, including outside their respective districts, in case of emergency.

- Natural resources and TM: like under the DRC laws, the Traditional Medicine Act should make express provisions allowing individuals to harvest medicinal plants free of charge.

Bibliography

Scholarly literature and reports

Abdullahi, Ali. "Trends and challenges of traditional medicine in Africa." *African Journal of Traditional, Complementary, and Alternative Medicines* 8 (2011): 115-123.

African Commission on Human and Peoples' Rights, Rules of Procedure of the African Commission on Human and Peoples' Rights, 2020.

African Commission on Human and Peoples' Rights, Resolution on State's obligation to regulate private actors involved in the provision of health and education services-ACHPR/Res.420 (LXIV), Egypt, 2019.

African Commission on Human and Peoples' Rights, General Comment N° 4 on the African Charter on Human and Peoples' Rights: the right to redress for victims of torture and other cruel, inhuman or degrading punishment or treatment, 2017.

African Commission on Human and Peoples' Rights, 42nd Activity Report, 2017.

African Commission on Human and Peoples' Rights, 41st Activity Report, 2016.

African Commission on Human and Peoples' Rights, General Comment N°. 3 on the African Charter on Human and Peoples' Rights: The right to life (Article 4), 2015.

African Commission on Human and Peoples' Rights, State party reporting guidelines for economic, social and cultural rights in the African Charter on Human and Peoples' Rights, 2012.

African Commission on Human and Peoples' Rights, Principles and Guidelines on the Implementation of Economic, Social and Cultural Rights in the African Charter on Human and Peoples' Rights, 2011.

African Commission on Human and Peoples' Rights, Resolution 141 on access to health and needed medicines in Africa, Abuja, 2008.

African Commission on Human and Peoples' Rights, Concluding observations and recommendations on the consolidated 2nd to 10th periodic report of the United Republic of Tanzania, 2008.

African Commission on Human and Peoples' Rights, Guidelines for national periodic reports, 1989.

African Commission's Recommendation on Periodic Reports, 1988.

African Court on Human and Peoples' Rights, Rules of Court, 2020.

African Court on Human and Peoples' Rights, Activity report 1 January–31 December, 2019, 2020.

African Court on Human and Peoples'Rights, Activity Report, 2018.

African Union Conference of Ministers of Health, Africa Health Strategy: 2007-2015, 2007.

Ahluwalia, Rashim et Méchin Bernard. *La médecine traditionnelle au Zaïre: fonctionnement et contribution potentielle aux services de santé.* Ottawa: CRDI, 1979.

Ahmadiani, Saeed, and Shekoufeh Nikfar, "Challenges of access to medicine and the responsibility of pharmaceutical companies: a legal perspective," *DARU Journal of Pharmaceutical Sciences* (2016): 2-7.

Akol, Angela, Moland Karen, Babirye Juliet, and Engebretsen Marie, "'We are like co-wives': Traditional healers'views on collaborating with the formal child and adolescent mental health system in Uganda." *BMC Health Services Research* (2018): 1-9.

Anochie Ph., Ndingkokhar B., Bueno J., Anyiam F., Linus Ndidi OssaiChidi L., Onyeneke E., and Onyeozirila A. "African medicinal plants that can control or cure tuberculosis." *International Journal of Pharmaceutical Sciences and Developmental Research 4*, no. (1) (2018): 1-8.

Antwi-Baffour, S., Bello A., Adjei D., and Abdulai S. "The place of traditional medicine in the African society: The science, acceptance and support." *American Journal of Health Research* 2, no. 2 (2014): 49-54.

Ariranga G. Pillay et al. "Three illegal and arbitrary decisions taken in bad faith by the SADC Council of Ministers and Summit of Heads of State and Government. Letter to the Executive Secretary of SADC," 2011. https://www.politicsweb.co.za/documents/three-illegal-and-ultra-vires-decisions (accessed July 12, 2019).

Asmelash, Henok. "Southern African Development Community (SADC) Tribunal." *MPILux Working Paper 10* (2017): 1-29.

Babb, D., Pemba L., Seatlanyane P., and Charalambous S. "Use of traditional medicine by HIV-infected individuals in South Africa in the era of antiretroviral therapy." *Psychology, Health & Medicine* (2007): 314-320.

Bahar, Jibriel. "The justiciability and enforcement of the right to health under the African Human Rights system." *Haramaya Law Review* (2012):29-50.

Bahati, Jacques. *Evaluating peace and stability in the Democratic Republic of Congo and the United States policy in the Great Lakes Region.* Washington: Africa Faith and Justice Network 2009.

Baumstark, Gabriel Alexander. *The human right to health and its relation to the WTO.* Stuttgart: Boorberg, 2016.

Bazu Masikini. "République Démocratique du Congo: droits et défis pharmaceutiques." *Université de Neuchâtel* (2013): 1-66.

Beijing Declaration adopted by the WHO Congress on Traditional Medicine, Beijing, 2008.

Bekker, Gina. "The African Commission on Human and Peoples' Rights and remedies for human rights violations." *Human Rights Law Review* 13, no 3 (2013): 499-528.

Besson, Samantha. "Human rights and constitutional law: patterns of mutual validation and legitimation." In *Philosophical foundations of human rights*, eds. Rowan Cruft, S. Matthew Liao, and Massimo Renzo, 279-299. Oxford: Oxford Scholarship Online, 2015.

Boerefijn, Ineke. *The reporting procedure under the Covenant on Civil and Political Rights. Practice and procedures of the Human Rights Committee.* Cambridge: Intersentia, 1999.

Bofoe, Lokangu. *La criminalité pharmaceutique en République Démocratique du Congo. Une véritable menace au droit à la santé.* Paris: L'Harmatan, 2019.

Bouso J. Carlos and Sánchez-avilés Constanza, "Traditional healing practices involving psychoactive plants and the global mental health Agenda," *Health and Human Rights 22*, no. 1 (2020): 145-150.

Brownlee, Kimberley. "Do we have a human right to the political determinants of health?" In *Philosophical foundations of human rights*, eds. Rowan Cruft, S. Matthew Liao, and Massimo Renzo, 502-514. Oxford: Oxford Scholarship Online, 2015.

Bulto, Takele. "Beyond the promises: resuscitating state reporting procedure under the African Charter on Human and Peoples' Rights." *Buffalo Human Rights Law Review 12* (2006): 57-92.

Burkina Faso, Periodic report within the framework of the implementation of article 62 of the African Charter on Human and Peoples' Rights, 2015.

Business Monitor International Ltd, Tanzania Pharmaceuticals and Healthcare Report Q3, 2016.

Chenwi, Lilian and Chirwa Danwood. "Direct protection of economic, social and cultural rights in international law." In *The protection of economic, social and cultural rights in Africa: International, regional and national Perspectives*, eds. Danwood Mzikenge Chirwa and Lilian Chenwi, 33-71. Cambridge: Cambridge University Press, 2016.

Chinkin, Christine. "Sources." In *International human rights law*, eds. Moeckli, Shah, Sivakumaran, 2nd ed., 75-95. Oxford: Oxford University Press, 2014.

Chirwa, DM. "Access to medicines and health care in Sub-Saharan African: A historical perspective." *Md. J. Int'IL.* 31 (2016): 21-43.

Chirwa, DM. "The right to health in international law: its implications for the obligations of state and non-state actors in ensuring access to essential medicine." *SAJHR 19*, no. 4 (2003): 541-566.

Coalition for an Effective African Court on Human and Peoples' Rights, African Court Coalition discussions: States withdrawals from article 34 (6) of the African Court Protocol, Official Bulletin Vol. 1, 2020.

Coburn, David and Coburn Elaine. "Health and health inequalities in a neo-liberal global world." In *The economics of health equity*, eds. Di McIntyre and Gavin Mooney, 13-35. Cambridge: Cambridge University Press, 2007.

Collen, Flood M. and Aeyal Gross. "Introduction: marrying human rights and health care systems: contexts for a power to improve access and equity." In *The right to health at the public/private divide. A global comparative study*, eds. Collen M. Flood and Aeyal Gross, 1-18. Cambridge: Cambridge University Presse, 2014.

Commission Nationale des Droits de l'Homme de la République Démocratique du Congo, Troisième rapport annuel d'activités de la Commission Nationale des Droits de l'Homme (Janvier à Décembre 2018), Kinshasa, 2019.

Commission Nationale des Droits de l'Homme, Rapport synthèse des visites des centres pénitentiaires et de détention effectuées en République Démocratique du Congo, 2018.

Committee on Economic, Social and Cultural Rights, concluding observations on the initial to third reports of the United Republic of Tanzania, 2012.

Committee on Economic, Social and Cultural Rights, General comment N°21, Right of everyone to take part in cultural life (art 15 (1) of the ICESCR, 2009.

Committee on Economic, Social and Cultural Rights, concluding observations: Democratic Republic of the Congo, 2009.

Committee on Economic Social and Cultural Rights, General Comment No. 16: The equal right of men and women to the enjoyment of all economic, social and cultural rights (art. 3 of the ICESCR), 2005.

Committee on Economic, Social and Cultural Rights, General Comment No. 14: The Right to the Highest Attainable Standard of Health (Art. 12), 2000.

Committee on Economic Social and Cultural Rights: Report on the second session, 1988.

Committee on Economic, Social and Cultural Rights, General comment No. 9: The domestic application of the Covenant, 1998.

Committee on Economic, Social and Cultural Rights, Provisional Rules of Procedure of the Committee, 1993.

Committee on Economic, Social and Cultural Rights, General comment N°. 3: The nature of States Parties' obligations (art. 2, para. 1, of the Covenant), 1990.

Committee on Economic, Social and Cultural Rights, General comment N°. 1: Reporting by States Parties, 1981.

Committee on the Elimination of Discrimination against Women, concluding observations on the combined seventh and eighth periodic reports of the United Republic of Tanzania, 2016.

Committee on the Elimination of Discrimination Against Women, concluding observations: Democratic Republic of the Congo, 2013.

Committee on the Elimination of Discrimination Against Women, General recommendation N°. 24: Article 12 of the Convention (Women and Health), 1999.

Committee on the Rights of the Child, concluding observations: Democratic Republic of the Congo, 2017.

Committee on the Rights of the Child, Concluding observations: United Republic of Tanzania, 2015.

Committee on the Rights of the Child, Concluding observations: United Republic of Tanzania, 2012.

Committee on the Rights of the Child, "Day of general discussion on 'resources for the rights of the child- Responsibility of states'", 2007.

Conclusions and Recommendations of the Committee on the Elimination of Racial Discrimination: Venezuela, 67th sess, UN Doc CERD/C/VEN/CO/18, 2005.

Coomans, Fons. "Identifying the key elements of the right to education: A focus on its core content." *Child Rights Information Network* (2007): 1-10.

Coomans, Fons. "The Ogoni case before the African Commission on Human and Peoples' Rights." *International and Comparative Law Quarterly* 52 (2003): 749-760.

Community Health Fund Act, 2001.

Cowell, Frederick. "The death of the Southern African Development Community Tribunal's human rights jurisdiction." *Human Rights Law Review* (2013): 153-165.

Democratic Republic of the Congo, 11th to 13rd reports to the African Commission on Human and Peoples' Rights, 2015.

Democratic Republic of the Congo, National report submitted in accordance with paragraph 15 (a) of the annex to Human Rights Council Resolution 5/1, 2009.

Democratic Republic of the Congo, combined second to fifth reports to the Committee on Economic Social and Cultural Rights, 2007.

Democratic Republic of the Congo, eighth to tenth periodic reports to the African Commission on Human and Peoples Rights, 2007.

Ebobrah, Solomon. "Human rights developments in African sub-regional economic communities during 2009." *African Human Rights Law Journal 10* (2010): 233-264.

Economic and Social Council, resolution 1988/4, 1988.

Economic and Social Council, resolution 1987/5, 1987.

Economic and Social Council, resolution 1985/17, 1985.

Elangi, Botoy. *Propriété intellectuelle et droits de l'homme: l'impact des brevets pharmaceutiques sur le droit à la santé dans le contexte du VIH/SIDA en Afrique.* Genève: Schulthess Médias Juridiques SA, 2007.

Executive Council, decision on the activities of the African Commission on Human and Peoples´ Rights, 2017.

Executive Council, decision on the 2016 Activity report of the African Court on Human and Peoples' Rights, 2017.

Executive Council, decision on the forty-second activity report of the African Commission on Human and Peoples' Rights, 2017.

Extraordinary SADC Summit of Heads of State and Government: Communiqué, Windhoek, 2011.

Extraordinary SADC Summit of Heads of State and Government: Communiqué, Kingdom of Swaziland, 2009.

Festo Balegele and 784 Others vs. Dar es Salaam City Council (Civil Case No. 299 of 1988).

Fetter Bruce, "Health care in twentieth century Africa: Statistics, theories and policies," *Africa Today* 40, no. 3 (1993): 9-23.

Forere, Malebakeng and Stone Lee. "The SADC Protocol on Gender and Development: duplication or complementarity of the African Union Protocol on Women's Rights?" *African Human Rights Law Journal* (2009): 434-458.

Forman Lisa, Caraoshi Luljeta, Chapman Audrey R, and Lamprea Everaldo. "Conceptualising minimum core obligations under the right to health: How should we define and implement the morality of the depths." *International Journal of Human Rights* (2016): 1-18.

General Assembly resolution A/RES/42/102, 1987.

Gittleman, Richard. "The African Charter on Human and Peoples' Rights: a legal analysis." *Virginia Journal of International Law* (1986): 667-714.

Gnegel, G. et ali, "Identification of falsified chloroquine tablets in Africa at the time of the COVID-19 pandemic." *American Journal of Tropical Medicine & Hygiene* 103, no. 1 (2020): 73-76.

Government of the Republic of South Africa and others vs. Grootboom and others 2001 (1) SA 46 (CC).

Guidelines for medicines and medical supplies donations for Tanzania Mainland, 2015.

Gumedze, Sabelo. "Bringing communications before the African Commission on Human and Peoples' Rights." *African Human Rights Law Journal 3*(2003): 118-148.

Habtom, GK. "Perceptions and attitudes of modern and traditional medical practitioners about traditional medical practice in Eritrea." *International Journal of Alternative and Complementary Medicine* 11, no. 1 (2018): 6-19.

Haidan Yuan, Qianqian Ma, Li Ye, and Guangchun Piao, "The traditional medicine and modern medicine from natural products." *Molecules* (2016): 1-18.

Health Laboratory, Practitioners Act, 2007.

Health Sector Reform Programme, 1998.

Heggenhougen, Harald Kristian. "Health services: official and unofficial." In *Tanzania - crisis and struggle for survival*, eds. Jannik Boesen et al., 309-317. Sweden: Scandinavian Institute of African Studies, 1986.

Hestermeyer, Holger. *Human rights and the WTO: The case of patents and access to medicines*. Oxford: Oxford University Press, 2007.

Hestermeyer, Holger. "Access to medication as a human right." *Max Planck UNYB* 8 (2004): 102-180.

Heyns, Christof. "The African regional human rights system: in need of reform?" *AHRL* 1, no 2 (2001): 155-174.

Hoecke, Mark Van. "Legal doctrine: which method (s) for what kind of discipline?." In *Methodologies of legal research. Which kind of method for what kind of discipline?*, ed. Mark Van Hoecke, 1-17. Oxford: Hart Publishing, 2013.

Human Rights Committee, concluding observations to DRC, 2017.

Human Rights Committee, General comment N°6: article 6 (right to life), 1982.

India, combined second, third, fourth and fifth periodic reports submitted by State parties under articles 16 and 17 of the Covenant, 2006.

International Federation for Human Rights, Practical guide: The African Court on Human and Peoples' Rights, towards the African Court of Justice and Human Rights, 2010.

International Institute for Democracy and Electoral Assistance, The proposed Draft Constitution of Tanzania, 2014.

Juma, Dan. "Access to the African Court on Human and Peoples' Rights: A Case of the poacher turned gamekeeper." *Essex Human Rights Review 4*, no. 2 (2007): 1-21.

Kabengele, E, Tshimungu Kandolo, Verloo Henck, Ngoy Bukonda, Ngianga-Bakwin, and Chastonay Phillipe. "Traditional/alternative medicines and the right to health: key elements for a convention on global health." *Health and Human Rights* 15, no. 1 (2013): 44-57.

Kabudi, P. "The judiciary and human rights in Tanzania: domestic application of international human rights norms." *Verfassung und Recht in Übersee / Law and Politics in Africa, Asia and Latin America* 24, no. 3 (1991): 271-281.

Kamgoui Victorine. *Médecine traditionnelle et droit de la santé pour une intégration du droit dans le système traditionnel*. Paris: L'Harmattan, 2017.

Kaniki, Andrew M. and Mphahlele Kutu. "Indigenous knowledge for the benefit of all: can knowledge management principles be used effectively?" *South African Journal of Library & Information Science 68*, 1 (2002): 1-15.

Kavanagh, Matthew M. "Constitutionalizing health: rights, democracy and the political economy of health policy." *Publicly Accessible Penn Dissertations*, 2017. https://repository.upenn.edu/edissertations/2863 (accessed October 14, 2018).

Kazadi Mpiana. *La position du droit international dans l'ordre juridique congolais et l'application de ses normes.* Paris: EPU, 2013.

Kohler JC, and Makey TK. "Why the COVID-19 pandemic should be a call for action to advance equitable access to medicines". *BM Med 18, 193* (2020): 1-3.

Krajewski Markus, "Human Rights and Austerity Programmes." *SSRN*, 2013. https://ssrn.com/abstract=2199625 (accessed January 18, 2019).

Kumbu Jean M, Kabamba Bob et Esambo Jean L. "La constitution de la République Démocratique du Congo." In *Mandats, rôles et fonctions des pouvoirs constitués dans le nouveau système politique de la République Démocratique du Congo. Journées d'information et de formation organisées à l'intention des parlementaires, députés provinciaux et des Hauts Cadres de l'administration*, ed. Programme des Nations Unies pour le Développement, 16-30. Kinshasa: PNUD, 2007.

Laura Niada, The human right to medicines in Sub-Saharan Africa, Thesis, University of Westminster, 2010, available Thesis NADIA LAURA.pdf (accessed June 18, 2020).

Le Roux-Kemp, Andra. "The recognition of health rights in constitutions on the African continent: a systematic review." *African Journal of International and Comparative Law 24*, no. 1 (2016):142–157.

Lee Bryant and Tarimo Kuki, "Analysis of the Government of Tanzania's Budget Allocation to the Health Sector for Fiscal Year 2017/18,"2018, 7183-7323_TanzaniaBudgetAllocationHealthSectorBrief.pdf (accessed January 12, 2019).

Limburg Principles on the implementation of the International Covenant on Economic, Social and Cultural Rights, 1987.

Magili, Phoibe. "The efficacy of the law and regulatory mechanisms in combating counterfeit drugs in Tanzania." *Mzumbe University* (2014): 1-74.

Mahomoodally, Fawzi. "Traditional medicines in Africa: An appraisal of ten potent African medicinal plants." *Evidence-Based Complementary and Alternative Medicine* (2013) 1-14.

Majamba Hamudi. "Environmental rights jurisprudence in Tanzania: Review of judicial precedents." *Lesotho Law Journal* (2005): 1-26.

Manento J.K and others vs. the Attorney General, 2006.

Manjoo, Rashida. "Women's human rights in Africa." In *The African regional human rights system: 30 years after the African Charter on Human and Peoples' Rights*, ed. Manisuli Ssenyonjo, 137-154. Netherlands: Leiden-boston, 2012.

Maria Jurua, "Access to drugs at risk: securing access to medicines for least developed countries," *Africa Development, 42*, no. 1 (2017): 101-120.

Mazyambo, Makengo. "Introduction aux droits de l'homme: théorie générale, instruments, mécanismes de protection." In *Mandats, rôles et fonctions des pouvoirs constitués dans le nouveau système politique de la République Démocratique du Congo. Journées d'information et de formation organisées à l'intention des parlementaires, députés provinciaux et des Hauts Cadres de l'administration*, ed. Programme des Nations Unies pour le Développement, 226-279. Kinshasa: PNUD, 2007.

Mbwambo, Z, Mahunnah R., and Kayombo Edmund. "Traditional health practitioner and the scientist: bridging the gap in contemporary health research in Tanzania." *Tanzania Health Research Bulletin* 9, no. 2 (2007): 115-120.

Mégret, Frédéric. "Nature of obligations." In *International human rights law*, eds. Moeckli, Shah, Sivakumaran, 2nd ed., 97-118. Oxford: Oxford University Press, 2014.

Mtei, Gemini and Makawia Suzan. "Universal health coverage assessment: Tanzania." *Global Network for Health Equity* (2014): 1-11.

Meyer, Christine. *Menschenrechte in Afrika: Regionaler Menschenrechtsschutz als Herausforderung an menschenrechtliches Universalitätsdenken.* Baden-Baden: Nomos, 2013.

Mhamba, Robert and Mbirigenda Shukrani. "The pharmaceutical industry and access to essential medicines in Tanzania." *Institute of Development Studies, University of Dar es Salaam* (2010): 1-23.

Ministère de la Santé Publique, Plan National de Développement Sanitaire 2016-2020: vers la couverture sanitaire universelle, 2016.

Ministère de la santé publique, Lignes directrices relatives aux dons de médicaments, 2015.

Ministère de la Santé publique, Liste nationale des médicaments essentiels, 2010.

Ministère de la Santé Publique, Plan National de Développement Sanitaire 2011-2015, 2010.

Ministère de la santé publique, Cartographie des systèmes d'approvisionnement et de distribution des médicaments et autres produits de santé, 2010.

Ministère de la Santé Publique, Stratégie de Renforcement du Système de Santé, 2006.

Ministry of Health, Community Development, Gender, Elderly and Children, The National Health Policy 2017, 2017.

Ministry of Health and Social Welfare, Health Sector Strategic Plan July 2015 – June 2020, 2015.

Ministry of Health and Social Welfare, Tanzania Human Resource for Health and Social Welfare Strategic Plan 2014–2019, 2014.

Ministry of Health and Social Welfare, National Health Strategy June 2013–July 2018, 2013.

Ministry of Health and Social Welfare, Standard treatment guidelines and essential medicines list, 4th ed, 2013.

Ministry of health and social welfare, Tanzania Global Health Initiative Strategy 2010-2015, 2011.

Ministry of Health and Social Welfare, Mapping of the medicines procurement and supply management system in Tanzania, 2008.

Ministry of Health and Social Welfare, Primary Health Services Development Programme 2007–2017, 2007.

Morsink, Johannes. *Inherent human rights: philosophical roots of the Universal Declaration.* Philadelphia: University of Pennsylvania Press, 2009.

Moyo, Admark. "Defending human rights and the rule of law by the SADC Tribunal: Campbell and beyond." *African Human Rights Law Journal* (2009): 590-614.

Mufusama Jean Pierre et ali, "Quality of the antimalarial medicine artemether–lumefantrine in 8 cities of the Democratic Republic of the Congo," *Drug Testing and Analysis 10* (2018): 1601-1603.

Mukadi Bonyi. *Droit du travail.* Bruxelles: CRDS, 2008.

Mulumba M, Kabanda D, and Nassuna V. "Constitutional provisions for the right to health in east and southern Africa." *Centre for Health, Human Rights and Development, Regional Network for Equity in Health in East and Southern Africa* (2010): 1-23.

Müller, Markus et Balagizi Innocent. "La médecine moderne ou traditionnelle: le besoin de coopération." *Tearfund*, no. 48 (2001): 1-5.

Mumbanika, Mbwisi. "The Protection of the right to health under the Constitution of the Democratic Republic of Congo." *Verfassung und Recht Übersee 4* (2014): 434-446.

Munalula, Mulela. "SADC Protocol on Gender and Development: Road map to equality?" *SADC Law Journal 1* (2011): 189-196.

Murray, Rachel. *Human rights in Africa from the OAU to the African Union.* Cambridge: Cambridge University Press, 2004.

Murray, Rachel and Elizabeth Mottershaw. "Mechanisms for the implementation of decisions of the African Commission on Human and Peoples' Rights." *Human Rights Quarterly 36*, no. 2 (2014): 349-372.

Mutua, Makau. "The African human rights system: a critical evaluation." *Human Development Occasional Papers* (2000): 1-39.

Mvita, Roger. "La nouvelle compétence de la cour constitutionnelle fondée sur la protection des droits humains. Une lecture critique de l'Arrêt R. Const. 0038 du 20 Août 2015." *Annuaire Congolais de Justice Constitutionnelle* (2016): 207-212.

Mvungi, Edmund. "Sixty years of the Universal Declaration of Human Rights and twenty years of the Bill of Rights in Tanzania." In *Justice and dignity for all. Current issues of human rights in Tanzania*, eds. Kennedy Gaston et al., 61-72. Dar es Salaam: Dar es Salaam University Press, 2010.

Mwilanya Néhemie. "Mécanismes nationaux de promotion et de protection des droits de l'homme." In *Mandats, rôles et fonctions des pouvoirs constitués dans le nouveau système politique de la République Démocratique du Congo. Journées d'information et de formation organisées à l'intention des parlementaires, députés provinciaux et des Hauts Cadres de l'administration*, ed., Programme des Nations Unies pour le Développement, 280-288. Kinshasa: PNUD, 2007.

Naldi, Gino. "Observations on the Rules of the African Court on Human and Peoples' Rights." *AHRLJ 14* (2014): 366-392.

Namibia, initial reports submitted by State parties under articles 16 and 17 of the Covenant, 2014.

Nathan, Laurie. "The disbanding of the SADC Tribunal: A cautionary tale." *Human Rights Quarterly 35*, no. 4 (2013): 870-892.

Ngbolua, Koto-te-Nyiwa et ali., "Medicinal plants from Democratic Republic of the Congo as sources of anticancer drugs," *Journal of Advanced Botany and Zoology 6* (2018):1-2.

Ngondankoy, Paul G. "Droit constitutionnel des droits de l'homme." In *Cours intensifs sur les droits de l'homme et le droit international pénal*, ed. Bakama Bope, 76-136. Kinshasa: Université Protestante au Congo, 2012.

Ngoy, Lumbu. "Contrôle et protection des droits sociaux fondamentaux en droit congolais: portée et état de la question." *Presse de l'Université Internationale du Congo* (2014): 274-310.

Nwobike, C. "The African Commission on Human and Peoples' Rights and the demystification of second and third generation rights under the African Charter: Social and Economic Rights Action Center (SERAC) and the Center for Economic and Social Rights (CESR) v. Nigeria." *African Journal of Legal Studies 2* (2005): 129-146.

OAU Assembly of Heads of State and Government, Decision on the declaration of the period 2001-2010 as the OAU decade for African traditional medicine, Zambia, 2001.

OAU Heads of State and Government, Abuja Declaration on HIV/AIDS, tuberculosis and other related infectious diseases, 2001.

Oberleitner, Gerd. "Right to health." In *Understanding human rights: manual of human rights education*, ed. Wolfgang Benedek, 147-170. Graz: European Training, and Research Centre for Human Rights and Democracy, 2012.

Obonye, Jonas. "Neutering the SADC Tribunal by blocking individuals' access to the tribunal." *International Human Rights Law Review 2* (2013): 294-321.

Okere, Obinna. "The protection of human rights in Africa and the African Charter on Human and Peoples' Rights: a comparative analysis with the European and American system." *Human Rights Quarterly 6*, no. 2 (1984): 141-159.

Okoloise Chairman. "Circumventing obstacles to the implementation of recommendations by the African Commission on Human and Peoples' Rights." *African Human Rights Law Journal* 1 (2018): 27-57.

Oppong, Frimpong. "Enforcing judgements of the SADC Tribunal in the domestic courts of member states. Monitoring regional integration in Southern Africa Yearbook 2010." *Trade Law Centre for Southern Africa* (2011): 115-142.

People's Republic of China, second periodic reports submitted by State parties under articles 16 and 17 of the Covenant, 2010.

Perehudoff, Katrina, Toebes B, and Hogerzeil H. "Essential medicines in national Constitutions: Progress since 2008." *Health and Human Rights Journal 18* (2016) 141-156.

Perehudoff, SK, Laing, Ro and Hogerzeil, HV, "Access to medicines in national constitutions." *Bulletin of the World Health Organization 88* (2010):800-800.

Peter, Chris. *Human rights in Tanzania: selected cases and materials.* Köln: Rüdiger Köppe Verlag, 1997.

Peter, Chris. "Justice and dignity for all: the state of human rights in Tanzania." In *Justice and dignity for all. Current issues of human rights in Tanzania,* eds., Kennedy Gaston et al., 7-60. Dar es Salaam: Dar es Salaam University Press, 2010.

Phooko, Moses. "No longer in suspense: clarifying the human rights jurisdiction of the SADC." *Tribunal, PER / PELJ* 18, no. 3 (2015): 531-569.

Politique Pharmaceutique Nationale, 2008.

Proudlock, Paula. "Children's socio-economic rights." In *Child law in South Africa,* ed. Trynie Boezaart, 291-308. Cape Town: Juta, 2009.

Raju, KD. "Patent linkages and its impact on access to medicines: challenges, opportunities for developing countries." In *Access to medicines and vaccines,* eds. Correa CM and Hilty RM, 329-369. Cham: Springer, 2022.

Report of the Special Rapporteur on the right of everyone to the enjoyment of the highest attainable standard of physical and mental health, 2013.

Report of the Special Rapporteur on the right of everyone to the enjoyment of the highest attainable standard of physical and mental health, 2006.

Report of the WHO Expert Committee, the selection and use of essential medicines, in WHO technical report series 914, 2002.

Republic of South Africa, initial reports submitted by State parties under articles 16 and 17 of the Covenant, 2017.

Republic of South Africa, combined second periodic report under the African Charter on Human and Peoples' Rights and initial report under the Protocol to the African Charter on the Rights of Women in Africa, 2015.

Republic of Uganda, Initial reports submitted by State parties under articles 16 and 17 of the Covenant, 2012.

Republic of Zimbabwe, 7th to 10th combined Report submitted to the African Commission on Human and Peoples' Rights, 2006.

Republic of Zambia, initial reports submitted by State parties under articles 16 and 17 of the Covenant, 2003.

Republic of Zimbabwe, second and third report in terms of article 62 of the African Charter on Human and Peoples' Rights, 1997.

Republic of Zimbabwe, initial reports submitted by State parties under articles 16 and 17 of the Covenant, 1995.

Ruppel, Oliver. "Regional economic communities and human rights in East and Southern Africa." In *Human rights law in Africa: Legal perspectives on their protection and promotion*, eds. Bösl A and Diescho J, 275-317. Windhoek: McMillan Education, 2009.

SADC Charter of the Fundamental Social Rights, 2003.

SADC Declaration on the fight against HIV and AIDS, 2003.

SADC Declaration on Gender and Development, 1997.

SADC Summit of Heads of state and Government: Communiqué, United Republic of Tanzania, 2019.

SADC Summit of Heads of State and Government: Communiqué, Victoria Falls, 2014.

Sakata M. Tawab. *Introduction au droit économique: droit de l'OHADA, transformation des entreprises publiques, état entrepreneur, établissements publics, sociétés du portefeuille, nationalisation, rétrocession, libéralisation et politique des prix, protection des consommateurs, droits de l'homme.* Kinshasa: Presse Universitaire de Kinshasa, 2013.

Sama Martyn and Nguyen Vinh-Kim. *Governing health systems in Africa.* Dakar: Council for the Development of Social Science Research in Africa, 2008.

San Giorgi, M. *The human right to equal access to health care.* Cambridge: Intersentia, 2012.

Schäfermann, S. et ali., "Substandard and falsified antibiotics and medicines against noncommunicable diseases in western Cameroon and north-eastern Democratic Republic of Congo," *American Journal of Tropical Medicine & Hygiene 103,* no. 2 (2020): 894-908.

Scheinman, David. "Traditional medicine in Tanga today: The Ancient and modern worlds meet." *Indigenous Knowledge Notes,* no. 51 (2002): 1-4.

Schiavetti, B. et al., "The quality of medicines used in children and supplied by private pharmaceutical wholesalers in Kinshasa, Democratic Republic of Congo: a prospective survey." *American Journal of Tropical Medicine and Hygiene 98* (2018): 898-900.

Semenya, Sebua and Maroyi Alfred. "Medicinal plants used for the treatment of tuberculosis by Bapedi traditional healers in three districts of the Limpopo province, South Africa." *African Journal of Traditional, Complementary and Alternative Medicines 10,* no 2. (2013): 316-323.

Sepúlveda, Magdalena. *The nature of the obligations under the International Covenant on Economic, Social and Cultural Rights.* Cambridge: Intersentia, 2003.

Sellin, Jennifer Anna. *Access to Medicines. The Interface between Patents and Human Rights: Does one size fit all?.* Cambridge: Intersentia, 2014.

Shemdoe, Georges and Mhando Loy. "National policies and legal frameworks governing traditional knowledge and effective intellectual property systems in Southern and Eastern Africa: The case of traditional healers in Tanzania." *African Technology Policy Studies Network* (2012): 1-39.

Sillo Hiiti. "Regulatory enforcement and the risk of counterfeit and substandard medicines in Africa: the case of Tanzania." Wired. 2013. https://medeor.de/images/themen/konferenz/HiitiSillo.pdf (accessed July 12, 2018).

Sixième rapport périodique soumis par la République Démocratique du Congo en application des articles 16 et 17 du Pacte, attendu en 2013, 2019.

Smith, E. Robert. *Medicinal Chemistry-Fusion of Traditional and Western Medicine.* Sharjah: Bentham Science Publishers, 2013.

Smits, Jan M. *The mind and method of the legal academic.* Camberley: Edward Elgar 2012.

Southern African Development Community Protocol on Health as amended, 2004.

Southern Africa Toward Economic Liberation: A Declaration by the Governments of Independent States of Southern Africa, 1980.

Ssenyonjo, M. "The influence of the International Covenant on Economic, Social and Cultural Rights in Africa." *Netherlands International Law Review* (2017): 259–289.

Ssenyonjo, M. "The protection of economic, social and cultural rights under the African Charter, in *The protection of economic, social and cultural rights in Africa: international, regional and national perspectives,* eds. Danwood Mzikenge Chirwa and Lilian Chenwi, 91-120. Cambridge: Cambridge University Press, 2016.

Sisai Wang. *Market access of traditional Chinese medicinal product in the EU under WTO legal framework.* Cham: Springer International Publishing 2020.

Stuttaford Maria et al. "The right to traditional, complementary, and alternative health care." *Global Health Action* (2014) 1-8.

Tanzania Food and Drugs Authority, Ten years of regulating food, medicines, cosmetics and medical devices 2003-2013: Milestones attained, 2013.

Temba, Ferdinand. "Right to health with focus on people with HIV and AIDS in Tanzania." *The Eastern African Law Review 42,* no. 2 (2015): 27-55.

Tobin, John. *The right to health in international law.* Oxford: Oxford University Press, 2012.

Toebes, Brigit. *The Right to Health as a Human Right in International Law.* Cambridge: Intersentia, 1999.

United Nations Conference on Trade and Development: The least developed countries Report, 2019.

UN Human Rights Office of the High Commissioner, Access to Medicines in the context of the Right to Health, 2015.

UN Human Rights Council, Resolution 12/24 on access to medicine in the context of the right of everyone to the enjoyment of the highest attainable standard of physical and mental health, A/HRC/RES/12/24, 2009.

UN GA Resolution A/RES/42/105 on "Reporting obligations of States parties to United Nations instruments on human rights", 1987.

UN GA Resolution A/RES/55/2, United Nations Millennium Declaration, 2000.

United Nations Research Institute for Social Development, The human rights-based approach to social protection, Issued Brief 02, 2016.

United Nations Joint Human Rights Office in the Democratic Republic of the Congo, Progress and obstacles in the fight against impunity for sexual violence in the Democratic Republic of the Congo, 2014.

United Nations Research Institute for Social Development, The human rights-based approach to social protection, Issued Brief 02, 2016, 1, file:///C:/Users/Besitzer/Google%20Drive/My%20PHD%20THESIS/IB2-Human-rights-based-approach.pdf (accessed November 11, 2018).

UN Security Council Resolution 1308 on the Responsibility of the Security Council in the Maintenance of International Peace and Security: HIV/AIDS and International Peace-keeping Operations, 2000.

United Republic of Tanzania, combined initial, second and third periodic reports submitted by States parties under articles 16 and 17 of International Covenant on Economic, Social and Cultural Rights, 2009.

United Republic of Tanzania, fourth periodic report to the Human Rights Committee, 2007.

United Republic of Tanzania, Consolidated 2nd to 10th periodic reports to the African Commission of Human and People's Rights, 2006.

United States Department of State, Country Reports on Human Rights Practices for 2017: Tanzania.

Urias Eduardo and Ramani Shyama V., "Access to medicines after TRIPs: Is compulsory licensing an effective mechanism to lower drug prices? A review of the existence evidence," *Journal of International Business Policy* (2020): 367-384.

Viljoen, Frans. "Regional institutional and remedial arrangements for the judicial enforcement of economic, social and cultural rights in Africa." In *The protection of economic, social and cultural rights in Africa: international, regional and national perspectives*, eds. Danwood Mzikenge Chirwa and Lilian Chenwi, 243-273. Cambridge: Cambridge University Press, 2016.

Viljoen, Frans. "State reporting under the African Charter on Human and Peoples' Rights: a boost from the south." *Journal of African Law 44*, no. 1 (2000): 110-118.

Wambali, Michael. "The Enforcement of basic rights and freedoms and the state of judicial activism in Tanzania." *Journal of African Law* (2009): 34–58.

Wikha, Tshibinda. "Guarantee mechanisms of "rights-claims" recognized by the constitution: right to health, state obligation." *African Law Study Library 4* (2010): 1-19.

Willcox, Merlin and Bodeker Gerard. "Traditional herbal medicines for malaria." *BMJ* (2004): 1156-1159

Winani, Stephen. "Community Health Fund scheme in Tanzania: An exploration of its challenges and opportunities in contribution towards universal health coverage." *Royal Tropical Institute* (2015) 1-49.

Wolf, Jonathan. "The content of the human right to health." In *Philosophical foundations of human rights*, eds. Rowan Cruft, S. Matthew Liao, and Massimo Renzo, 491-502. Oxford: Oxford Scholarship Online, 2015.

"World Bank. Tanzania Public Expenditure Review 2020. © World Bank," 2020, Tanzania-Health-Sector-Public-Expenditure-Review-2020.pdf (accessed January 15, 2020).

WHO Medical Product Alert N°4/2020: Falsified Chloroquine products circulating in the WHO region of Africa (Update of 9 June), 2020.

World Health Organization. Declaration of Astana: Global Conference on Primary Health Care, Astana, 2018.

World Health Organization, Member State mechanism on substandard/spurious/ falsely-labelled/falsified/ counterfeit medical products, Seventieth World Health Assembly, A70/23 Provisional agenda item 13.6, 2017.

World Health Organization, Mental health action plan 2013–2020 (2013).

World Health Organisation regional office for Africa, Progress Report on decade of traditional medicine in the African region, 2011.

World Health Organisation, Traditional Medicine Strategy 2014-2023, 2010.

World Health Organisation and Office of the United Nations High Commissioner for Human Rights, The right to health, Fact Sheet N°31, 2008.

World Health Organisation, Counterfeit medicines, Fact Sheet N°275, 2006.

World Health Organisation, General guidelines for methodologies on research and evaluation of traditional medicine, 2000.

World Health Organisation Regional Committee for Africa, Promoting the role of traditional medicine in health systems: a strategy for the African Region, 2000.

Yahaya Sekaya, Aryeija Warren, and Bitwari Unice. "Traditional medicine in Uganda: historical Perspective, challenges and advances." *IK Notes*, no. 67 (2004): 1-4.

Yamane, Hiroko. *Interpreting TRIPS Globalisation of intellectual property rights and access to medicines*. Oxford: Hart Publishing, 2011.

Yamin Alicia. "The future in the mirror: incorporating strategies for the defence and promotion of economic, social, and cultural rights into the mainstream human rights agenda." *HRQ 27*, no. 4 (2005): 1200-1244.

Yeshanew Sisay. "Approaches to the justiciability of economic, social and cultural rights in the jurisprudence of the African Commission on Human and Peoples' Rights: Progress and perspectives." *African Human Rights Law Journal* (2011): 317-340.

Zargaran A, Karimi M, and Rezaeizadeh H, "COVID-19: Natural Products and Traditional Medicines; Opportunity or Threat?," *Trad Integr Med, 6*, no. 1 (2021):1-2.

Zweigert, K. and Kötz, H. *An introduction to comparative law*. 3rd ed. Translated by Tony Weir. Oxford: Oxford University Press, 1998.

List of Laws and Regulations

African Charter on Human and Peoples' Rights, 1986.

African Charter on the Rights and Welfare of the Child, 1999.

African Union Convention for the Protection and Assistance of Internally Displaced Persons in Africa, 2012.

African Youth Charter, 2009.

Arrêté ministériel N°1250/CAB/MIN/SP/010/ CPH/OMP/2015 modifiant et complétant l'Arrêté ministériel n°1250/CAB/MIN/ S/AJ/01 du 14 mars 2000 portant conditions d'octroi des autorisations d'ouverture et de fonctionnement des établissements pharmaceutiques, 2015.

Arrêté ministériel 1250/CAB/MIN/SP/008/CPH/OBF/2015 portant réglementation du commerce des produits pharmaceutiques en RDC, 2015.

Arrêté ministériel 1250/CAB/MIN/SP/007/CPH/OBF/2015 portant création de la commission d'homologation des produits pharmaceutiques et autres produits de santé, 2015.

Arrêté ministériel 1250/CAB/MIN/SP/009/CPH/OBF/2015 portant des lignes directrices dans le domaine pharmaceutique en RDC, 2015.

Arrêté ministériel 1250/CAB/MIN/SP/011/CPH/OBF/2015 modifiant et complétant l'arrêté ministériel N°1250/CAB/MIN/S/AJ/MS/013/2001 portant dispositions relatives à l'enregistrement et à l'autorisation de mise sur le marché des produits pharmaceutiques, 2015.

Arrêté ministériel N°1250/CAB/MIN/SP/069/CJ/OMK/2010 portant renouvellement de la suspension des importations de certains médicaments, 2010.

Arrêté ministériel N° 1250/ CAB/MIN/S/AJ/DJK/12/2002 portant création et organisation d'un programme national de promotion de la médecine traditionnelle et des plantes médicinales, 2002.

Arrêté ministériel N° 1250/ CAB/MIN/S/CJ/KIZ/32/2002 portant organisation de l'exercice de la profession de praticien de la médecine traditionnelle, 2002.

Arrêté Ministériel 1250/CAB/MIN/S/AJ/MS/012/2001 Portant dispositions relatives à l'enregistrement et à l'autorisation de mise sur le marché des produits pharmaceutiques, 2001.

Basic Rights and Duties Enforcement Act, 1995.

Charter of the United Nations, 1945.

Circulaire N°001 /CAB/MIN/BUDGET/2012 du 2 Août Contenant les instructions relatives à l'exécution de la loi de finances N°12/002 du 20 Juillet 2012.

Commission for Human Rights and Good Governance Act, 2001.

Constitution of the Democratic Republic of Congo as amended, 2006.

Constitution of the URT as amended, 1977.

Constitution du 24 Juin 1967.

Constitution of the World Health Organization, 1948

Constitutional Review Act, 2011.

Constitutive Act of the African Union, 2001.

Convention on the Rights of Persons with disabilities, 2008.

Convention on the Rights of the Child, 1990.

Convention on the Elimination of All Forms of Discrimination Against Women, 1981.

Covenant of the League of Nations, 1919.

Declaration of Alma-Ata on International Conference on Primary Health Care, Alma-Ata, 1978.

Décret N° 06/130 portant statut spécifique des médecins des services publics de l'Etat, 2006.

Décret portant code de procédure civile, 1960.

Décret portant art de guérir au Congo -Belge, 1952.

Disabled Persons Act, 1982.

Environmental Health Practitioners Act, 2007.

HIV and AIDS Act, 2008.

ILO Social Security (Minimum Standards) Convention n° 102, 1952.

International Convention on the Protection of the Rights of all Migrant Workers and Members of their Families, 2003.

International Convention on the Elimination of all Forms Racial Discrimination, 1969.

International Covenant on Civil and Political Rights, 1976.

International Covenant on Economic, Social and Cultural Rights, 1976.

International Labour Organization, Social Security (Minimum Standards) Convention n° 102, 1952.

Law of the Child Act, 2009.

Loi N° 18/021 portant statut des anciens Présidents de la République élus et fixant les avantages accordés aux anciens chefs de corps constitués, 2018.

Loi N° 18/038 portant statut du personnel de l'enseignement supérieur, universitaire et de la recherche scientifique, 2018.

Loi N°18/001 modifiant et complétant la Loi n° 007/2002 du 11 juillet 2002 portant code minier, 2018.

Loi N° 18/035 fixant les principes fondamentaux relatifs à l'organisation de la santé publique, 2018.

Loi N°023/2002 du 18 novembre 2002 portant code judiciaire militaire telle que modifiée et complétée par la Loi organique n° 17/003 modifiant et complétant la Loi n° 023-2002 du 18 Novembre 2002 portant code judiciaire militaire, 2017.

Loi N° 16/013 portant statut des agents de carrière des services publics de l'Etat, 2016.

Loi N° 015/2002 portant code de travail telle que révisée par Loi n° 16/010 du 15 Juillet 2016 modifiant et complétant la Loi n° 015-2002 portant code du travail, 2016.

Loi N° 16/009 fixant les règles relatives au régime général de la sécurité sociale, 2016.

Loi N° 15/015 fixant le statut des chefs coutumiers, 2015.

Loi N° 14/003 relative à la conservation de la nature, 2014.

Loi N°13/013 portant statut du personnel de carrière de la police nationale, 2013.

Loi N° 09/001 portant protection de l'enfant, 2009.

Loi N° 08/011 portant protection des droits des personnes vivant avec le VIH/SIDA et des personnes affectées, 2008.

Loi N° 15/013 portant modalités d'application des droits de la femme et de la parité, 2015.

Loi N°11/2002 portant code forestier, 2002.

Loi n°82-001 sur la Propriété Industrielle, 1982.

Loi organique N° 18-020 relative à la liberté des prix et à la concurrence, 2018.

Loi organique N° 16/027 portant organisation, compétence et fonctionnement des juridictions de l´ordre administratif, 2016.

Loi organique N° 13/011-B Portant organisation, fonctionnement et compétences des juridictions de l'ordre judiciaire, 2013.

Loi organique N° 08/016 portant composition, organisation et fonctionnement des entités territoriales décentralisées et leurs rapports avec l'Etat et les provinces, 2008.

Loi organique N° 06/020 portant statut des magistrats, 2006.

Medical Practitioners Act, 2007.

Mental Health Act, 2008.

National Essential Medicine List for Tanzania, 2007.

National Health Insurance Fund Act, 1999.

National Institute for Medical Research Act, 1979.

National Social Security Fund Act, 1997.

Natural Wealth and Resources (Permanent Sovereignty) Act, 2017.

Optional Protocol to the International Covenant on Economic, Social and Cultural Rights, 2013.

Ordonnance N° 20/017 fixant les attributions des ministères, 2020.

Ordonnance N° 11/023 modifiant et complétant le décret n° 04/029 du 17 mars 2004 portant création et organisation du Programme National Multisectoriel de Lutte Contre le Sida, 2011.

Ordonnance-Loi 91-018 Portant création d'un ordre des pharmaciens en République du Zaïre, 1991.

Ordonnance 72-359 Portant mesures d'exécution de l'Ordonnance-Loi 72-046 sur l'Exercice de la pharmacie, 1972.

Ordonnance-Loi 72-046 sur l'exercice de la pharmacie, 1972

Ordonnance n° 344 sur le régime pénitentiaire, 1965.

Ordonnance 71-81 sur l'exercice de l'art de guérir et les conditions et modalités d'application, 1958.

Ordonnance N° 27 bis Hyg. sur l'Exercice de la pharmacie au Congo-Belge, 1933.

Ordonnance de l'Administrateur Général du Congo, 1886.

Persons with Disabilities Act, 2010.

Pharmacy Act, 2011.

Prisons Act, 1967.

Protocol on Tribunal in the Southern African Development Community, 2011.

Protocol to the African Charter on Human and Peoples'Rights on the establishment of an African Court on Human and Peoples' Rights, 2004.

Protocol to the African Charter on Human and Peoples' Rights on the Rights of Women in Africa, 2005.

Public Health Act, 2009.

Regulation (EU) 2019/6 of the European Parliament and of the Council on veterinary medicinal products and repealing Directive 2001/82/EC, 2018.

SADC Protocol on Employment and Labour 2014.

SADC Protocol on Gender and Development as amended, 2008.

SADC Protocol on Health, 1999.

Tanzania Food and Drug Authority, Guidelines for application for registration of traditional medicinal products, 2014.

Tanzania Food, Drugs and Cosmetics Act, 2003.

Tanzanian Reciprocal Enforcement of Foreign Judgements Act, 2002.

Towards a Southern African Development Community. A Declaration made by the Heads of State and Government of Southern Africa at Windhoek, 1992.

Treaty for the Establishment of the East African Community as amended, 2000.

Treaty of the Southern African Development Community as amended, 1993.

Treaty establishing the Economic Community of West African States as revised, 1975.

Universal Declaration of Human Rights, 1948.

Vienna Convention on the Law of Treaties, 1969.

Worker's Compensation Act, 2015.

World Health Organisation Framework Convention on Tobacco Control, 2005

List of cases law

Application N° 006/2012: African Commission on Human and Peoples' Rights vs. Republic of Kenya, 2017.

Application 009/2016: Diakite Couple vs. Republic of Mali, 2017.

Application 003/2014 Ingabine Victoire Umuhoza vs. Republic of Rwanda, 2014.

Application 006/2012: African Commission on Human and Peoples' Rights vs. Republic of Kenya, 2012.

Applications N° 009/2011 and N° 011/2011, 2011.

Arrêt R. Const. 0038 RH 010/CC, 2015.

Case N° SADC (T) 01/2010.

Case N° (T) 03/2009.

Case N°. 2/2007 Mike Campbell (Pvt) Ltd and 78 Others vs. The Republic of Zimbabwe, 2007.

Case N° SADCT: 2/07, Mike Campbell (PVT) limited and William Michael Campbell vs. the Republic of Zimbabwe, 2007.

Communication 323/06: Egyptian Initiative for Personal Rights and Interrights vs. Egypt, 2011.

Communication 321/2006: Law Society of Zimbabwe et al/ Zimbabwe, 2006.

Communication 241/01: Purohit and Moore vs. Gambia, 2001.

Communication 54/91-61/91-96/93-98/93-164/97_196/97-210/98: Malawi African Association and others vs. Mauritania, 2000.

Communication 147/95-149/96: Sir Dawda k. Jawara vs. Gambia, 2000.

Communication 137/94-139/94-154/96-161/97: International PEN, Constitutional Rights Project, Civil Liberties Organisation and Interights vs. Nigeria, 1998.

Communication 155/96: Social and Economic Rights Action Center (SERAC) and Center for Economic and Social Rights (CESR) vs. Nigeria, 1996.

Communication 25/89, 47/90, 56/91, 100/93: Free Legal Assistance Group, Lawyers' Committee for Human Rights, Union Interafricaine des Droits de l'Homme, les Témoins de Jehovah/Zaïre, 1993.

Law Society of South Africa and Others vs. President of the Republic of South Africa and Others, 20382/2015, 2018.

Legal and Human Rights Centre and Others vs. Attorney General (1) (Miscellaneous Civil Case N° 77 of 2005).

Republic Prosecutor vs. Siza Pembe Maneno (Case N°. 61), 2001.

Tanganyika Law Society vs. Ministry of Foreign Affairs and international cooperation of the URT and the Attorney General of the URT, 2019.

Tanganyika Law Society and the Legal and Human Rights Centre vs. the United Republic of Tanzania, 2013.

www.ingramcontent.com/pod-product-compliance
Ingram Content Group UK Ltd.
Pitfield, Milton Keynes, MK11 3LW, UK
UKHW021014120926
8556IPUK00040B/1125

9 783631 887592